W9-CBY-265

Metadata Fundamentals
for All Librarians

Priscilla Caplan

AMERICAN LIBRARY ASSOCIATION

Chicago

2003

While extensive effort has gone into ensuring the reliability of information appearing in this book, the publisher makes no warranty, express or implied, on the accuracy or reliability of the information, and does not assume and hereby disclaims any liability to any person for any loss or damage caused by errors or omissions in this publication.

Trademarked names appear in the text of this book. Rather than identify or insert a trademark symbol at the appearance of each name, the authors and the American Library Association state that the names are used for editorial purposes exclusively, to the ultimate benefit of the owners of the trademarks. There is absolutely no intention of infringement on the rights of the trademark owners.

METADATA is a trademark of the Metadata Company. American Library Association uses the term *metadata* in a descriptive sense, meaning "data about data." American Library Association is not in any way affiliated with the Metadata Company.

Design and composition by ALA Editions in Minion and Avant Garde using QuarkXPress 5.0 for the PC

Printed on 50-pound white offset, a pH-netural stock, and bound in 10-point coated cover stock by Victor Graphics

The paper used in this publication meets the minimum requirements of American National Standard for Information Sciences—Permanence of Paper for Printed Library Materials, ANSI Z39.48-1992. ∞

Library of Congress Cataloging-in-Publication Data

Caplan, Priscilla.
    Metadata fundamentals for all librarians / Priscilla Caplan.
        p.   cm.
    Includes bibliographical references and index.
    ISBN 0-8389-0847-0
    1. Metadata. 2. Information organization.   I. Title.
Z666.5.C37 2003
025.3—dc21   2002151683

Copyright © 2003 by the American Library Association. All rights reserved except those which may be granted by Sections 107 and 108 of the Copyright Revision Act of 1976.

Printed in the United States of America

07 06 05 04 03   5 4 3 2 1

CONTENTS

FIGURES

PREFACE

This book is intended as an introduction to metadata for librarians and others working in a library environment. I hope it will also be useful to educators and students in library and information science. Part I discusses concepts and issues applicable to all metadata schemes, while part II describes a number of individual metadata schemes. For each scheme, I try to note the types of resources and uses for which it was designed, how the scheme is described, the major sections and elements of the scheme, what syntax or content rules apply, and some applications that use the scheme. This book will not teach anyone how to catalog or describe information resources according to any particular metadata scheme, but it will give an overview of how various metadata schemes differ, what they have in common, and how they are designed to serve different purposes.

This is not a comprehensive catalog of metadata schemes. It was difficult to select which schemes to include and which to leave out. In general I tried to include schemes that those working in libraries or in an academic environment would be most likely to encounter. I can imagine being faulted for insufficient attention to museum information, or to multimedia standards, or to high-level collection description, to name only a few areas. I would encourage anyone with an interest in schemes not covered in this book to use some of the metadata clearinghouses listed in the readings for chapter 1 to locate more information about them.

In this text, the names of metadata elements taken from defined metadata schemes are spelled with initial capital letters: Title, Online Provider, Technical Infrastructure of Complex Object. If the scheme is defined as an SGML or XML DTD or schema, metadata elements may be referred to by their tag names in angle brackets: <title>, <classDecl>, <taxonomy>. Values of metadata elements are given in quotes: the value of Record Type may be "work" or "image." Names and values of attributes are also given in quotes: the value of the "id" attribute is "12345." When describing what information is given in metadata schemes themselves, the attributes by which metadata elements are described are also given in quotes: each element is defined by "name," "label," "definition," and "vocabulary" attributes.

ACKNOWLEDGMENTS

I would like to thank Ellen Purcell at the Florida Center for Library Automation for her help in producing the figures in this book.

I am also grateful to the following colleagues who reviewed portions of the manuscript: Murtha Baca at the Getty Research Institute, Karen Coyle at the California Digital Library, Michael Fox at the Minnesota State Historical Society, Rebecca Guenther at the Library of Congress, Stephanie Haas at the University of Florida Libraries, and Gertrude Koh at Dominican University. Their comments greatly improved the text and saved me from several embarrassing errors. Needless to say, any remaining errors are all my own.

Finally, I would like to thank Charles Husbands at the Harvard University Library, who once suggested it might be more productive for me to learn something about library cataloging than to continue to complain that I didn't understand it.

Metadata Basics

1

WHAT IS METADATA?

Although metadata is a topic of major interest in library and information science, the term itself comes from the field of computer science. In computer terminology, the prefix "meta" is commonly used to mean "about," so a *metalanguage* is a language used to describe other languages, and *metadata* is data used to describe other data. The first published use of the word in the sense of data about data may have been in the first edition of NASA's *Directory Interchange Format Manual* published in 1988.[1]

Interestingly, the term *METADATA*, spelled with an initial capital or all capitals, was actually coined by Jack E. Myers in the late 1960s and registered in 1986 as a trademark of the Metadata Company, which provides software and services related to medicine and health care. According to the trademark, *metadata* as one word refers to current and future products of that company, and more generic senses of the word must be represented by the terms "meta data" or "meta-data." For this reason, the IMS Global Learning Consortium, Inc., calls its metadata specification the "IMS Meta-data Specification." Most other metadata initiatives have not been so fastidious, and some have publicly taken the position that the term "metadata" has entered the public domain.

By the early 1990s, the term *metadata* was being used in the sense of the information necessary to make computer files useful to humans, particularly in relation to scientific, social science, and geospatial datasets. One of the first specifications to call itself metadata was the Federal Geographic Data Committee's Content Standard for Digital Geospatial Metadata, version 1 of which was issued in 1994. The stated purposes of the standard were to help a user "determine the availability of a set of geospatial data, to determine the fitness of the set of geospatial data for an intended use, to determine the means of accessing the set of geospatial data, and to successfully transfer the set of geospatial data."[2]

With the rise of Internet computing and the Web, the term *metadata* began to be used in the context of describing information objects on the network. Even text files, which unlike numeric datasets are easily human-understandable, may still require metadata to be found, placed in the context of authorship and date, or otherwise managed or controlled. The term entered the working vocabulary of mainstream librarianship around 1995 with the creation and promotion of the Dublin Core Metadata Element Set. The organizers of the first Dublin Core workshop were active participants in the World Wide Web Consortium (W3C), an (at that time) infant organization concerned with managing the development of the equally infant Web. As such, the early Dublin Core initiative served as an agent of cross-fertilization between the library and Web communities, and was able to energize the library community with new concepts and terminology.

Librarians were quick to realize that they had been creating data about data, in the form of cataloging, for centuries. However, there is inconsistent use of the term "metadata" even within the library community, some using it to refer to the description of both digital and nondigital resources, and others restricting it to electronic resources only. An example of the latter is a website maintained by the International Federation of Library Associations (IFLA), which says of metadata: "The term refers to any data used to aid the identification, description and location of networked electronic resources."[3]

Although the more restrictive interpretation is probably closer to the original computer science concept, it is certainly more useful to think of metadata as descriptive of all types of information resources, including print publications. Many collections consist of both digital and nondigital objects, and even digital objects often trace their ancestry to an artifactual original. One would hate to have to argue that a cataloging record describing an e-journal was a form of metadata, while a record describing the print version of the same publication was not.

Another often assumed constraint is that metadata itself must be electronic, regardless of the nature of the object described. In practical terms this is not terribly restrictive, as most resource description today is created and stored in digital form. However, this would imply that a MARC record is metadata, while a catalog card not yet converted into MARC format is not. This bothers some, while others would contend this is exactly the distinction that is intended. It is interesting to note that publishers appear to be more inclusive in this respect than many librarians. According to the Association of American Publishers, "Metadata is information that describes content. An everyday example is a card catalog in a library, an entry in a book catalog, or the information in an online index."[4]

As a final variation on the term, we note that the W3C appears to have adopted the most restrictive definition of all: "Metadata is machine understandable information for the web."[5] The requirement that metadata be machine-understandable is almost the exact inverse of the original need expressed by scientists and social scientists dealing with numeric datasets, who needed metadata to make their computer data human-understandable. This definition also expresses a more subtle requirement that metadata is "for the web," disqualifying not only the card and book catalogs allowed by the publishers, but also disqualifying resource description accessible via all other Internet protocols and all non–web-based computer systems.

It should be abundantly clear by now that there is no right or wrong interpretation of *metadata*, but that anyone using the term should be aware that it may be understood differently depending on the community and context within which it is used. In this text a fairly liberal definition is employed. *Metadata* is here used to mean structured information about an information resource of any media type or format. This definition is mute on whether the structured information is electronic or not, or whether the resource described is electronic, network-accessible, or web-accessible. It also does not care whether the metadata is intended for human or machine consumption. However, it does place two constraints on what qualifies as metadata. First, the information must be structured, which is to say it cannot be a randomly accumulated or represented set of data elements, but must be recorded in accordance with some documented metadata scheme.

Second, the metadata must describe an information resource. We will beg the question of what precisely is an information resource in the same manner that the 1995 Dublin Core workshop begged the definition of a "document-like object," the idea being that a reasonable person will know one when he or she sees one. However, metadata is also a topic of intense interest in business, manufacturing, and electronic commerce. Metadata is needed to describe screws and widgets, packaged sets of screws and widgets, and transactions involving packaged sets of screws and widgets. The structured descriptions necessary to control the manufacture, inventory, and trade of such items are certainly metadata, and any number of initiatives are interested in furthering metadata definition and exchange in this context. These are, however, excluded from the scope of this book, not because they are uninteresting but because this author is almost entirely ignorant of them.

Overall, the most useful discussions of metadata are not concerned with what it applies to but rather with what it is intended to accomplish. A good example is a glossary published by the Getty Research Institute, where metadata is defined to include "data associated with either an information system or an information object for purposes of description, administration, legal requirements, technical functionality, use and usage, and preservation."[6] Similarly, the U.K. Office for Library and Information Networking (UKOLN) says that metadata "is normally understood to mean structured data about digital (and nondigital) resources that can be used to help support a wide range of operations. These might include, for example, resource description and discovery, the management of information resources (including rights management) and their long-term preservation."[7]

TYPES OF METADATA

Recognition of the many uses of metadata has led to the construction of a very broad typology of metadata as being descriptive, administrative, or structural. These categories refer to the functional use and intent of the metadata rather than to inherent qualities of the metadata elements, as all metadata by definition is descriptive of something.

Descriptive metadata is understood to serve the purposes of discovery (how one finds a resource), identification (how a resource can be distinguished from other, similar resources), and selection (how to determine that a resource fills a particular need, for example, for the DVD version of a video recording). Descriptive metadata may also be used for collocation (bringing together all versions of a work) and acquisition (obtaining a copy of the resource, or access to one). Traditional library cataloging viewed as metadata is primarily descriptive, as are such schemes as the Dublin Core and the VRA (Visual Resources Association) Core.

Other functions that fall under the broad heading of descriptive metadata include evaluation, linkage, and usability. Evaluation may be narrative and subjective, such as a book or movie review, or may be more formally expressed by content ratings, which utilize rating schemes maintained by some authority. Examples of content ratings include the movie rating scheme (G, PG, PG-13, etc.) maintained by the Motion Picture Association of America and the Internet Content Rating Association labels.

Linkage is the expression of relationships between the thing described and other things or sets of things. The number of potentially relevant relationships is limitless. A book, for example, may be related to earlier and later editions, to translations and other versions, and to other books by the same author or on the same topic. A journal article is related to the journal in which it appears, to the other articles in the same issue, and to the publications that it cites. A digital object may be related to other objects expressing the same content in different formats or media. A building, a photograph of the building, a scanned TIFF image of the photograph, a PhotoShop PSD file derived from the TIFF, an artist's enhanced version of the PSD, a page of HTML that embeds the artist's PSD, and the website that incorporates the HTML page as part of its content are all related to each other in ways that can be defined and expressed in metadata.

The ability to express relationships between digital objects is particularly important, in part because of the possibility of using an actionable link (hyperlink) between them, and in part because variant formats and versions proliferate in the digital environment. The National Research Council Committee on an Information Technology Strategy for the Library of Congress noted that the "plasticity" of digital objects "will require that considerably more attention be given to issues of relationships than has been required for physical artifacts."[8]

Digital objects also require more metadata relating to usability. Although most people can be expected to use a printed document without assistance, that same content encoded as an SGML file is likely to require some explanation. Library cataloging rules allow the recording of high-level usability information, such as the hardware and software needed to make use of an electronic resource. The Text Encoding Initiative (TEI), which is concerned with encoding texts in SGML not only for the purpose of reading but also for linguistic and literary analysis, allows a detailed description of precisely how the textual content has been marked up. Metadata schemes concerned with documenting datasets must include extensive information on the logic and structure of the data elements included.

Administrative metadata is information intended to facilitate the management of resources. It can include such information as when and how an object was created, who is responsible for controlling access to or archiving the content, what control or processing activities have been performed in relation to it, and what restrictions on access or use apply.

As noted, the distinction between descriptive and administrative metadata is not clear-cut and often depends on the perspective of the user of the metadata. An accession number, for example, would be considered administrative metadata when used in the acquiring institution's processing of the item; however, to the extent that the accession number is a unique identifier for the item, it can also serve the descriptive function of identification. Similarly, restrictions on access could be used by a searcher who wants only items that are immediately available, helping to serve the function of selection. Despite such ambiguity, the distinction is in practice a useful one, as administrative and descriptive metadata are often defined in different schemes and used in different systems by different people. For example, descriptive metadata is usually available in publicly accessible search systems, while the viewing of administrative metadata may be restricted to only the staff responsible for managing the data resources.

The category of administrative metadata can be further subdivided into nonexclusive subclasses, including rights management metadata, preservation metadata, and technical metadata. Rights management and preservation metadata are named for the functions they are intended to support. Technical metadata documents characteristics of digital files, often down to a highly detailed level, such as whether a TIFF file is physically segmented in tiles or strips. Technical metadata is an important component of preservation metadata, because it is necessary to know the detailed physical characteristics of a file in order to reconstruct it or migrate it to another format.

Structural metadata can be thought of as the glue that holds compound digital objects together. A book, for example, may have many chapters, each consisting of a set of pages, each page represented by a separate digital file. Structural metadata is required to record the relationships between physical files and pages, between pages and chapters, and between chapters and the book as a whole. Presentation software uses structural metadata to display tables of contents and to deliver such functions as going directly to a requested chapter, or to turn pages forward or backward in order. Structural metadata ties together the components of a multimedia entity, such as associating audio with text in order to synchronize a narrator's voice with the transcript of an oral history. Structural metadata also documents the order and format of data elements in a numeric or statistical dataset, such as a census. As the purpose of structural metadata is to enable use of some entity, it has something in common with descriptive usability metadata. The distinction, if there is one, is that usability metadata is intended primarily for human consumption while structural metadata is generally used in machine processing.

METADATA SCHEMES

It is possible to think of single metadata elements in isolation. For example, a bookshelf may contain a row of books with the titles printed vertically on the spines. The titles are a form of metadata and certainly improve discovery over taking down and examining every volume. (In fact, the practice of printing titles on book spines began only in the first half of the eighteenth century; until then, external metadata in the form of lists mapping books to shelf locations was required.[9]) However, we generally think in terms of metadata *schemes*, which are sets of metadata elements and rules for their use that have been defined for a particular purpose. In common usage, the terms *scheme* and *schema* are used interchangeably with this general definition. *Schema*, however, has another meaning in relation to computer database technology as the formal organization or structure of a database, and another specialized meaning in relation to XML. For that reason, in this text, we prefer the term *scheme*.

Specific metadata schemes are discussed in some detail in part II of this text. A few of the descriptive schemes that are referred to frequently in part I are introduced briefly here.

The *Dublin Core Metadata Element Set* (Dublin Core) is a simple set of fifteen descriptive data elements intended to be generally applicable to all types of resources. Developed by the Dublin Core Metadata Initiative (DCMI), it is now ANSI/NISO Standard Z39.85. The reference description of the element set is at http://dublincore.org/documents/dces/, and the home page for the DCMI is available at http://dublincore.org.

The *Visual Resources Association Core Categories* (VRA Core) was developed primarily to describe items held in visual resources collections, which typically hold surrogates (photographs, slides, and/or digital images) of original works of art and architecture. The element set is defined at http://www.vraweb.org/vracore3.htm, and the home page for the Visual Resources Association is http://www.vraweb.org/.

The *Encoded Archival Description* (EAD) was developed as a way of representing archival finding aids in electronic form. Finding aids are a form of archival description that generally begin with narrative information about the collection as a whole and provide progressively more detailed descriptions of the components of the collection. The official website for the EAD is at http://www.loc.gov/ead/ead.html.

AACR2/MARC cataloging isn't exactly a metadata scheme in the sense that the preceding metadata element sets are schemes. However, together, the suite of rulesets and format specifications used in traditional library cataloging do functionally constitute a metadata scheme. These include the International Standard Bibliographic Description (ISBD), the *Anglo-American Cataloguing Rules*, second edition, revised (AACR2R), the MARC21 specifications, and a number of related documents. ISBD information can be found at http://www.ifla.org/VI/3/nd1/isbdlist.htm. AACR2 is published by the American, Canadian, and British library associations and is available only in paper and CD-ROM. MARC21 and related specifications can be found at http://lcweb.loc.gov/marc/.

Semantics, content rules, and syntax are three aspects of metadata that can be specified in metadata schemes.

Semantics refers to the meaning of the items of metadata (metadata elements) themselves. A metadata scheme will normally specify the metadata elements that are included in the scheme by giving each of them a name and a definition. The scheme should also indicate whether each element is required, optional, or conditionally required (e.g., "mandatory if applicable") and whether the element may or may not be repeated.

Content rules specify how values for metadata elements are selected and represented. The semantics of a metadata scheme may establish the definition of an element named "author," but the content rules would specify such information as which agents qualify as authors (selection) and how an author's name should be recorded (representation). The *Anglo-American Cataloguing Rules*, for example, specify that the commonly known form of a person's name should be used, and then give a number of subrules on how to ascertain the commonly known form. A different set of content rules might specify a standard format, such as last name, first initial, middle initial, while yet another set of rules might require the metadata creator to supply a unique identifier for the author obtained from some authority file.

The *syntax* of a scheme is how the elements are to be encoded in machine-readable form. Practically speaking, processing systems designed to search, display, or otherwise act upon metadata may have internal storage formats quite different from the metadata format. The specified syntax of a scheme serves more to provide a common exchange format for interchanging metadata between parties than to proscribe how data are stored in any local system. For this reason, the syntax of a metadata scheme may be called a *communications format, exchange format, transport syntax,* or *transmission syntax.*

Logically, the semantics, content rules, and syntax are independent but related aspects of a metadata scheme. In practice, any particular scheme may contain, conflate, or omit these components in any combination. For example, some metadata schemes are defined as SGML or XML structures, inextricably entangling semantics with syntax. Other metadata schemes fail to specify any syntax, or offer implementers the choice of multiple approved syntaxes. Some schemes have no content rules, refer to external content rules, or are designed to allow the use of any content rules as long as the ruleset is noted.

Often the semantics, content rules, and syntax specified by a metadata scheme are incomplete, are not very proscriptive, or offer the implementer many choices. In this case the rules of the scheme alone are not enough to guarantee that metadata created by different individuals, or even by the same individual at different times, will be consistent. It is common for those using metadata schemes to follow guidelines that are more proscriptive than the scheme itself. These may be local to a particular project or department creating metadata, or may be shared by a national or international community. *Profiles* (also called *application profiles*) are formally developed specifications that limit and clarify the use of a metadata scheme for a specific user community. Whether informal guidelines or formal profiles, additional rulesets are generally needed to supplement metadata schemes as published.

Even within the limited universe of libraries, cultural heritage institutions, publishers, and information services, a fairly large number of metadata schemes are employed, and there is wide variation in their content and format. For example, the Dublin Core includes for each element a name, identifier, definition, and comment. *Qualifiers* (terms that restrict the meaning of an element or indicate how the value is represented) are specified in a separate document, and there are no prescribed content rules. Mappings from Dublin Core elements to other metadata element sets have been done, but are independent of the Dublin Core itself.

Name: Title

Identifier: Title

Definition: A name given to the resource

Comment: Typically, a Title will be a name by which the resource is formally known.

In contrast, the VRA Core version 3.0 includes for each element a name, qualifiers, a definition, and a loose tie to content rules in the form of a "Data values" field, which is defined as containing recommendations for use of controlled vocabularies or standardized lists. The VRA Core specification also includes mappings to Dublin Core and other metadata schemes.

RECORD TYPE

Qualifiers: None

Definition: Identifies the record as being either a WORK record, for the physical or created object, or an IMAGE record, for the visual surrogates of such objects

Data Values (controlled): work, image

VRA Core 2.0: None

CDWA: None

Dublin Core: TYPE

Interestingly, there is no standard for metadata schemes governing what they must contain and how it should be represented. There is, however, an ISO standard for data elements (ISO/IEC 11179 Specification and standardization of data elements) that addresses units of information found in files and databases.[10] The purpose of ISO 11179 is to make data elements understandable and shareable. Part 1 of the six-part standard establishes a framework for understanding data elements and for using the rest of the standard. Part 2 concerns the use of classification schemes. Part 3 defines required and optional attributes for describing data elements. Part 4 gives rules and guidelines for writing definitions of data elements. Part 5 focuses on how to assign names and identifiers, and part 6 concerns registries of data elements.

Because metadata elements for describing information resources are a subset of the universe of all data elements, ISO 11179 should apply to at least that portion of a metadata scheme that defines data elements. However, developers of metadata schemes used in libraries and cultural heritage institutions do not overall seem to have taken much cognizance of it. Most of the interest in ISO 11179 in these communities has come from those interested in the development of metadata registries.

LEVELS OF DESCRIPTION

The preceding sections have been deliberately vague and even inconsistent about what metadata actually describes, using such terms as "object," "thing," "item," and "resource." In fact, metadata can be used to describe many different types or levels of entity, from abstract concepts to physical objects. One of the fundamental aspects of definition for a metadata scheme or element is specifying which type(s) of entities the scheme or element can apply to.

A popular and useful model for the types of entities that can be described bibliographically is given in the IFLA Functional Requirements for Bibliographic Records.[11] This model, known as FRBR (pronounced fur-bur), defines four levels of entity: work, expression, manifestation, and item. A *work* is an abstract concept defined as "a distinct intellectual or artistic creation." Shakespeare's *Othello* is a work, as is Handel's *Messiah*. Works are realized in expressions, or specific renderings of the work, such as a particular edition of *Othello*, or a particular score of the *Messiah*. There can be, and often are, many *expressions* of a work, including different editions, translations, abridgements, and arrangements. Performances of musical and dramatic works are considered expressions along with scores and scripts. However, a modification that introduces significant new intellectual or artistic aspects is considered to constitute a new work, as is the adaptation of a work from one art form to another. Hence, Verdi's opera *Othello* is a work in its own right, with its own set of expressions in the form of scores, libretti, and performances.

A *manifestation* is defined as "the physical embodiment of an expression of a work," or all copies of an expression produced on the same medium in the same physical form. A performance of Verdi's *Othello* might, for example, be recorded on film, DVD, VHS videotape, CD, and various formats of audiotape. Each of these constitutes a separate manifestation. An expression of a textual work can be represented by manifestations including regular print, large-type print, and microfilm.

The final entity in the model is the *item*, defined as "a single exemplar of a manifestation, " a single physical object or set of physical objects (e.g., a recording on two compact discs). In general, all items for a particular manifestation would be the same, although "actions external to the intent of the producer" might introduce variations, such as a library rebinding a copy of a monograph.

The FRBR model can be useful in helping to clarify what we are trying to do with metadata. For example, a reader looking for content probably cares first and foremost if he or she can find the right version of the resource at all, and only secondarily whether it is available in paper. Expression-level description would serve this need. On the other hand, the metadata creator probably has a single instance of the resource in hand and may have a preference for describing what is easily known. This would lead to a system of manifestation-level description. Administrative users, such as preservationists, are concerned with managing specific physical objects, so metadata schemes for such purposes would tend to focus on the item.

Most metadata schemes have elements pertaining to more than one of the FRBR entities. Without a rigorous data model underlying the scheme, this can lead to confusion and complexity. For example, a MARC21 bibliographic record has defined places to put information pertaining to works, expressions, manifestations, and items. AACR2 cataloging rules with some exceptions call for creating a separate bibliographic record for each format of a publication, corresponding roughly to each manifestation in IFLA terms. This has led to a number of practical problems for both catalogers and catalog users when there are multiple manifestations. The bibliographic information for the work must be repeated redundantly in each cataloging record, adding to the burden of cataloging, while the catalog user is confronted with a multiplicity of retrieved records and forced to figure out what distinguishes them from each other. A number of approaches to addressing this problem have been proposed, including a multitiered record structure in which the data elements descriptive of the work are separated from elements descriptive of the expression and manifestation.

As useful as the FRBR model is when thinking about problems like these, the model itself does not cover all the types of entity that metadata must deal with. Intentionally limited by its framers to entities described by the traditional bibliographic record, the FRBR model does not cover entities larger than the single work, such as the collection. Collection-level description is important not only for archival collections (those defined by provenance and curatorship) but also for aggregations of network-accessible materials that form collections based on such characteristics as being linked to from a single website, being accessed via a single retrieval system, or even being described by a single pool of item-level metadata. Another concept that has some potential usefulness, particularly for rights management purposes, is that of the *superwork*, which is all works descended from a common origin. Both Shakespeare's and Verdi's *Othello*s would belong to the family of the superwork *Othello*.

Electronic resources also challenge FRBR. A manifestation is defined as all copies in the same medium in the same physical form, but what constitutes identity of medium is left unexplored. Is online disk storage a medium, or do various forms of disk storage, such as SCSI and SSA, count as different media? Is the same physical disk or tape a different medium if it is online or offline? Common sense tells us that there is a level of discrimination beyond which metadata creators are unlikely to know, and users unlikely to care, about differences in media.

The point is, however, that good metadata schemes should have underlying them some explicit model of the types of entities they are meant to describe, and of the possible relationships between them. It is also important to recognize (as the FRBR model does) that nonbibliographic entities are also relevant. Other types of entity include agents (persons and corporate bodies), events, places, and even transactions. Metadata schemes focusing on the description of resources often include elements pertaining to each of these entity types. The traditional cataloging record, for example, includes some information about agents (for example, the name and birth and death dates of the author of a book) and some about events (e.g., the date and place of publication). However, the person who is an author is an entity in his or her own right, and it would be possible to create a metadata record describing that person in far more detail than is allowed in a cataloging record. Linking between metadata records for different types of entities is as necessary, and often as much of a problem, as linking metadata records for related resources.

NOTES

1. E. Paul Shelley and B. David Johnson, "Metadata: Concepts and Models," in *Proceedings of the Third National Conference on the Management of Geoscience Information and Data, organised by the Australian Mineral Foundation, Adelaide, Australia, 18–20 July 1995*, 4.1-5, available at http://www.ainet.com.au/web%20pubs/Papers/AMF95/Shelley&Johnson.html. Accessed 1 June 2002.
2. Federal Geographic Data Committee, *Content Standard for Digital Spatial Metadata (CSDSM)*, version 2, 1998, available at http://www.fgdc.gov/metadata/contstan.html. Accessed 1 June 2002.
3. International Association of Library Associations and Institutions, *Digital Libraries: Metadata Resources*, available at http://www.ifla.org/II/metadata.htm. Accessed 1 June 2002.
4. MICI Metadata Information Clearinghouse (Interactive) (home page). Accessed 1 June 2002. Available at http://www.metadatainformation.org/.
5. Metadata and Resource Description (home page of the W3C Metadata Activity). Accessed 1 June 2002. Available at http://www.w3.org/Metadata. The Metadata activity was superseded by the Semantic Web activity with a home page at http://www.w3.org/2001/sw/.
6. Murtha Baca, ed., *Introduction to Metadata: Pathways to Digital Information*, version 2.0, available at http://www.getty.edu/research/institute/standards/intrometadata. Accessed 1 June 2002.

7. Metadata (page of the UKOLN website). Accessed 1 June 2002. Available at http://www. ukoln.ac.uk/metadata/.

8. National Research Council, Committee on an Information Technology Strategy for the Library of Congress, *LC21: A Digital Strategy for the Library of Congress* (Washington, D.C.: National Academy Press, 2001), available at http://books.nap.edu/catalog/9940.html? onpi newsdoc072600. Accessed 1 June 2002.

9. Henry Petroski, *The Book on the Bookshelf* (New York: Alfred A. Knopf, 1999).

10. These standards are available in print from the International Organization for Standardization (http://www.iso.ch). The best source for web-accessible versions and additional information about this family of standards is the European Commission's Diffuse Project (http://www.diffuse.org/). See Diffuse's summary page for ISO/IEC 11179 at http://www. diffuse.org/meta.html#ISO11179.

11. IFLA Study Group on the Functional Requirements for Bibliographic Records, *Functional Requirements for Bibliographic Records: Final Report* (Munich: K. G. Saur, 1998), available at http://www.ifla.org/VII/s13/frbr/frbr.htm. Accessed 1 June 2002.

READINGS

Hodge, Gail. *Metadata Made Simpler*. Bethesda, Md.: NISO Press, 2001. Available at http://www.niso.org/news/Metadata_simpler.pdf.

> A good general introduction to metadata schemes and issues, published in hard copy by NISO Press and available on the Web from the NISO website.

IFLA Study Group on the Functional Requirements for Bibliographic Records. *Functional Requirements for Bibliographic Records: Final Report* (Munich: K. G. Saur, 1998). Available at http://www.ifla.org/VII/s13/frbr/frbr.htm.

Jones, Wayne, et al., eds. *Cataloging the Web: Metadata, AACR, and MARC21.* ALCTS Papers on Library Collections and Technical Services no. 10 (Lanham, Md., and London: Scarecrow, 2002).

> Short papers from the Preconference on Metadata for Web Resources, 6–7 July 2000, at the ALA Annual Conference in Chicago.

Tillett, Barbara B. "Bibliographic Relationships." In *Relationships in the Organization of Knowledge,* ed. Carole A. Bean and Rebecca Green (Dordrecht: Kluwer Academic Publishers, 2001), 9–35.

> More about FRBR.

There are several excellent clearinghouses of metadata schemes and related documents. This is by no means an inclusive list:

The Canadian Heritage Information Network, CHIN, maintains a portal to metadata standards in several areas, with some emphasis on museum information (http://www.chin.gc.ca/English/Standards/metadata_description.html).

The Diffuse Project, funded by the European Commission's Information Society Technologies Programme (http://www.diffuse.org/). This site maintains pointers to a large number of metadata-related standards and specifications in a wide range of subject areas.

IFLA maintains a listing of metadata schemes and related documents of interest to the library sector (http://www.ifla.org/II/metadata.htm).

MICI Metadata International Clearinghouse (Interactive), a site maintained by the Association of American Publishers (http://www.metadatainformation.org/). It focuses primarily on metadata of interest to publishers.

2

Syntax, Creation, and Storage

EXCHANGE SYNTAX

We begin this discussion of metadata management with a review of some formats commonly used for representing metadata in machine-readable form. In some cases metadata is stored and processed in local systems in these formats. More commonly, metadata is stored in local database systems but exchanged with other systems using these formats as transport syntaxes. In that case the local system will need to import or export metadata in one or more of these formats.

MARC

The most commonly used syntax in the library environment is, of course, MARC. MARC, standing for Machine-Readable Cataloging, was developed by the Library of Congress (LC) in the mid-1960s, primarily to enable the computer production of catalog cards that could subsequently be distributed through the Cataloging Distribution Service. The existence of MARC, however, completely transformed library systems, both technically and organizationally. MARC enabled the rise of the bibliographic utilities (OCLC, RLIN, WLN) and wide-scale shared cataloging. It made integrated library systems possible and enabled a competitive market in commercial turnkey library management systems. Shared cataloging and similar library systems in turn reinforced a library culture of communication, cooperation, and respect for standards.

For all the influence of MARC, it is important to remember that MARC itself is not a metadata scheme, but one complex component of the multifaceted scheme that comprises traditional library cataloging. It is a "complex" component because, when people refer to MARC, they are generally referring to at least two things: a structure for machine-readable records defined in ANSI/NISO Standard Z39.2, and the set of encoding rules documented in the *MARC21 Format for Bibliographic Data* and other LC publications. (USMARC was renamed MARC21 in 1988 as part of the effort to harmonize the U.S., Canadian, and U.K. MARC formats.)

Standard Z39.2 defines a data transmission format consisting of three parts: a twenty-four-character record *leader* segmented into nine data elements, each of which has some meaning as a code or a count; a record *directory* containing one twelve-character entry for each data field to follow indicating its name, length, and starting position; and a variable number of fields. Each field is defined as either a *control field* (also known as a fixed field) or a *data field* (also called a variable field). A fixed field has a predefined number of bytes that, like the leader, are segmented into data elements with meanings specific to that field. A variable field begins with two one-byte flags known as *indicators*, followed by textual content subdivided into subfields, ending with a field terminator character. Subfields are flagged by a special character known as a *subfield delimiter* (an unprintable ASCII character generally represented as a vertical bar or a dollar sign) followed by a one-character code indicating the type of subfield. Both fixed and variable fields are named in the directory with a three-character *tag*. Figure 2-1 shows the basic MARC structure of leader, directory, control fields, and data fields.

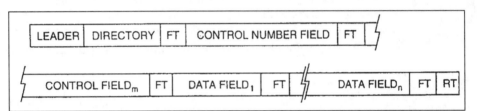

FIGURE 2-1   Structure of a MARC record. Reprinted, by permission, from ANSI/ NISO Z39.2-1994 (2001) Information Interchange Format, 3. © 1994 by NISO Press, National Information Standards Organization. FT indicates a Field Terminator, and RT a Record Terminator.

Note that in this record structure, the name of the field does not occur adjacent to the field data, but rather is given in the record directory along with the starting position of the unlabeled data. However, when MARC data are represented on screen or in print, the field tag is usually shown as a label before the start of the field data. Spacing is also added around subfields for readability:

245 14 $a The sound and the fury / $c by William Faulkner.

Standard Z39.2 defines this rather complex structure, but it has nothing to say about the meanings of the field tags, indicators, and subfields represented in any given bibliographic record. These are defined in documentation issued by the Library of Congress— the *MARC21 Format for Bibliographic Data* and a shorter, web-accessible version called the *MARC21 Concise Format for Bibliographic Data* (http://www.loc.gov/marc/biblio graphic/ecbdhome.html). Z39.2 specifies that a variable field has a three-character tag, two indicator positions, and a variable amount of data subdivided into subfields. The MARC21 documentation specifies that the tag for a main entry personal name field is 100; that the first indicator of this field can take the values 0, 1, or 3, depending on the type of name; that the second indicator is undefined and should always contain a blank; that subfield a contains the surname and/or forename, and so on. Figure 2-2 shows a page from the *MARC21 Concise Format for Bibliographic Data* defining the use of the 100 field.

Together, Z39.2 and the MARC21 publications constitute a transport syntax for the content recorded in traditional library cataloging, indicating how data should be represented for exchange. In fact, MARC21 is a mixture of syntax, semantics, and content rules. It defines the meaning of many data elements not otherwise defined in the library cataloging rules, and it contains or references authority lists for the content of many data elements. Additionally, MARC21 contains processing rules, as indicator values are often used to control sorting, display, or other processing related to field content. For example, an indicator value may flag that a particular label should appear before the field data, or that a certain number of characters be ignored for filing purposes.

MARC is often criticized for being prohibitively complicated. In fact, Z39.2 was designed for an older model of data processing and probably is unnecessarily complex; it is unlikely we would design a record structure like this today. However, the indicator and subfield structure of fields is inherently no more complicated than more modern XML representations of the same information. MARC is complicated because of the enormous amount of content it can convey and the complexity of the content rules used in conjunction with it.

Another criticism of MARC is perhaps more valid—that it is a niche format, used only within the library market, without general-purpose parsing and processing software. Although this is true, note that there are few examples of generic, widely used record structures for textual information before XML. Because of MARC, libraries have for many years been able to exchange cataloging records with one another and with the bibliographic utilities with far more ease than most other businesses have been able to communicate with one another.

HTML

Most users of this text are probably familiar with the basic form of an HTML document. *Tags*, the names of HTML elements, are enclosed within angle brackets. Most tags work in pairs, with an opening tag and a closing tag that are the same except that the closing tag begins with a slash:

<B> text to be displayed in bold </B>

An HTML document begins with an <html> tag (element) and ends with a </html> tag. Within this, documents are generally divided into two more sections, the <head> and the <body>. The <title> tag and <meta> tags appear within the <head> section of the document; the actual content of the web page should appear in the <body>. A very simple web document, then, might look like this:

<HTML>

<HEAD>

MARC 21 Concise Bibliographic: Main Entry Fields (1XX)

Fields 1XX contain a name or a uniform title heading used as a main entry in bibliographic records. Except for the definitions of indicator positions and subfield codes that are field specific, the content designation for each type of name and for uniform titles is consistent for Main Entry (100-130), Series Statement (440-490), Subject Access (600-630), Added Entry (700-730), and Series Added Entry (800-830) fields.

- 100 - MAIN ENTRY--PERSONAL NAME (NR)
- 110 - MAIN ENTRY--CORPORATE NAME (NR)
- 111 - MAIN ENTRY--MEETING NAME (NR)
- 130 - MAIN ENTRY--UNIFORM TITLE (NR)

Information for Translators and Other Users
Items highlighted in red indicate changes made after the 2000 edition of the *MARC 21 Concise Formats* was published and are included in the 2001 printed edition of the *MARC 21 Concise Formats*.

100 - MAIN ENTRY--PERSONAL NAME (NR)

A personal name used as a main entry in a bibliographic record.

Indicators

- First - Type of personal name entry element
  - 0 - Forename
    The name is a forename or is a name consisting of words, initials, letters, etc., that are formatted in direct order.
  - 1 - Surname
    The name is a single or multiple surname formatted in inverted order or a single name without forenames that is known to be a surname.
  - 3 - Family name
    The name represents a family, clan, dynasty, house, or other such group and may be formatted in direct or inverted order.
- Second - Undefined
  - # - Undefined

Subfield Codes

- $a - Personal name (NR)
  A surname and/or forename; letters, initials, abbreviations, phrases, or numbers used in place of a name; or a family name.
- $b - Numeration (NR)
  A roman numeral or a roman numeral and a subsequent part of a forename when the first indicator value is 0.
- $c - Titles and other words associated with a name (R)
- $d - Dates associated with a name (NR)
  Dates of birth, death, or flourishing, or any other date associated with a name.

FIGURE 2-2   Page from the *MARC21 Concise Format for Bibliographic Data*. From Library of Congress, Network Development and MARC Standards Office, *MARC21 Concise Format for Bibliographic Data* 2001, concise edition. Available at http://www.loc.gov/marc/bibliographic/ecbdhome.html.

```
<TITLE>Weather Report for Monday</TITLE>

<META NAME="title" CONTENT="Weather Report for Monday">

</HEAD>

<BODY>

<P>Warmer and slightly cloudy with a 20% chance of afternoon
thunderstorms.</P>

</BODY>

</HTML>
```

Metadata can be embedded in HTML documents using <meta> tags. There are two forms of the <meta> tag, which does not have a closing tag:

```
<META HTTP-EQUIV= "text string1" CONTENT="text string2">

<META NAME="text string1" CONTENT="text string2">
```

Both forms allow metadata to be embedded in documents, but the first form also indicates that when a document is requested, a webserver should use "text string 1" as a response header with "text string 2" as its value. The second form is more commonly used for recording metadata. In this case, the name of the metadata element is recorded as "text string 1" and the value of the element as "text string 2."

```
<META NAME="author" CONTENT="Smith, John">
```

Any label can be supplied as the value of the attribute "name," but it is only useful to the extent that it is recognized by search systems. Many Internet search engines recognize at least a few of the Dublin Core elements, and a local search engine can be programmed to recognize elements from any scheme. Recommended practice is to preface the metadata element name with an indication of the scheme from which it is taken, and use the <link> tag to relate the prefix to a web-accessible definition of the scheme:

```
<META NAME="DC.Creator" CONTENT="Smith, John">

<LINK REL= "schema.DC" HREF= "http://purl.org/DC/elements/1.0/">
```

A complete example of embedded HTML metadata might then be:

```
<HTML>

<HEAD>

<TITLE>Weather Report for Monday</TITLE>

<META NAME="DC.Title" CONTENT="Weather Report for Monday">

<META NAME="DC.Creator" CONTENT="National Weather Service">

<META NAME="DC.Date" CONTENT="2001-12-01">

<LINK REL="schema.DC" HREF="http://purl.org/DC/elements/1.0/">

</HEAD>
```

```
<BODY>
```

\<P>Warmer and slightly cloudy with a 20% chance of afternoon thunderstorms.\</P>

```
</BODY>
```

```
</HTML>
```

SGML

HTML is actually an implementation of the more generalized markup language SGML (ISO 8879:1986 Information processing—Text and office systems—Standard Generalized Markup Language). SGML is formally a *metalanguage*, or a language for describing other languages. SGML specifies generic syntax rules for encoding documents (such as the rule that tag names occur in angle brackets), but does not specify any particular set of tags; rather, it gives the means for anyone to define his or her own set of tags and rules for their use. This is done by creating a *document type definition*, or DTD. One DTD, for example, might be called "HTML" and specify that allowable tags include <title>, <meta>, <link>, <head>, <body>, and <p>, and that <title>, <meta>, and <link> tags must occur only within <head>, while <p> must occur only within <body>.

As illustrated by HTML, SGML markup encodes some data content between start and end tags and other data content as the value of *attributes*, which follow the name of the opening tag. For example, the <meta> tag shown here has an attribute "name" whose value follows the equals sign:

<META NAME="title" ...>

Attributes may be defined as optional or required, and a list of allowable attribute values may be specified. An SGML element can be defined to have both textual data and one or more attributes, only text, or only attributes. Elements can also be defined to take other elements as content, in which case the outer element is called a *wrapper*, while the nested elements are *subelements*. For example, the wrapper element <date> may take <month>, <day>, and <year> as subelements:

<date>

    <month>02

    <day>12

    <year>2002

</date>

An element can also be defined to take no text or subelements as data, in which case it is known as an *empty element*. A line break, for example, can be indicated by an empty element inserted in the text where the line should break:

<lb></lb>

SGML is in many ways a good encoding syntax for metadata. It was designed to handle variable-length textual data gracefully. An unlimited number of elements (tags and attributes) can be defined, and their names can be descriptive of their contents. The Encoded Archival Description (EAD), for example, uses the tag <titleproper> for the title proper, which is certainly more mnemonic than the MARC equivalent, "245 sub-field a." SGML is inherently hierarchical and can enforce rules of hierarchy, making it a perfect medium for expressing the types of hierarchical relationships found within collections and among works, expressions, manifestations, and items. SGML inheritance allows elements at a lower level of hierarchy to inherit information encoded at higher levels of the hierarchy, so descriptive data do not have to be repeated. In addition, the ability of SGML elements to contain within them other elements makes it possible to delimit metadata in very flexible ways. For example, in this portion of an EAD finding aid, the title statement (<titlestmt>) contains a title proper and an author:

<titlestmt>

<titleproper>A Guide to the Paul A. M. Dirac Collection</titleproper>

<author>Processed by Burt Altman and Charles Conaway</author>

</titlestmt>

However, because the EAD DTD allows it, it would also be possible to delimit some or all personal names, in order to treat them specially for indexing or display:

<titlestmt>

<titleproper>A Guide to the <persname>Paul A. M. Dirac</persname> Collection</titleproper>

<author>Processed by Burt Altman and Charles Conaway</author>

</titlestmt>

The semantics of any metadata scheme could be represented in SGML by creating an appropriate DTD. The Library of Congress actually created a DTD for encoding MARC21 data in SGML while preserving all MARC21 tagging. Using this DTD, a title encoded in MARC21 like this:

245 04 $a The health of dairy cattle / $c edited by Anthony H. Andrews.

could be encoded in SGML like this:

<mrcb245 i1=0 i2=4><mrcb245-a>The health of dairy cattle /<mrcb245-c> edited by Anthony H. Andrews.

A number of metadata schemes are actually defined as SGML DTDs. That is, rather than using syntax-independent names and definitions for each metadata element, the elements are defined in terms of SGML tags and attributes. When a metadata scheme is defined by a DTD, supporting tools are useful, as not everyone involved in resource description can be expected to understand a DTD. One useful tool is a *tag library*, a document that lists all the SGML elements and attributes alphabetically, along with their definitions and human-readable rules for their use. Figure 2-3 shows an entry in the EAD Tag Library, version 1.0.

\<div\> Text Division

Description:

A generic element that designates a major section of text within \<frontmatter\>. Examples of these text divisions include a title page, preface, acknowledgments, or instructions for using a finding aid. Use the \<head\> element to identify the \<div\>'s purpose.

May contain:

address, blockquote, chronlist, div, head, list, note, p, table

May occur within:

div, frontmatter

Attributes:

ALTRENDER	#IMPLIED, CDATA
AUDIENCE	#IMPLIED, external, internal
ID	#IMPLIED, ID

Example:

```
<frontmatter>
<titlepage>
    [other possible elements and text... ]
</titlepage>
<div><head>Acknowledgements</head>
<p>The University of Ishtaba Manuscript Library wishes to acknowledge the
generosity of the family of Edgar Holden for an endowment in support of
the processing and maintenance of this collection and the Clark Foundation
for grant funding in support of the encoding of this and other finding
aids using the Encoded Archival Description standard.</p></div>
    [other possible elements and text... ]
</frontmatter>
```

FIGURE 2-3   Example of an XML tag library. From the *Encoded Archival Description: Tag Library,* version 1.0. Chicago: The Society of American Archivists, 1998. Reprinted by permission of the Society of American Archivists.

XML

Despite the many strengths of SGML, it has one significant disadvantage: it is a difficult language for programs to process. Because of this, relatively few software applications have been designed to support the creation, storage, modification, and web display of SGML-encoded text, and those that do exist are complex. XML can be thought of as a subset of SGML designed with tighter rules, fewer features, and fewer options, in order to make it easier to process. For example, in SGML, end tags can be omitted under certain circumstances, and attribute values may or may not be enclosed within quotation marks. In XML, if an element has an end tag, that tag must be used and an attribute value must always appear in quotation marks. The preceding SGML example would have to be encoded differently in XML:

\<mrcb245 i1="0" i2="4"\>\<mrcb245-a\>The health of dairy cattle /\</mrcb245a\>
\<mrcb245-c\>edited by Anthony H. Andrews.\</mrcb245-c\>\</mrcb245\>

Other differences are intended to make XML more suitable for use on the World Wide Web. For example, XML tag names are case sensitive (that is, <META> and <meta> are two different data elements) and can contain non-ASCII UNICODE characters. This makes XML better adapted for an international environment in which usage of the roman alphabet cannot be assumed.

The development of XML and related specifications is an active initiative of the World Wide Web Consortium (W3C).[1] Related specifications approved or under development include an XML linking language (XLink); an XML query language (XQuery); a stylesheet specification (XSL, Extensible Stylesheet Language); and XHTML, an XML-compatible reformulation of HTML. An important related activity is the development of XML Schema, an alternative way of defining document types that supports more structural rules and more content validation than the DTD. The Library of Congress has developed an XML Schema called MARCXML for MARC21 records. According to that schema, the title field noted earlier would be encoded:

<datafield tag="245" ind1="0" ind2="4">

    <subfield code="a">The health of dairy cattle /</subfield>

    <subfield code="c">edited by Anthony H. Andrews.</subfield>

</datafield>

XML is important because it is becoming the language of the Web. Browsers are incorporating support for XML-encoded documents, and many applications have arisen to support XML encoding, storage, retrieval, and display. Some of the more recently developed metadata schemes, such as the Data Documentation Initiative (DDI), have been defined as XML DTDs, and schemes like the EAD, initially developed as SGML DTDs, have been migrated to use XML DTDs. It is likely that future metadata schemes will be defined using XML Schema rather than DTDs.

RDF

The Resource Description Framework, or RDF, is an attempt to represent metadata on the Web with sufficient rigor that it is not only machine-readable, but also machine-understandable. Formally, RDF is a data model for representing resources, their properties, and the values of those properties, and in theory this data model could be expressed in any number of syntaxes. However, when we think of RDF, we generally think of its XML representation, and most of the RDF specification concerns the grammar of expressing (or "serializing") the RDF data model in XML.[2]

Fundamental to RDF is the notion of namespaces, which can be thought of as web-accessible versions of metadata schema. Every metadata element in an RDF description should be prefaced with a label associating it with a particular namespace. This accomplishes two purposes: first, the element name is associated with a way of obtaining its definition, and second, elements from multiple metadata schemes can be used together without ambiguity to describe a single resource.

The Dublin Core description of the weather report shown earlier embedded in HTML could be represented in simple RDF as shown here:

```
<?xml version="1.0"?>
<!DOCTYPE rdf:RDF SYSTEM "http://dublincore.org/documents/
2001/04/11/dcmes-xml/dcmes-xml-dtd.dtd">
<rdf:RDF xmlns:rdf="http://www.w3.org/1999/02/22-rdf-syntax-ns#"
    xmlns:dc="http://purl.org/dc/elements/1.1/">
<rdf:Description about="http://[URL of weather report page]">
    <dc:title>Weather Report for Monday</dc:title>
    <dc:creator>National Weather Service</dc:creator>
    <dc:date>2001-12-01</dc:date>
</rdf:Description>
</rdf:RDF>
```

The RDF record begins by declaring two namespaces—the RDF specification itself and the Dublin Core—and associating these with the arbitrary labels "rdf" and "dc," respectively. This tells us that any element name prefixed with "rdf" is defined in the document at http://www.w3.org/1999/02/22-rdf-syntax-ns#, and any element name prefixed with "dc" is defined in the document at http://purl.org.dc/elements.1.1/.

Following this, we have an RDF <description> element, which groups statements pertaining to a single resource. The "about" attribute identifies the resource by giving its identifier, in this example a URL. Finally, we have three Dublin Core elements appropriately prefixed with "dc."

RDF can be embedded within HTML; the proper browser treatment is to ignore it, but some browsers may actually try to display the content. It is more common for the RDF to be created as a stand-alone external document. An HTML page can refer to its RDF description by means of a <link> tag:

```
<HTML>
<HEAD>
<TITLE>Weather Report for Monday</TITLE>
<LINK REL="meta" HREF="[URL of the RDF description]">
</HEAD>
<BODY>
<P>Warmer and slightly cloudy with a 20% chance of afternoon
thunderstorms.</P>
</BODY>
</HTML>
```

RDF imposes additional structural constraints on XML, which can be seen as a benefit or a disadvantage depending on what one is trying to accomplish. RDF is also more verbose. Some metadata applications will want to define their transport syntax in

RDF to take advantage of its potential machine-understandability, while other applications will prefer simple XML.

METADATA CREATION AND STORAGE

When metadata is created by individuals, it is generally done with the aid of some software application. In libraries, where AACR2/MARC metadata creation is a mature activity, there are two basic models for processing. In the first, resource description is done through the shared cataloging systems of one of the bibliographic utilities. Both OCLC and RLIN support the creation of MARC/AACR2 cataloging records, and OCLC through the CORC (Cooperative Online Resource Catalog) system (now a part of OCLC Connexion) supports a set of metadata semantics that can be represented either in MARC or as Dublin Core. Because these systems have accumulated huge central databases, it is possible to search for and often find an existing record applicable to the resource being described, which can then be "claimed" as the library's own record, with or without modifications. Records created in this manner can be exported from the central system and imported into a library's local system for display in the local catalog. This shared cataloging reduces the time, expertise, and expense required to create records and cuts down on data entry errors.

In the second model, records are created through the library's integrated library system (ILS) and may or may not later be contributed to a bibliographic utility. Most systems support the local input and edit of MARC cataloging records, and some vendors have begun adding support for other metadata schemes as well. Both the local ILS and the bibliographic utilities have relatively sophisticated interfaces for entering and verifying the correctness of MARC data, or at least for the content designation of that data. For example, the programs can check that a field contains only valid indicator values and valid subfield encoding. Although programs cannot check that the actual text entered is correct and follows the appropriate rulesets, many ILSs have fairly sophisticated capabilities for spell-checking and for verifying name and subject headings against the appropriate authority files.

MARC metadata is rarely stored in Z39.2 format. Most systems will deconstruct the data elements into relational database tables. Separate keyword and string indexes are generally built from the base data to optimize retrieval. Despite this, library systems are extremely cognizant of MARC structure, and special handling routines aware of the semantics of indicator values and subfields are commonplace.

Although library systems have been supporting the creation and maintenance of MARC records for decades, the need to create other forms of metadata is relatively new, and systems to support this are less mature and show wider variation. Many of these are developed in-house rather than purchased from commercial vendors, although generalized SGML and XML editing tools may also be used. Newer versions of general-purpose word-processing programs support XML documents, but use of special authoring programs is preferred. The current generation of authoring tools tends to handle both SGML and XML, and provides such functionality as using a DTD to create a template for data entry, checking to ensure entered data is well-formed XML, checking to ensure entered data are valid (conform to the DTD), displaying nested markup with appropriate indentation, and using stylesheets to tailor views of the data. Another common approach for simple metadata structures is to use a web form as a template for data entry. The data are then validity checked and converted into storage format—for example, rows in a relational database table. Some metadata initiatives have sponsored the development of data entry tools or have promoted tools developed by independent third parties. Many of these tools, however, are better for initial data creation than for ongoing maintenance of the data over time.

Once the SGML or XML metadata is created, it must be stored, indexed for retrieval, and reformatted for display. There are two fundamentally different approaches to the storage and retrieval of SGML/XML data from database systems: data-centric and document-centric. In the data-centric approach, the SGML/XML markup is seen as fundamentally a transport syntax. The database system provides tools for importing and exporting marked-up data, but stores the data elements themselves in relational or object-oriented structures. Data-centric systems are commonly used for storing business or scientific data that may be exchanged in SGML/XML but have no other use for markup. Document-centric systems are generally used when the markup is integral to the content itself—for example, for publishing systems for books and articles. These systems generally use native SGML or XML databases that can actually preserve the entire structure of the document. Content management systems are application packages that integrate all functions pertaining to the document-centric approach, including authoring, storage and maintenance, query, and presentation.

Metadata can be managed under either approach. It is quite valid to view the SGML/XML markup as only a transport syntax for metadata records, and to store and retrieve the metadata elements from a traditional data management system, such as a relational database. It is also valid to see metadata records as documents in their own right, best handled within content management systems. This is especially true of the more complex SGML/XML-based schemes, such as the EAD, in which the metadata has many of the characteristics of textual documents.

ILS vendors are beginning to add to their systems the capability to create, index, and display SGML/XML-based metadata schemes, and even to allow libraries to define their own local schemes. These modules are not as mature as the MARC-based modules, but they appear to be a focal point for development. Although at this time these are generally "add-on" products, available at additional cost, we can expect them to become more integrated with the base systems and to more closely integrate the handling of MARC and other metadata as non-MARC schemes become more prevalent.

NOTES

1. Extensible Markup Language (XML) (home page of the W3C XML Activity), available at http://www.w3.org/XML/. Accessed 3 June 2002.
2. Resource Description Framework (RDF) Model and Syntax Specification, W3C Recommendation 22 February 1999, available at http://www.w3.org/TR/REC-rdf-syntax/. Accessed 3 June 2002.

READINGS

Furrie, Betty. *Understanding MARC Bibliographic: Machine-Readable Cataloging.* 5th ed., 1998. Available at http://www.loc.gov/marc/umb/.

> A simple introduction to MARC basics written for the reader with no prior knowledge of MARC.

MARC Standards (page of the Library of Congress Network Development and MARC Standards Office website). Available at http://lcweb.loc.gov/marc/.

> This site contains extensive, authoritative documentation related to MARC, including links to the *MARC21 Concise Format* documents and code lists, information about proposed and recent changes to MARC21, and representations in SGML and XML.

Miller, Eric. "An Introduction to the Resource Description Framework." *D-Lib Magazine* (May 1998). Available at http://www.dlib.org/dlib/may98/miller/05miller.html.

> An early but easily understandable introduction to RDF. For more complete and more recent documentation, see the website of the W3C's RDF activity at http://www.w3.org/RDF/.

Text Encoding Initiative Consortium. *A Gentle Introduction to XML* (extracted from *TEI P4: Guidelines for Electronic Text Encoding and Interchange,* 2002). Available at http://www.tei-c.org/Guidelines2/gentleintro.pdf.

> This introduction to XML is also part of the introduction to TEI P4, but was used so frequently by itself it was published as a separate document. There is also "A Gentle Introduction to SGML" in the introduction to the third edition of the TEI guidelines, available on the Web through the University of Virginia (see http://etext.lib.virginia.edu/tei-tocs1.html).

Vocabularies, Classification, and Identifiers

3

Earlier we said that metadata schemes consist of semantics, syntax, and content rules. Content rules govern how the value of a metadata element is recorded. They can specify how the value of an element is determined (for example, the rules for determining main entry in AACR2), the format in which a value is represented (for example, the ISO 8601 standard for representing dates), or the set or range of values an element can take (for example, an authority list).

In this chapter we examine three special types of content: controlled vocabularies, classification, and identifiers.

VOCABULARIES

In ordinary language, a person's vocabulary is the set of words and phrases he uses to express himself. Everyone has a different vocabulary. The vocabulary of a three-year-old child is quite different from the vocabularies of her parents, and the vocabulary of a mathematician is different from that of a nurse, an auto mechanic, or a librarian.

In the language of metadata, a *vocabulary* is the universe of values that can be used for a particular metadata element. For some elements, such as titles, there are few restrictions on the terms that can be used. For other elements, the possible values may be strictly limited. A controlled vocabulary in the broadest sense is the sum of the limitations on the values a metadata element may take. In a narrower sense, a controlled vocabulary is a predefined set of allowable values. The VRA Core, for example, specifies that the valid data values for the Record Type field are "work" and "image." This is a small controlled vocabulary. The *Art and Architecture Thesaurus* (AAT) is a more elaborate controlled vocabulary, containing about 125,000 terms related to art, architecture, and material culture.

The main methods for implementing controlled vocabularies are term lists, author-ity files, and thesauri, which are used by metadata creators to assign terms (words or phrases) from the vocabulary. Simple *term lists* can be used when the number of terms is relatively small and their meanings relatively unambiguous. Authority files and the-sauri are used for larger and more complex vocabularies. *Authority files* are compilations of authorized terms used by an organization or in a particular database. Authority files do not show relationships between terms (except perhaps to map from unused terms to valid terms) and so are most appropriate for flat (nonhierarchical) vocabularies, such as the names of persons and organizations. A *thesaurus* is an arrangement of a controlled vocab-ulary in which all allowable terms are given and relationships between terms are shown.

Relationships defined by thesauri include equivalence, homography, hierarchy, and association.[1] Equivalence occurs when different terms (including synonyms and spelling variants) represent the same concept. One term is chosen as the descriptor, and the equivalent terms are listed as "Use for" terms. In the AAT, for example, the descrip-tor "single-family dwellings" has a long list of "Use for" terms, including "single family homes," "single family houses," and "single family dwellings." Homography involves a string of letters that has multiple meanings. A thesaurus will disambiguate homographic descriptors, usually by adding some qualifying term, for example, "Radius (bone)."

Hierarchy is represented by use of broader terms (BT) and narrower terms (NT). For example, "Photograph albums" and "Scrapbooks" may be narrower terms of the broader term "Albums." These are particularly useful in searching, as material indexed under a broader term may be relevant to a more specific search: a user finding nothing under "Scrapbooks" may want to search "Albums" as well. Related terms (RT) are des-ignated when a searcher interested in one concept is likely to be interested in another. Related-term relationships are reciprocal (if A is related to B, B is related to A) and should not be hierarchical or they would be expressed as BT/NT relationships. The Library of Congress Subject Headings (LCSH) lists "Presidents" and "Ex-presidents," "Art objects" and "Antiques,"and "Aquatic sports" and "Boats and boating" as related terms.

Controlled vocabularies are used to improve retrieval. In natural language the same concept can often be expressed by several different words or phrases. Computer chips may be called microchips or integrated circuits; civil liberties may be called civil rights; dedications of buildings may be called building dedications. The situation is exacer-bated when audiences with different vocabularies are involved. What is a boo-boo to a child is a bruise to his parents and a hematoma to a nurse. When the full text of docu-ments is available for indexing, there is a reasonable chance that synonyms and alternate expressions will appear within the text. Metadata records, on the other hand, are terser, and metadata creators must make careful choices about the data values they supply or the searcher could miss relevant resources. A controlled vocabulary seeks to assign a single index term to every concept, and thereby to collocate like materials together under the same descriptors.

This is useful, of course, only insofar as the language of the searcher is or can be made congruent with the controlled vocabulary. A vocabulary designed for medical professionals should select different terms than one designed for mathematicians. Even within a single target audience, however, it can be difficult for searchers to anticipate the chosen term. If nothing else, the constraints of vocabulary design in some cases dis-courage the use of natural language; a searcher looking for works on dog breeding may not intuitively think to search for "dogs—breeding." There may be no clearly preferred term within a group of natural synonyms. Also, the broader the audience, the less likely there will be consensus on any term, and the more difficult it will be for those who maintain the controlled vocabulary to keep up with new concepts and changing terminology in popular use. In LCSH, works on campaign finance reform will be found under "Campaign funds," because the subject heading vocabulary has not caught up with user interest in the more specific topic.

There are three basic methods for ameliorating dissonance between the searcher's vocabulary and the indexer's. The first is to make the controlled vocabulary itself available to the user. Many libraries still leave bound copies of the LCSH "red books" in public catalog areas for library patrons to use. In the online environment, retrieval systems can link to online term lists or thesauri, or incorporate thesaurus search and display in query construction. The Colorado Digitization Project (CDP), for example, has created term lists of Colorado subject terms and Colorado author names. These lists are searchable from the CDP website, and searchers can cut-and-paste terms from the lists into the form for searching the CDP union catalog.[2]

A second method is to incorporate records that show term relationships into retrieval. A user searching "Vietnam war" in my library's catalog will retrieve this cross-reference:

VIETNAM WAR 1961 1975

*Search under:

Vietnamese Conflict, 1961-1975

In some systems, the user's search is automatically redirected. There is some disagreement whether this helps the searcher by saving a step or contributes to confusion by yielding a result set with no apparent relationship to the search term.

A third technique relies on searchers finding some relevant material with any search. They can then examine the metadata record to see what terms were applied in fields with controlled vocabularies and do subsequent searches on those terms to retrieve more relevant materials. Some retrieval systems facilitate this by treating the contents of these fields as hyperlinks that are automatically used as search arguments when clicked.

These methods are increasingly ineffective in today's networked environment. In a paper environment, users were forced to search one file at a time, with the consequence that they were always aware of which database (card catalog, book index, etc.) they were searching, and had a reasonable chance of acquiring some familiarity with the vocabularies of those resources. Now, a user sitting at a single computer terminal can select from hundreds of databases and often has the option of searching across several different databases simultaneously. The searcher is far more likely to encounter multiple controlled vocabularies and far less likely to be familiar with the vocabularies he or she is encountering. Additionally, the Internet/Web environment is truly global, exacerbating the problem of multiple vocabularies with that of multiple languages. These problems are inspiring many research and development efforts to devise approaches to vocabulary interoperability. Some of these approaches include techniques for mapping between vocabularies, providing *entry vocabularies* (indexes) to controlled vocabularies, and using classification systems or other types of conceptual mappings as entry points to term-based retrieval.

Despite impediments to using controlled vocabularies in searching, it is generally acknowledged that use of controlled vocabularies in retrieval systems has the potential to improve both precision and recall. Many metadata schemes encourage or require the use of controlled vocabularies for the values of at least some metadata elements. Generally there must be some mechanism for specifying the vocabulary used as well as the term(s) taken from it. In the EAD, for example, all tags that may have values taken from controlled vocabularies allow the attribute "source":

<controlaccess>

<subject source="lcsh">Fishery law and legislation—Minnesota.</subject>

</controlaccess>

CLASSIFICATION

Classification schemes are another form of controlled vocabulary. Classification schemes group related resources into a hierarchical structure, or tree. Each node on the tree is designated with a code, called a *notation*, which may be alphabetic, alphanumeric, or numeric. Textual definitions, descriptors, or both are associated with the notations, providing an explanation of the classification code as well as a textual mode of entry into the hierarchy.

Classification schemes may be general (applying to all knowledge) or specific to a particular discipline, subject, national literature, or other focus. In all cases, the classification begins with the relevant universe of knowledge and successively divides it into classes and subclasses. For example, the National Library of Medicine (NLM) classification has two main classes—preclinical sciences and medicine—that are divided into eight and thirty-three major subclasses, respectively. Each subclass is further subdivided as appropriate. In any classification scheme, a class must be subdivided into subclasses according to some characteristic or principle of subdivision. A classification of artworks, for example, could group works by genre, by artist, or by period. Which is the chosen characteristic for the higher-level classes will determine whether all works by Michelangelo fall together or are dispersed among other paintings, sculptures, and so on.

The two main types of classification systems are known as enumerative and faceted. An *enumerative classification* system attempts to list all possible subjects and their notations in a hierarchy, and each work that is classified occupies a single location within the hierarchy. The Library of Congress Classification (LCC) and the Dewey Decimal Classification (DDC) are both enumerative systems, as are most of the classification systems devised in the nineteenth century. Figure 3-1 shows a section of the LCC outline for subclass QL (Zoology); general works on butterflies would be classified as QL 544.

Faceted classification systems define broad general properties of subjects, called *facets*, and require the classifier to identify, within each class, all defined facets appropriate to the work and then to combine these in a prescribed way. The Universal Decimal Classification (UDC), which is widely used in Europe, is a faceted system.

In libraries, classification schemes do double duty as ways of organizing knowledge and ways of organizing books on shelves. The classification notation serves as the basis

```
Subclass QL

QL1-991                  Zoology
QL1-355                    General
                             Including geographical distribution
QL360-599.82               Invertebrates
QL461-599.82                 Insects
QL605-739.8                Chordates.  Vertebrates
QL614-639.8                 Fishes
QL640-669.3                 Reptiles and amphibians
QL671-699                  Birds
QL700-739.8                Mammals
QL750-795                 Animal Behavior
QL791-795                   Stories and anecdotes
QL799-799.5               Morphology
QL801-950.9              Anatomy
QL951-991               Embryology
```

FIGURE 3-1   Library of Congress Classification Outline for subclass QL, Zoology.

for *call numbers*, which denote the shelving locations of library materials. However, classification notation and call numbers should not be confused: the first locates a work within a hierarchical representation of knowledge, while the latter uniquely identifies items. Unlike classification schemes, call number schemes must have some method of disambiguating multiple works on the same topic and multiple copies of the same work.

Classification has the potential for great utility in the online environment, although this remains largely unexploited. Classification has been used by major Internet portals like Yahoo! to organize electronic resources. Systems with the ability to allow classification-based searching and to present search results in classified order would enable the user to browse a virtual shelf. The ability to browse a classification system itself could provide an entry point for searching and a context for search terms. Classification notation is language-neutral and could provide a bridging mechanism between different vocabularies or even different languages. Unfortunately, just as few systems make thesauri available for browsing online, fewer still give access to classification schemes, possibly because until recently, few schemes were available electronically. The availability of DDC and LCC in machine-readable form may improve this situation.[3]

IDENTIFIERS

Identifiers are another special form of metadata. A bibliographic identifier is a string intended to uniquely identify a logical bibliographic entity. Some types of identifiers are derived from bibliographic data, but most types are assigned by an authority (the *naming authority*). The naming authority must ensure that the identifiers assigned are unique within the scope of the identifier system (also called a *namespace*).

Different identifier systems have different scopes, in terms of both the types of materials they can be assigned to and the types of entities they apply to. Some identifiers pertain to works, while others pertain to manifestations or items. For example, barcodes and ISBNs (International Standard Book Numbers) are two types of identifiers. For a barcode, the assigning authority is the barcoding library, and each barcode uniquely identifies an item in that library's collection. For the ISBN, the assigning authority for U.S. publications is the U.S. ISBN Agency, and each ISBN uniquely identifies an edition of a publication in some format (roughly a manifestation). In general, the narrower the scope of the naming authority, the lower the level of entity the identifiers apply to.

Several types of identifiers are commonly used in bibliographic systems. The ISBN applies to monographic publications in all formats. It is a ten-character string divided into four sections separated by hyphens or spaces, for example, ISBN 90-70002-04-3. The International ISBN Agency coordinates the work of national and regional ISBN agencies that assign ISBN prefixes to different publishers. Publishers are then responsible for assigning unique ISBN strings to their own publications. Hardcover and paperback editions of books must be assigned different ISBNs, as must different electronic formats (e.g., RocketBook or PDF).

The ISSN is an international code applying to serial publications. The ISSN is an eight-character identifier. The first seven digits identify the title and the eighth is a check digit that can be a number or the letter "X." The ISSN is always displayed as two groups of four characters separated by a hyphen: ISSN 1140-3853. The ISSN uses a system of distributed assignment similar to that of the ISBN. Both the ISSN and the ISBN are international (ISO) and U.S. national (ANSI/NISO) standards.

The BICI (Book Item and Contribution Identifier) and the SICI (Serial Item and Contribution Identifier) are national standard identifiers that apply to component parts of books and serials, such as chapters, issues, and articles. They are based on the ISBN and ISSN, respectively, using those codes to identify the title and then going on to identify the part within the title. Unlike most identifiers, BICIs and SICIs are not assigned and registered but are derived from the bibliographic data for the item. For example, an article by Nikhil Hutheesing, "Keeping the Seats Warm" in *Forbes,* January 1, 1996, vol. 157, no. 1, p. 62, is identified by the SICI: 0015-6914(19960101)157:1<62:KTSW>2.0. TX;2-F. Here the ISSN 0015-6914 identifies the journal title, the parenthetical "(19960101)" is derived from the chronology (date) of the issue, "157:1" is derived from the enumeration (volume and issue), "<62:KTSW>" is derived from the starting page and title, and the remainder of the string is a series of required coded values for such things as checksum and format.

The ISBN, ISSN, BICI, and SICI can be assigned to publications in both printed and electronic forms. The Digital Object Identifier (DOI) is primarily intended for digital publications. The DOI has two parts, a prefix and a suffix. Prefixes are assigned by a distributed system of registration agencies, which are distinguished not by geographical area, as for the ISSN and ISBN, but by the user communities they serve and the services they offer. The prefix always begins with "10." and identifies the content producer who registered the DOI, while the suffix is an arbitrary string identifying the actual content. For example, the HTML version of the *DOI Handbook* has the DOI "10.1000/102." The prefix "1000" indicates the DOI was assigned by the International DOI Foundation (IDF), while the suffix "102" identifies the publication specifically. The PDF version of the same handbook has the DOI "10.1000/106."

The DOI is widely used by publishers for digital content because it is actionable; that is, it functions as a clickable hotlink in a browser. This is because the DOI can be *resolved* (translated) into a URL by a resolution system run by the IDF. As a result, the DOI is commonly used for reference linking and similar purposes. For example, one journal article may cite as a reference a previously published journal article, giving the DOI of the earlier article as part of the citation. When a reader clicks on that DOI, the identifier is routed to the IDF's DOI resolver, where the identifier is looked up and an associated URL retrieved. The reader's request is then redirected to the target of the URL. There is no inherent reason why other types of identifiers could not have similar systems of resolution, and, in fact, the European Union currently is experimenting with the development of a resolution system for the SICI. However, the infrastructure to support resolution has always been part of the DOI system.

The Uniform Resource Locator (URL) is not formally an identifier using the definition given earlier, because a URL designates the location of a physical item rather than the identity of a logical entity. The URL specifies an access service (commonly HTTP, but also possibly FTP, TELNET, or others) and the location of an item within that service. Because it is common for digital objects to be moved from one server to another, an object may have many URLs over its lifetime, and the same content will have different URLs as it is made available through different services.

The Internet Engineering Task Force (IETF), the organization that oversees standards development for the Internet, has for some time recognized the limitations of URLs and the need to support a variety of true identifiers in the networked environment. IETF working groups have developed the Uniform Resource Name (URN) framework as an architecture to accommodate this. A URN is an identifier that, like the DOI, can be resolved to one or more URLs. Also like the DOI, the URN consists of two parts: a string designating the naming authority and a string assigned by the naming authority to designate the identified object. Other types of identifiers fit within the URN framework as long as they can be appropriately expressed in the URN syntax. An ISBN, for example, can be expressed as a URN as "URN:ISBN:0-395-36341-1." The prefix "URN" is required to identify the string as a URN, "ISBN" identifies the naming authority, and "0-395-36341-1" is the object identifier assigned by the ISBN authority.

In the URN framework, there would be some global mechanism for routing URNs to the appropriate resolution services for the particular naming authority. At this time, such a global mechanism does not exist, nor is there native browser support for URNs as opposed to URLs. Therefore, many metadata schemes that require actionable identifiers for specific data elements specify the use of Uniform Resource Identifiers (URIs). In the IETF framework, both URLs and URNs are forms of URI. Specifying URIs as metadata content permits the use of URLs in the short term and URNs in the longer term.

Identifiers are perceived as crucial to managing content in the digital environment. In addition to identifiers just mentioned, any number of identifiers are in use or under development for particular types of materials. Some of these include the International Standard Technical Report Number (ISRN) for technical reports; the International Standard Recording Code (ISRC) for identifying sound and audiovisual recordings on CD and other media; the International Standard Music Number (ISMN) for printed music publications; the International Standard Musical Work Code (ISWC) and International Standard Audiovisual Number (ISAN), both of which identify works as opposed to particular publications or manifestations; and the International Standard Textual Work Code (ISTC) under development for identifying textual works.

NOTES

1. National Information Standards Organization, NISO Z39.19-1993(R1998), *Guidelines for the Construction, Format, and Management of Monolingual Thesauri* (Bethesda, Md.: NISO Press, 1998), available at http://www.niso.org/standards/resources/Z39-19.pdf. Accessed 6 June 2002.
2. William A. Garrison, "Retrieval Issues for the Colorado Digitization Project's Heritage Database," *D-Lib Magazine* 7, no. 10 (October 2001), available at http://www.dlib.org/dlib/october01/garrison/10garrison.html. Accessed 6 June 2002.
3. Diane Vizine-Goetz, *Using Library Classification Schemes for Internet Resources*, available at http://www.oclc.org/oclc/man/colloq/v-g.htm. Accessed 10 June 2002.

READINGS

Lynch, Clifford A. "Identifiers and Their Role in Networked Information Applications." *ARL: A Bimonthly Newsletter of Research Library Issues and Actions* 194 (October 1997). Available at http://www.arl.org/newsltr/194/identifier.html.

Metadata Resources (page of the UKOLN Metadata Resources Clearinghouse) has a fairly comprehensive bibliography related to identifiers and URIs. Available at http://www.ukoln.ac.uk/metadata.resources/.

Milstead, Jessica L. *Use of Thesauri in the Full-text Environment.* 1998. Available at http://www.jelem.com/useof.htm/. Accessed 10 June 2002.

Sevonius, Elaine. "Use of Classification in Online Retrieval." *Library Resources and Technical Services* 27, no. 1 (January/March 1983): 76–80.

> Two papers exploring uses of thesauri and classification, respectively, in the online retrieval environment.

Approaches to Interoperability

4

In the network environment, applications are concerned with many types of interoperability. Interoperability may mean that two applications share a common communications protocol, that one client can interact with many servers, or that data can be reused in different contexts. When we talk about interoperability in relation to metadata, we are generally talking about *search interoperability*, or the ability to perform a search over diverse sets of metadata records and obtain meaningful results. The metadata may have been created according to the same scheme but by different individuals or organizations, or it may represent the application of multiple schemes.

UNION CATALOGS

One way to achieve search interoperability is to build a central database of metadata from multiple sources. Traditional MARC-based library union catalogs are one good example of this. Union catalogs can be implemented at any level from institutional (for example, a public library with many branches) to international (for example, OCLC's WorldCat). Many statewide and regional resource-sharing consortia support union catalogs or specialty files, such as union lists of serials.

There are several different models for implementing union catalogs. Under one model, participating libraries send copies of their own cataloging records to some organization that maintains a central searchable catalog. For example, MELVYL, the old union catalog of the University of California (UC), received weekly or monthly updates from as many as twenty-nine different data sources, including the cataloging departments of the UC libraries, the California State Library, and affiliated institute libraries.[1] Under another model, records may be created directly in the union catalog database and then copied into the holding library's own local system. In either of these approaches, records for the same title contributed to the union database by different institutions may be maintained as duplicates or may be consolidated into a single master record showing multiple holding locations. A third technique creates a kind of pseudo–union catalog by building a union index over multiple catalog files, rather than by maintaining a consolidated catalog database. When entries are selected from the index, records from the source catalogs are displayed.

Union catalogs of this sort are relatively effective because the library community as a whole shares a common data format (MARC21) and a more or less common set of cataloging rules. Not only are the records in the central file relatively homogeneous, but they are similar to those stored in the contributing local library catalogs, so the search and retrieval facilities in the union catalog are likely to be familiar to the searcher.

It is also possible but more complicated to build union catalogs from non-homogeneous sources of metadata. One approach is to convert from the various metadata schemes to a common format for storage and indexing. The Dublin Core has proved useful as a kind of "least-common-denominator" set of elements into which richer schemes can be mapped for this purpose. This approach was taken by the Colorado Digitization Project (CDP), which maintains a union database of metadata contributed by Colorado archives, historical societies, libraries, and museums (http://coloradodigital.coalliance.org). Participating institutions are allowed to send metadata in several different formats, but they have to provide a specification for mapping their own data elements to a common set of elements based on Dublin Core. The CDP centrally converts contributed metadata records into the common format before loading them into the union catalog.

Another example is provided by sites that have implemented the Open Archives Initiative (OAI) Metadata Harvesting Protocol. The Open Archives model is a variation on the traditional union catalog in which metadata from the various contributing sites is collected by harvesting rather than by contribution (a pull rather than push model), somewhat similar to the way an Internet spider collects HTML content. The metadata harvesting protocol itself is a simple protocol in which queries and responses are carried over HTTP. A harvester application can query a metadata repository for a list of the metadata formats supported by the repository, a list of record sets supported by the repository, and/or a list of the identifiers of all the records within a repository or record set. The application can also request the repository to export a single metadata record or group of records. An OAI-compliant data provider must be able to respond to these requests and export metadata in at least one format, an XML rendition of unqualified Dublin Core, although other formats can be supported by agreement between the data provider and the harvester. In this case the work of converting to the common format is done by each participating data provider rather than at the central site as with CDP.

Metadata embedded in the HTML source of documents and web pages can also be harvested into a union database and indexed for retrieval by Internet search engines. As with all other types of union search, the more consistent the data, the better the retrieval. Several states, including Washington and Illinois, have developed guidelines for using <META> tags for statewide GILS (Government Information Locator Service) projects. State webcrawlers visit government agency sites and look for specific <META> tags to index.

Not all heterogeneous union catalogs convert metadata to a common format. In another model, the source metadata records are maintained in their original schemes and formats, but are searched as though they were a single file. The Library of Congress's American Memory is a good example of this approach (http://memory.loc. gov). The American Memory website offers access to over 7 million items from more than one hundred collections. Although most of these collections were digitized from LC holdings, other institutions were funded to contribute digital collections as part of the LC Ameritech competition from 1997 to 1999. Participating institutions were allowed to store their digital content locally, but had to send metadata in one of four schemes (MARC, Dublin Core, TEI header, or Encoded Archival Description) to LC. Separate files were maintained for different types of metadata, and separate sets of indexes were built for each file. When a user enters a search on the entire collection, he or she actually sees the combined results of searches on each of the indexes. Selecting an index entry for display causes the full-source metadata record to be retrieved and formatted for display.[2]

CROSS-SYSTEM SEARCH

In the union catalog approach, a union database (or, in some cases, union index) of metadata is maintained, and a central search and retrieval system is used to access data from it. In the cross-system search approach, metadata records are stored in multiple, distributed databases and retrieved using the search facilities associated with each database system.

ANSI/NISO Z39.50 (also ISO 23950) is an international standard protocol that allows one system (the origin or client) to request that a search be performed in another system (the target or server) and receive results back in a format that the first system can display.[3] Z39.50 specifies a dialog that allows the origin to establish a connection with the target, communicate a search, request that hits be returned in a particular format, request the number of records to be returned at one time, and so on. However, the real genius of Z39.50 lies in recognizing that it is not necessary to translate from the search language of every system to that of every other system. Instead, Z39.50 requires every search to be expressed in a common, abstract syntax, so every system only needs to know its own search language and that of Z39.50. (You can think of the first approach as a speaker of one language having to learn every other spoken language in order to communicate with people in the rest of the world, and the Z39.50 approach as each speaker knowing only two languages, her own and Esperanto.) The Z39.50 client translates the user's search to the common request language, and the Z39.50 server translates from the common request language to the syntax of the server's search system.

Z39.50 accomplishes this language independence through the use of *attribute sets*, or lists of abstract search characteristics for particular types of searching. The "bib-1" attribute set is most commonly used for bibliographic search.[4] Bib-1 includes six types of attributes named Use, Relation, Position, Structure, Truncation, and Completeness. The Use attribute identifies the set of access points against which the search term can be matched. For example, Use attribute "1" denotes a personal name, "2" denotes a corporate name, and "3" denotes a conference name. Other types of attributes specify how searching should be done. The Position attribute, for example, specifies where a search term must occur in a field, with "1" indicating the search term must occur at the beginning of a field and "3" indicating the search term can occur in any position in the field.

Z39.50 allows a single user interface to be built in front of heterogeneous distributed systems. It is also used as a means of performing broadcast search (also called federated searching), the simultaneous searching of multiple services. Several commercially available Z39.50 gateway products "speak" the HTTP protocol on one end and function as Z39.50 clients on the other.[5] A user connecting to the gateway with his browser will be offered a menu of target services and is generally allowed to search all services together or select any subset of them to search. Results are most often listed by target, although some products attempt to merge result sets from different targets into a single list.

Gateways such as these are popular in situations in which an institution wants to offer search interoperability among a preselected set of resources. Many consortia have implemented Z39.50-based "virtual" union catalogs as an alternative to "physical" union catalogs sharing a central union database. Z39.50 gateways are also used to integrate searching across different types of bibliographic resources (for example, library catalogs and A&I databases) or across repositories of different metadata types, such as MARC and Dublin Core.

Although the goal of implementing such gateways is to provide seamless searching across disparate resources, experience has demonstrated a number of limitations to Z39.50-based approaches. Part of the problem lies with software: Z39.50 is a complex protocol for systems to implement, and as a result there are many partial and/or imperfect implementations. Inconsistent retrieval can also occur when different search systems do not have comparable functionality. For example, one system may have an "Author" index (Use attribute 1003), while a second system has a "Name" index (Use attribute 1002). If the first system transmits a Z39.50 query on "Author," the results will depend on how that search is configured in the second system. If it rejects the search because there is no equivalent index, the searcher will miss relevant materials. If it maps the search to the "Name" index, the searcher will get false retrievals.

A promising approach to improving interoperability is the adoption of Z39.50 profiles. A profile stipulates specific functions that Z39.50 client and server software must support, specific configurations it must use, and specific indexes that must be available for searching. Any set of information servers that conform to the same profile should have reasonably good search interoperability. The Bath Profile is an internationally registered profile for library applications.[6] A U.S. National Profile based on the Bath Profile is under development by NISO.

Although profile development has so far focused on bibliographic data, the issues are similar for other forms of metadata. The Digital Library Federation sponsored a demonstration project to implement a Z39.50-based search facility over distributed collections of EADs. Participants agreed to support a common set of indexes, or "Common Access Points," for cross-system searching in addition to the indexes they provided for local use. Although consistent retrieval was hindered by the fact that different institutions applied EAD markup differently, the project concluded that the distributed search model was feasible.[7]

Other limitations of Z39.50 cannot be addressed through profiles. Z39.50 interfaces rarely support the full range of functionality available through the native interface of a system and may not be adequate for sophisticated searchers. It has also been widely perceived that Z39.50 does not scale for broadcast searching of a very large number of resources. Because acknowledged connections must be established between the client and all servers, initialization can be slow, especially when one or more servers are unavailable and the client must wait for a timeout interval to pass.

Another problem is simply the limited number of information resources accessible through Z39.50. Z39.50 servers are difficult to develop and maintain, partly because of the range of functionality the protocol supports, but also because of the age of the standard. For example, the protocol requires data to be transmitted in a complex encoding scheme that is no longer widely used and that few programmers know. For these and other reasons, many providers of online information services have chosen not to support Z39.50 access.

Some of these problems are being addressed by a subgroup of the Z39.50 Implementors Group (ZIG) that is working on a "next generation" Z39.50, called Z39.50-International Next Generation (ZING).[8] ZING would take advantage of more web-friendly technologies, such as HTTP, XML, and SOAP (a simple XML-based protocol for exchanging messages), while eliminating lesser-used or outdated features of the standard. The hope is that by modernizing the mechanics of the Z39.50 protocol while retaining the great power of its abstract semantics, Z39.50 can be made more attractive to information providers.

In sum, a primary advantage of Z39.50 is that it relieves the client software of the need to know the access protocol and search syntax of every remote system to be searched. A major disadvantage is that a Z39.50 client can talk only to a Z39.50 server, and not all online information services provide Z39.50 servers. A number of software products have been developed to get around the latter problem by supplementing Z39.50 connections with other methods of searching information services.

Many information services available on the Web use search parameters passed in the query portion of a URL. For example, a general keyword search for documents on hay fever would have the following syntaxes in PubMed, Google, and the University of Chicago library catalog, respectively:

http://www.ncbi.nlm.nih.gov/entrez/query.fcgi?cmd=Search&db=PubMed&term=hay+fever

http://www.google.com/search?q=hay+fever

http://ipac.lib.uchicago.edu/ipac/ipac?uofc=on&db=uofc&sp1=.gk&se=hay+fever&tm=summary

Software designed for broadcast search could take a user's input search request, translate it into these three queries, and send each query to the appropriate target service. Usually such applications will have separate scripts or program modules for each target service that they are able to search. Of course, the normal response of a web-accessible information service to a URL-based query is to display a formatted list of hits, not to return a file of source records. Therefore, these programs generally have to do "screen-scraping," or format-recognition on returned displays, to isolate returned hits or error messages. Such programs are vulnerable to small changes in output formatting, as well as to more major changes in the search syntax of any particular information service. As a consequence, they require a higher level of ongoing maintenance than Z39.50-based services.

An increasing number of information services are offering XML gateways, interfaces that accept XML-formatted queries and return result sets as XML-formatted records. Although the required query languages, like URL-based search parameters, still vary from system to system, this technique has the advantage that results are sent as records so screen-scraping is not required.

Several broadcast search applications combine the ability to do Z39.50 searches with modules to implement URL-based searching, XML gateway searching, and other search techniques in order to be able to provide the largest number of targets. These include library system vendor products, such as Ex Libris's MetaLib and Endeavor's Encompass, and local development projects, such as the California Digital Library's Searchlight (http://searchlight.cdlib.org/cgi-bin/searchlight). Searchlight uses both Z39.50 and web search techniques to offer broadcast searching of library catalogs, journal databases, and other information resources.

CROSSWALKS

Interoperability between different metadata schemes is facilitated by the use of *crosswalks*, or authoritative mappings from the metadata elements of one scheme to those of another. The Library of Congress's mapping from Dublin Core to MARC, for example, specifies that the Contributor element in unqualified Dublin Core maps to the MARC 720 field with blank indicators; that the value of Contributor should appear in 720 subfield a; and that the literal string "contributor" should appear in 720 subfield e.[9] An excerpt from LC's Dublin Core/MARC/GILS Crosswalk is shown in figure 4-1.

Creator
An entity primarily responsible for making the content of the resource.

MARC 21:

Unqualified:

- 720 ##$a (Added Entry--Uncontrolled Name/Name) with $e=author

Qualified:

- Personal: 700 1#$a (Added Entry--Personal Name) with $e=author
- Corporate: 710 2#$a (Added Entry--Corporate Name) with $e=author
- Conference: 711 2#$a (Added Entry--Conference Name) with $e=author
- Role: 720 ##$e (Added Entry--Uncontrolled Name/Relator term)
- Role (Personal): 700 1#$e (Added Entry--Personal Name/Relator term)
- Role (Corporate): 710 2$e (Added Entry--Corporate Name/Relator term)

Note: The above qualifiers have not been approved by DCMI.

GILS:

- Originator

FIGURE 4-1 Excerpt from LC's crosswalk between Dublin Core, MARC, and GILS. (The Library of Congress, Network Development and MARC Standards Office, Dublin Core/MARC/GILS Crosswalk, available at http://lcweb.loc.gov/marc/dccross.html)

Crosswalks are lateral (one-way) mappings from one scheme to another. Separate crosswalks would be required to map from scheme A to scheme B and from scheme B to scheme A. In general, even with pairs of crosswalks, round-trip mapping is not supported without some loss or distortion of information. That is, if a metadata record were "crosswalked" from scheme A to scheme B and back to scheme A, it is unlikely that the resulting record would be identical to the original.

Crosswalks have been developed between most of the major metadata schemes for describing information resources. The Library of Congress maintains mappings for MARC21, including crosswalks to and from Dublin Core, the FGDC Content Standards for Geospatial Metadata, the Global Information Locator Service (GILS), and ONIX. Crosswalks to and from other schemes are often maintained by the organizations responsible for those schemes. Some metadata schemes, such as the VRA Core and the IEEE Learning Object Metadata, even include crosswalks to other schemes as part of their own documentation.

A primary use of crosswalks is to serve as base specifications for physically converting records from one metadata scheme to another for record exchange, contribution to union catalogs, or metadata harvesting. Crosswalks can also be used by search engines to query fields with the same or similar content in different databases. An underappreciated but very significant use of crosswalks is to aid humans in understanding new metadata schemes. Someone encountering an unfamiliar scheme can use a crosswalk between that and a more familiar scheme to make inferences about the meaning and use of the metadata elements.

The development of crosswalks is complicated by the fact that there is no standard format for representing metadata schemes, so different schemes may specify different properties of elements or call the same properties by different names.[10] The first step in crosswalk creation is to put the source and the target schemes into similar formats so that like properties are expressed in similar fashion. Following that, differences in the properties of the elements themselves must be reconciled. For example, one scheme may have a repeatable subject element while another has a nonrepeatable subject field in which multiple subject terms are separated by semicolons. Crosswalks must specify how to handle such one-to-many and many-to-one mappings. An element in a source scheme may have no comparable element in the target scheme, or it may map equally well to two or more target elements. There may be differences in data representation (for example, whether names are inverted) or in content rules (for example, whether a controlled vocabulary is required).

The most difficult issues to resolve concern true semantic differences. For example, when the Dublin Core was first established, there was no field in MARC to which the Dublin Core Creator element could accurately be mapped. MARC name fields were formally defined in terms of main and added entries, two AACR2 cataloging concepts wholly absent from Dublin Core semantics. To enable development of a Dublin Core to MARC crosswalk, a new 720 field (Added Entry—Uncontrolled Name) had to be added to the USMARC format.[11]

METADATA REGISTRIES

A *metadata registry* is a tool for recording authoritative information about metadata elements from multiple sources. By recording the names, definitions, and properties of metadata elements, metadata registries facilitate the identification, reusability, and interoperability of metadata elements. As more and more metadata schemes have come into use in particular information domains, interest has been increasing in metadata registries as data management tools.

Very few operational metadata registries actually exist. Most metadata registries in use or development today are based on the ISO/IEC 11179 standard, Specification and Standardization of Data Elements. Different parts of this standard cover basic attributes of data elements, how to formulate names and definitions of data elements, and how to establish registration authorities and metadata registries. This standard was developed not because of a proliferation of metadata schemes in the sense that we are describing, but to manage multiple database systems within an organization or a group of organizations, each with its own schema or sets of named elements. The metadata registry is intended to allow some higher-level organization to bring all this information together in a consistent fashion, allowing elements to be identified, understood, and reused.

One of the best known 11179-based metadata registries is the Australian Institute of Health and Welfare Knowledgebase (http://www.aihw.gov.au/knowledgebase/), which includes element definitions related to health, community services, and housing assistance. The major ISO/IEC 11179-based implementation in the United States is the Environmental Protection Agency's Environmental Data Registry, or EDR (http://www.epa.gov/edr/). The EDR describes environmental data both within and outside the EPA and contains (as of September 2002) 9,751 data elements from 1,419 information sources submitted by fifty-five different organizations. A search of "zip," for example, retrieves more than one hundred metadata elements defined in various databases, including ZIP_CODE (identifier 1-24175:1) for "The Zone Improvement Plan (ZIP) Code and the four-digit extension of the physical address location of the establishment" from the "DNB Company" table in the Dun and Bradstreet database in Envirofacts, and ZIP_CODE (identifier 1-24556:1) for "Zone Improvement Plan (ZIP) code in the address associated with the facility mailing address" from the "RCR Mailing Location" table in the Resource Conservation and Recovery Information System in Envirofacts.

Registries being developed for metadata schemes for information resource description are more accurately called cognizant of ISO/IEC 11179 than compliant with it. Three quite different approaches to registries have been taken by ROADS, the DCMI, and the DESIRE project.

ROADS (Resource Organisation And Discovery in Subject-based services) is a project of the eLib (Electronic Libraries) Programme of the Joint Information Systems Committee (JISC) in the United Kingdom. ROADS provides software that allows participants to set up subject gateways based on metadata records entered according to standard templates. Templates exist for documents, images, sound, collections, and other material types. The ROADS Metadata Registry is simply a listing of the templates and the elements they contain (http://www.ukoln.ac.uk/metadata/roads/templates/). It is not a registry in the ISO/IEC 11179 sense as there is no search access by element name and no ability to compare element usage in different templates. However, it does provide a place for the official versions of various templates to be registered, or publicly recorded.

The development of a metadata registry to support the Dublin Core Metadata Initiative is an active project of the DCMI's Registry Working Group (http://www.dublincore.org/groups/registry). The Working Group is interested in the development of two tools, a Vocabulary Management System and a Registry. The former is seen as a tool for the DCMI and would assist in the management and evolution of Dublin Core elements by providing information about all current and past terms and term definitions, providing a means for approving new terms, and similar functions. The Registry is conceived as a tool for end-users (both humans and software) to obtain comprehensive information about DC terms, term usage, and relationships. The Registry tool will provide a multilingual interface and multilingual descriptions of terms.

A broader approach has been taken by the DESIRE Metadata Registry (http://desire.ukoln.ac.uk/registry/). DESIRE (Development of a European Service for Information on Research and Education) was a collaboration between institutions in the Netherlands, Norway, Sweden, and the United Kingdom funded from 1998 through 2000. Unlike most ISO/IEC 11179-based registries, the DESIRE registry was designed to manage metadata elements from multiple namespaces (schemes). A demonstrator was built containing elements from three versions of the Dublin Core, an extended form of Dublin Core used by the BIBLINK project, selected ROADS templates, and a few other schemes.

An interesting aspect of the DESIRE approach was to test the automatic generation of crosswalks using the ISO Basic Semantics Register (BSR). The BSR is an internationally agreed-upon compilation of data elements designed to allow systems development in a multilingual environment. In the DESIRE project, instead of attempting unilateral mappings from the elements of each scheme to those of every other scheme, each element was instead mapped to a neutral semantic concept (in ISO terminology, a *semantic unit*). Mappings between any two schemes A and B could be effected by mapping the elements of scheme A to the corresponding BSR semantic units, then mapping the BSR semantic units to corresponding elements in scheme B. This approach should seem familiar to anyone who understands Z39.50.

There is active research in creating machine-understandable registries as well as human-understandable ones (see the section on the Semantic Web in chapter 5). Although metadata registries are still in their infancy, it is expected that registry technologies will mature and that, over time, the importance of metadata registries will increase in response to the growing problems of multiple metadata schemes with all their versions and variants.

BARRIERS TO INTEROPERABILITY

Regardless of the method used to search across multiple resources, differences in the underlying metadata will cause difficulties in retrieval and presentation, and it is a fair generalization that the more dissimilar the metadata, the more problematic retrieval will be. Issues that most commonly arise include the following:

1. *Semantic differences:* There is no necessary correspondence in meaning between the metadata elements of different schemes. Differences may be blatant (for example, no corresponding element at all), or they may be subtle. The Title element in the Dublin Core, for example, is any name given to a resource, while the Title Proper (245) in AACR2/MARC can be assigned only by following an elaborate and well-defined set of rules. Whether title elements in these two schemes are considered equivalent depends on how much error one is willing to accept. In another example, GILS has an Author

element, while Dublin Core and VRA Core have the more general Creator, and AACR2/MARC has main and added entries, which are both more general (in that they accommodate different types of roles) and more specific (in that there are restrictions on who can appear as main or added entries). The EAD has an Author element, but it is used to record the author of the EAD itself, not of the collection the EAD is describing.

2. *Differences in practice:* Different communities have different traditions of descriptive practice. Metadata created by staff of different institutions, such as libraries, archives, museums, and historical societies, will differ even for the most basic elements. Librarians, for example, generally insist on a title element and will make up titles for works that have none. Museum curators, on the other hand, prefer to omit titles for three-dimensional artifacts, relying instead on subject-rich descriptions. The principles and rules of archival description differ markedly from those of bibliographic description. There is no concept of author in an archival finding aid, though personal, corporate, and family names can be tagged wherever they are relevant.[12]

3. *Differences in representation:* Even where element definitions are identical, data can be recorded in different forms depending on representation rules. For example, if one set of metadata records represents authors in the form "Public, John Q." and another uses "Public, J.Q.," a keyword search on "John Public" will retrieve records only from the first store. Intelligent search interfaces can ameliorate some common discrepancies. For example, a broadcast search interface called Flashpoint developed at Los Alamos National Laboratories will prompt a user to repeat an author search using initials if no hits are retrieved on a query that includes a full first name.[13]

4. *Different vocabularies:* Incompatible vocabularies are a common problem when users attempt to search across metadata from different subject domains and/or types of organizations, such as libraries, art museums, natural history museums, and historical societies. These institutions are likely to use different subject vocabularies, and some may use highly specialized vocabularies. A library will index works using the common name "Red fox," while a museum of natural history will use the scientific name "Vulpes vulpes."

5. *Items versus collections:* Special problems arise when users attempt to combine metadata describing unitary objects (such as MARC bibliographic records or Dublin Core records) with EADs or other complex, multilevel descriptive schemes. If a complex collection-level scheme such as EAD is mapped to a common, Dublin Core–based format, the richness and hierarchy of the description are lost. Conversely, the EAD may not contain enough subject description at the item level to allow meaningful descriptions of items to be derived from it.

6. *Multiple versions:* The complexities raised by multiple versions have many nuances. One common problem is created by different treatment of reproductions. If, for example, a digitized photograph of a building is being described, such metadata elements as the creator and date of creation will differ depending on whether the focus of resource description is on the building, the photograph, or the image file.

7. *Multiple languages:* Although individual collections may be predominately monolingual, the network is inherently international, and cross-system search in the Internet environment increasingly raises problems of multiple languages. The traditional approach is to use controlled vocabularies for access and multilingual thesauri for translation. Multilingual metadata registries may also be needed to establish equivalence between element names.

NOTES

1. Karen Coyle, "The Virtual Union Catalog: A Comparative Study," *D-Lib Magazine* 6, no. 3 (March 2000), available at http://www.dlib.org/dlib/march00/coyle/03coyle.html. Accessed 26 July 2002.
2. Carolyn R. Arms, *Access Aids and Interoperability,* 1997, available at http://memory.loc.gov/ammem/award/docs/interop.html. Accessed 11 June 2002.
3. ANSI/NISO Z39.50-1995 Information Retrieval: Application Service Definition and Protocol Specification (Washington, D.C.: NISO Press, 1995), available at http://www.niso.org/standards/resources/Z39-50.pdf. Accessed 11 June 2002.
4. *Bib-1 Attribute Set,* available at http://lcweb.loc.gov/z3950/agency/defns/bib1.html. Accessed 11 June 2002. See also *Attribute Set Bib-1 (Z39.50-1995) Semantics,* available at ftp://ftp.loc.gov/pub/z3950/defs/bib1.txt.
5. See, for example, OCLC's SiteSearch (http://www.sitesearch.oclc.org/), Blue Angel Technology's MetaStar Gateway (http://www.blueangeltech.com/), and Fretwell-Downing's Zportal (http://www.fdgroup.co.uk/fdi/zportal/overview.html).
6. "The Bath Profile: An International Z39.50 Specification for Library Applications and Resource Discovery, Release 1.1," available at http://www.ukoln.ac.uk/interopfocus/bath/1.1/. Accessed 11 June 2002.
7. MacKenzie Smith, "DFAS: The Distributed Finding Aid Search System," *D-Lib Magazine* 6, no. 1 (January 2000), available at http://www.dlib.org/dlib/january00/01smith.html. Accessed 11 June 2002.
8. "ZING Z39.50-International: Next Generation," available at http://www.loc.gov/z3950/agency/zing/zing.html. Accessed 11 June 2002.
9. Library of Congress Network Development and MARC Standards Office, "Dublin Core/MARC/GILS Crosswalk," 2001, available at http://lcweb.loc.gov/marc/dccross.html. Accessed 12 June 2002.
10. Margaret St. Pierre and William P. LaPlant, Jr., "Issues in Crosswalking Content Metadata Standards," 1998, available at http://www.niso.org/press/whitepapers/crsswalk.html. Accessed 12 June 2002.
11. [MARBI], Proposal No. 96-2 (1996), available at http://lcweb.loc.gov/marc/marbi/1996/96-02.html. Accessed 12 June 2002.
12. William Garrison, "Retrieval Issues for the Colorado Digitization Project's Heritage Database," *D-Lib Magazine* 7, no. 10 (October 2001), available at http://www.dlib.org/dlib/october01/garrison/10garrison.html. Accessed 12 June 2002.
13. Dan Mahoney and Mariella Di Giacomo, "Flashpoint @ LANL.gov: A Simple Smart Search Interface," *Issues in Science and Technology Librarianship* (summer 2001), available at http://www.library.ucsb.edu/istl/01-summer/article2.html. Accessed 12 June 2002.

READINGS

Arms, William Y., et al. "A Spectrum of Interoperability: The Site for Science Prototype for the NSDL." *D-Lib Magazine* 8, no. 1 (January 2002). Available at http://www.dlib.org/dlib/january02/arms/01arms.html.

> How researchers approached metadata interoperability for the National Science Digital Library.

Coyle, Karen. "The Virtual Union Catalog: A Comparative Study." *D-Lib Magazine* 6, no. 3 (March 2000). Available at http://www.dlib.org/dlib/march00/coyle/03coyle.html.

> This article compares the implementation of a virtual union catalog using Z39.50 with the MELVYL physical union catalog.

Lynch, Clifford A. "Metadata Harvesting and the Open Archives Initiative." *ARL Bimonthly Report* 217 (August 2001). Available at http://www.arl.org/newsltr/217/mhp.html.

> An explanation of the Open Archives Metadata Harvesting Protocol, how it was developed, and why it is important.

Moen, William E., and Teresa Lepchenske. *Z39.50: Selected List of Resources.* Available at http://www.unt.edu/wmoen/Z3950/BasicZReferences.htm.

> This bibliography is not entirely up-to-date but complements the bibliography on the Z39.50 Maintenance Agency website.

St. Pierre, Margaret, and William P. LaPlant, Jr. *Issues in Crosswalking Content Metadata Standards.* 1998. Available at http://www.niso.org/press/whitepapers/crsswalk.html.

> A discussion of the incompatibilities in the representation of different metadata schemes and how these lead to problems in developing crosswalks.

Z39.50: A Primer on the Protocol. Bethesda, Md.: NISO Press, 2002. Available at http://www.niso.org/standards/resources/Z3950_primer.pdf.

> Extensive web-accessible information is available on Z39.50, including any number of introductions and primers. This is one of the most recently published.

Z39.50 International Standard Maintenance Agency: Library of Congress Network Development and MARC Standards Office (home page of the Z39.50 Maintenance Agency). Available at http://www.loc.gov/z3950/agency/.

> The official maintenance site for Z39.50, this page links to the Library of Congress Gateway to Z39.50-accessible catalogs as well as to a bibliography, a list of software products that support Z39.50, and other related resources.

Metadata and the Web

5

The most common way to associate metadata with web-accessible content is to embed the metadata in the digital object that it describes. If the object is an HTML document, metadata can be embedded by use of <meta> elements, as discussed in chapter 2. The metadata can then be harvested and indexed by Internet search engines.

INTERNET SEARCH ENGINES

Internet search engines use software programs called *spiders* or *webcrawlers* to find, gather, and index web content. Google uses a spider called Googlebot, for example, and AltaVista uses a program called Scooter. An organization running a spider for a specific purpose, such as to harvest pages on a corporate Intranet or to harvest all government websites in a state, can limit the spider to visiting specific addresses. More often, however, once spiders are seeded with an initial list of web addresses to visit, they expand the list dynamically by extracting and following the URLs found in the pages they harvest. Spiders will also revisit sites periodically so that new and changed content can be harvested. The major Internet search engines have complex algorithms for determining when to revisit a site that take into account the frequency with which the web pages are updated.

When a spider has found a harvestable web page, it will create and save a summary of the page, and it will extract the words on the page and save them into an index database. When a user does a search using Google or some other Internet search engine, it is actually this index that is searched, not the source web pages themselves, and it is the stored summary that is displayed. That is why entries retrieved by search engines are not always current and sometimes point to pages that are no longer available.

It should be noted that not all web pages are harvestable. Webmasters can prevent their sites from being harvested by including a file called "robots.txt" in the webserver directory. It is also possible to specify that a certain page should not be indexed by embedding a <meta> tag in the format: <META NAME="ROBOTS" CONTENT= "NOINDEX">. Most legitimate search engines support the robots.txt method of prohibiting indexing, but not all search engines support the <meta> tag method.

Most search engines have some method for ranking retrievals so that the entries most likely to be relevant are displayed first. Usually the algorithm takes into consideration the location of the search terms on the indexed pages, with terms occurring near the top of the page or within an HTML <title> tag weighted more heavily. Search engines will also use the frequency of term occurrence in calculating relevancy, although if a term occurs too frequently, the entire page may be dropped from the index, as noted in the discussion of spamming later in this section. Other factors that can affect relevancy rankings are link analysis and clickthrough measurement. *Link analysis* identifies how often pages are linked to from other pages, weighting more frequently linked-to pages more heavily, like a web version of a citation index. This is how Google produces its rankings. *Clickthrough measurement* keeps track of how users respond to the lists of hits returned by the search engine in response to their queries. Pages that are selected more frequently can rise in the rankings.

Internet search engines are wonderful tools. A single search engine can index a billion web pages or more, exposing researchers to huge amounts of content. However, users can expect huge retrieval sets as well—searching Google for "Internet search engines" returns nearly two million entries—so relevance ranking is extremely important. Use of metadata in the form of <meta> tags has the potential to improve both the accuracy of retrieval and the relevance ranking of results. In theory, authors could supply accurate information about the content of their web pages in <meta> tags, and search engines could use the content of these tags in indexing and ranking.

In practice, however, use of <meta> tags for page indexing varies from search engine to search engine. Currently, most major Internet search engines will index terms found in the Description field, and some will index terms found in the Keywords field. However, few search engines use the content found in these fields in calculating a page's relevancy ranking. This occurs because the search engines do not trust author-supplied metadata. Among commercial websites, there is intense competition for high ranking in retrieval, and unethical practices like spamming are widespread. *Spamming* is overloading a web page with keywords in order to affect search engine retrieval. To make these keywords invisible to the user, they are often entered in the same color as the page's background or are entered as the content of <meta> tags. A distributor of auto parts, for example, could repeat words like "automotive" hundreds of times in an attempt to increase the ranking of his or her home page. Worse, a pornography site could include terms like "automotive supplies" among its keywords in order to be included in the result sets of people searching for auto parts. For this reason, many search engines ignore <meta> tags for ranking, and some, like Google, ignore them for indexing as well.

It is unfortunate that misuse of metadata by an unethical minority can prevent the effective use of metadata by the majority. One long-term approach to the problem is to develop mechanisms for verifying the quality and authenticity of metadata. Metadata schemes could include defined places to record metadata about the metadata, such as the creator's identity and the completeness and quality of the data recorded. Encrypted checksums calculated over documents and their embedded metadata can indicate whether changes were made to either since the time of creation. Ultimately, the use of digital signatures is likely to be required for establishing trusted metadata. *Digital signatures* are data used to identify and authenticate the creator and content of a file using public-key encryption. This is particularly important for such applications as e-commerce and rights management where the integrity of metadata is crucial. The W3C Digital Signatures Activity is addressing digital signatures for metadata as well as for XML documents.[1]

DOMAIN-SPECIFIC SEARCH ENGINES

The major general Internet search engines, such as Google, AltaVista, HotBot, and Excite, make only minimal use of metadata embedded in <meta> tags. This is unfortunate, because <meta> tags allow terms to be designated as specific data elements, such as author or subject. When doing a search on Google or similar search engines, the user can only do a general keyword search; she cannot specify an author, a title, or a subject search. This contributes to the problem of too many retrievals with too little precision.

However, there is no barrier in general to using search engine technology with structured metadata embedded in HTML. Organizations wishing to index particular sets of websites have the choice of several commercial and noncommercial search engines that can be configured to index the content of <meta> elements. Some of these are Ultraseek, Berkeley's Swish-E, Microsoft's Index Server, Blue Angel Technologies' MetaStar, Verity, and LiveLink Search and Spider.

A good example of organizational use of structured metadata with search engines is provided by state government. A number of states have statewide initiatives to facilitate public access to government information by developing central portals to information resources. One technique in use in Washington, Illinois, Utah, and several other states is to encourage state agencies to embed metadata in their web pages using a state-specified core set of elements taken from the GILS (Government Information Locator Service) specification (see chapter 11). Many of the states have developed web-based metadata generators to make it easier for agency staff to create the appropriate <meta> tags. These interfaces present web forms for data entry that incorporate or link to the controlled vocabularies required for specific fields. When data entry is complete, the programs construct and display the appropriate <meta> tags, which can then be cut and pasted into the HTML for the web page.[2]

The agency websites are spidered by a state-run harvester configured to recognize and index the <meta> tags supported by the state. Use of structured metadata allows the public to search for specific types of data as well as the full text of the web pages. The Washington State interface, for example, allows searching of seventeen specific metadata elements, such as the title of the document, the originating department, the agency program, and subject keywords.

METADATA AND NON-HTML FORMATS

Most Internet search engines index only static HTML pages. However, a huge amount of web-accessible content is not maintained as static HTML. Known as the *hidden Web* or *deep Web*, such content includes specialized databases, such as library catalogs, census data, and newsbanks, which are made available on the Web only as dynamically for-matted pages in response to search requests. It also includes images, sound, video, and other nontextual files. It has been estimated that the size of the hidden Web is about five hundred times larger than the size of the surface Web indexed by search engines.[3] Given the near impossibility of universal access to the hidden Web, most approaches to getting at these materials are subject-specific. Lists of searchable resources may be maintained, as on library portals, and some desktop tools can be configured to search sets of resources simultaneously. In some areas, particularly those of commercial interest, selected content has been aggregated into storehouses.

Use of metadata is another possible approach to making some of the content of the hidden Web accessible. It is possible for metadata to be embedded into digital objects that are not in HTML format. Adobe Acrobat 5.0 and up, and other Adobe products such as InDesign and Illustrator, include support for Adobe's eXtensible Metadata Platform (XMP), which allows textual metadata to be embedded in PDF documents. The technology allows XML files called XMP packets to be embedded in the documents. XMP files can describe entire documents or component parts of documents; for example, a report that includes a photograph may have one embedded XMP file for the textual report and another for the photograph.

XMP files consist of a header and trailer with metadata in between. The metadata itself must be expressed in RDF-compliant XML. Adobe has defined some default XMP schemas for various types of materials, but any schema can be defined, so long as it con-forms to the XMP specification. To make use of the metadata, indexing programs must scan the document for embedded XMP files and extract the metadata for indexing.

Nontextual formats can contain textual metadata in header files. TIFF format image files can contain metadata in the TIFF header. The header points to a list of Image File Directories (IFDs), which are each essentially lists of tags. Each tag has a numeric value, a datatype, and a byte offset at which the data are located (a structure with some simi-larity to MARC). Most predefined header information is technical metadata detailing characteristics of the physical file, such as bits per sample, compression, and orientation. However, there are also tags for the document name, image description, date and time of creation, and artist. Local data elements can be defined with tags numbered 32768 and above.

Other image formats may also contain embedded metadata. The JPEG header can contain application-specific fields (called APP markers) with data inserted by different application programs. For example, Photoshop can insert structured metadata in the APP13 marker. Although it is possible for programs to extract metadata content from image headers for indexing, this is not done by any of the major Internet search engines. Those that do index images use textual clues external to the images themselves, includ-ing the content of the "alt" attribute of the HTML <img> tag, text appearing near the image on the page, or the filename of the image itself.

Audio formats, such as WAV and MP3, allow some elements of descriptive metadata to be recorded in the headers. The MPEG Audio Tag ID3v1 has fixed positions for recording title, artist, album, year, a comment, and the genre of the recording, which is taken from an authority list of coded values. MPEG-7 and MPEG-21 both present a framework for providing descriptive metadata for multimedia productions (see chapter 17). As with image headers, however, this metadata is not used by the Internet search engines.

CHANNELS

A *channel* is a website that can automatically send updated information for immediate display or viewing on request. Channels are used in *webcasting* (also called *netcasting*), which is the prearranged updating of news, stock quotes, or other selected information over the Web. Webcasting is a form of push technology in which the webserver pushes information to the user, although channels must be preselected and most of the pushing is triggered by request from the client browser. Figure 5-1 shows use of channels in My Netscape (http://my.netscape.com) where each rectangular box on the screen is the presentation of a channel. In that application, channels can be added, removed, and rearranged by the user resulting in a truly customized information service.

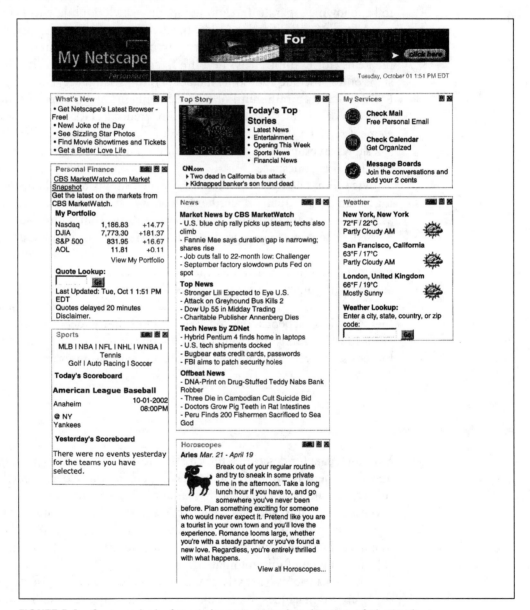

FIGURE 5-1 Screen shot of my.netscape.com showing use of channels.

Content is selected for channels based on metadata, and several schemes have arisen for defining channels and their content. Early specifications include the Meta Content Framework (MCF) developed and promoted by Apple Corporation, and Microsoft's Channel Definition Format (CDF). Currently, however, the dominant format is RSS, a fairly lightweight XML-based specification. RSS exists in several versions, not all of which are compatible. RSS (RDF Site Summary) 0.9, a very simple, ten-element format, was released by Netscape in 1999 for use in My Netscape. Shortly thereafter followed RSS (Rich Site Summary) 0.91 with fourteen additional elements, and RSS 0.92 with several optional features. In December 2000, RSS (RDF Site Summary) 1.0 incorporated RDF namespaces into RSS 0.9 as a technique to avoid further proliferation of base data elements. RSS (Rich Site Summary) 0.9x and RSS (RDF Site Summary) 1.x appear now to be following separate development paths, which doubtless will change further.

All the RSS specifications allow the definition of channels, each described by a title, a description, and a link to an external web page. Channels, in turn, can contain multiple items (for example, news headlines), again described by titles and links. Some versions of RSS include additional metadata ratings, language, and copyright information. RSS 1.0 defines a minimum of data elements in the base specification, but allows the inclusion of modules—external schema referenced as RDF namespaces—to expand the element set. The standard module for descriptive metadata is the Dublin Core. Figure 5-2 shows an example of a channel defined using RSS 1.0, including elements from the Dublin Core namespace.

Viewed in one light, channels can be seen simply as mechanisms for communicating certain web content. In another light, however, the metadata carried in such formats as RSS is important for resource discovery and selection. More and more content is syndicated, or sold by content producers to distributors for redistribution in channels, and the trend in syndication is toward aggregators who resell content from a wide range of providers. An important value added in these services is the ability to select appropriate content with some granularity in order to customize packages for resale. Some aggregators even allow their clients to create their own custom filters. The ability to provide these services depends on the existence of fairly detailed metadata, consistently encoded. The ability to embed fairly sophisticated resource description in channel formats such as RSS, then, has direct practical and commercial value.

THE SEMANTIC WEB

Most metadata for describing information resources is created by humans to be used by humans. There is an assumption that a person will actively search for information (directly or indirectly by creating search profiles to run automatically), will filter and select search results, and will analyze connections between different pieces of information. Many in the Web community, however, including Tim Berners-Lee, who is commonly credited with inventing the Web, believe that in the future, machines should be able to do much of this automatically.

The Semantic Web activity of the W3C is focused on representing semantic data on the Web in machine-processable ways. According to the Semantic Web Activity Statement, "The Semantic Web is an extension of the current Web in which information

```
<?xml version="1.0"?>

<rdf:RDF
  xmlns:rdf="http://www.w3.org/1999/02/22-rdf-syntax-ns#"
  xmlns="http://purl.org/rss/1.0/"
>

  <channel rdf:about="http://www.xml.com/xml/news.rss">
    <title>XML.com</title>
    <link>http://xml.com/pub</link>
    <description>
      XML.com features a rich mix of information and services
      for the XML community.
    </description>

    <image rdf:resource="http://xml.com/universal/images/xml_tiny.gif" />

    <items>
      <rdf:Seq>
        <rdf:li resource="http://xml.com/pub/2000/08/09/xslt/xslt.html" />
        <rdf:li resource="http://xml.com/pub/2000/08/09/rdfdb/index.html" />
      </rdf:Seq>
    </items>

    <textinput rdf:resource="http://search.xml.com" />

  </channel>

  <image rdf:about="http://xml.com/universal/images/xml_tiny.gif">
    <title>XML.com</title>
    <link>http://www.xml.com</link>
    <url>http://xml.com/universal/images/xml_tiny.gif</url>
  </image>

  <item rdf:about="http://xml.com/pub/2000/08/09/xslt/xslt.html">
    <title>Processing Inclusions with XSLT</title>
    <link>http://xml.com/pub/2000/08/09/xslt/xslt.html</link>
    <description>
     Processing document inclusions with general XML tools can be
     problematic. This article proposes a way of preserving inclusion
     information through SAX-based processing.
    </description>
  </item>

  <item rdf:about="http://xml.com/pub/2000/08/09/rdfdb/index.html">
    <title>Putting RDF to Work</title>
    <link>http://xml.com/pub/2000/08/09/rdfdb/index.html</link>
    <description>
     Tool and API support for the Resource Description Framework
     is slowly coming of age. Edd Dumbill takes a look at RDFDB,
     one of the most exciting new RDF toolkits.
    </description>
  </item>

  <textinput rdf:about="http://search.xml.com">
    <title>Search XML.com</title>
    <description>Search XML.com's XML collection</description>
    <name>s</name>
    <link>http://search.xml.com</link>
  </textinput>

</rdf:RDF>
```

FIGURE 5-2 Example of a channel defined using RSS 1.0. From "RDF Site Summary (RSS) 1.0," available at http://groups.yahoo.com/group/rss-dev/files/specification.html. Copyright © 2000 by the Authors. Permission to use, copy, modify and distribute the RDF Site Summary 1.0 Specification and its accompanying documentation for any purpose and without fee is hereby granted in perpetuity, provided that the above copyright notice and this paragraph appear in all copies. The copyright holders make no representation about the suitability of the specification for any purpose. It is provided "as is" without expressed or implied warranty.

is given well-defined meaning, better enabling computers and people to work in cooperation. It is the idea of having data on the Web defined and linked in a way that it can be used for more effective discovery, automation, integration, and reuse across various applications."[4] An earlier W3C note on web architecture describes the Semantic Web as "a Web that includes documents, or portions of documents, describing explicit relationships between things and containing semantic information intended for automated processing by our machines."[5]

Two of the main tools for creating the Semantic Web are RDF and ontologies. RDF is key because it allows metadata to be represented as assertions that can be specified wholly in terms of URIs, or links to the definitions of the subject, object, and predicate of the assertion. For example, RDF can make the assertion that document A (subject) is created by (predicate) John Smith (object), where the object is represented as a link to an authority record or document portion identifying Mr. Smith, the predicate is represented as a link to the creator element in the Dublin Core Metadata Specification, and the subject is represented as a link to the document. Computer programs can follow these links to obtain additional information about John Smith or about creators.

Ontologies, the second key component, are necessary to allow computers to make inferences about the meanings of terms. Ontologies are documents that formally define semantic relationships among concepts. Somewhat similar to thesauri, ontologies are concerned with concepts rather than terms. They generally include taxonomies defining classes of objects and their relationships, and inference rules for extending these relationships.

The idea behind the Semantic Web is that software agents can be written to use assertions specified in RDF along with ontologies and their inference rules to make connections between pieces of information that are not explicitly related. Unfortunately, when the Semantic Web is described, it is usually with rather prosaic examples. Automated agents are made to sound like office secretaries, automatically making appointments and travel arrangements. Many researchers, however, believe that the Semantic Web, which will greatly enhance our ability to use information, will prove even more transformative than the current World Wide Web, which so dramatically enhanced our ability to obtain information. In any case, all agree that one of the greatest challenges to achieving the vision of the Semantic Web lies not in the development of ontologies, inference engines, or intelligent agents, but rather in encouraging authors to provide meaningful metadata along with their web resources.

NOTES

1. W3C Technology and Society Domain, XML Digital Signatures Activity Statement, available at http://www.w3.org/Signature/Activity.html. Accessed 13 June 2002.
2. As an example of a GILS-compliant metadata generator, see the Utah HTML Metatag Builder at http://www.utah.org/GILS/uttagbuilder.htm.
3. Michael K. Bergman, "The Deep Web: Surfacing Hidden Value," *Journal of Electronic Publishing* 7, no. 1 (August 2001), available at http://www.press.umich.edu/jep/0701/bergman.html. Accessed 13 June 2002.
4. W3C Technology and Society Domain, Semantic Web Activity Statement, available at http://www.w3.org/2001/sw/Activity. Accessed 14 June 2002.
5. Tim Berners-Lee, Dan Connolly, and Ralph R. Swick, "Web Architecture: Describing and Exchanging Data," W3C Note 7 (June 1999), available at http://www.w3.org/1999/04/WebData. Accessed 14 June 2002.

READINGS

Ackermann, Ernest, and Karen Hartman. *Searching and Researching on the Internet and the World Wide Web.* 2nd ed. Wilsonville, Ore.: Franklin, Beedle, 1997. See also the online companion pages at http://www.webliminal.com/search/.

A comprehensive instructional guide to the use of directories, virtual libraries, search engines, and other tools for performing research on the Web. Among many other topics, this resource describes how specific search engines calculate relevance ranking, counter spamming, and perform other functions.

Berners-Lee, Tim, James Hendler, and Ora Lassila. "The Semantic Web." *Scientific American* (May 2001).

A clear explication of the vision of the Semantic Web by some of the visionaries most instrumental in its conception and design.

Lynch, Clifford A. "Authenticity and Integrity in the Digital Environment: An Exploratory Analysis of the Central Role of Trust." Available at http://www.clir.org/pubs/reports/pub92/lynch.html.

A thought-provoking discussion of authenticity, integrity, and provenance in the networked information environment.

6 Library Cataloging

Librarians have been engaged in resource description for as long as there have been libraries. Evidence exists of classification systems in use in Assyrian and Babylonian libraries in the seventh century BC.[1] The origin of modern Anglo-American cataloging, however, is generally traced to Sir Anthony Panizzi's compilation of cataloging rules for the British Museum in the mid-nineteenth century. There followed a succession of cataloging codes over the next one hundred fifty years, created first by influential individuals, such as Charles Jewett and Charles Cutter, and later by organizations, such as the American Library Association and the Library of Congress.

CATALOGING PRINCIPLES

Cutter's *Rules for a Dictionary Catalog* (first published in 1876 as *Rules for a Printed Dictionary Catalogue*) laid out principles of bibliographic description that heavily influenced all future cataloging codes. Cutter's famous statement that "the convenience of the user must be put before the ease of the cataloger," known as the *principle of user convenience*, underlies many of the rules in use today. It dictated an alphabetical rather than classified arrangement of the catalog and led to the principle of common usage, requiring that catalogers choose terms for subject and name headings that users would be most likely to look under.

Cutter also articulated what he believed were the objectives of the catalog:[2]

Objects

1. To enable a person to find a book of which any of the following is known:
   a. the author

b. the title

c. the subject

2. To show what the library has

d. by a given author

e. on a given subject

f. in a given kind of literature

3. To assist in the choice of a book

g. as to its edition (bibliographically)

h. as to its character (literary or topical)

For every objective, Cutter then laid out the cataloging devices that were the means of achieving them. For example, to enable a user to find a book when the author is known and to show what the library has by a given author, the cataloger makes an author entry with the necessary references. To assist in choosing a book by edition, the cataloger gives the edition and imprint, with notes if needed.

Cutter's *Rules* were followed by a succession of cataloging codes, including but by no means limited to the American Library Association (ALA) rules in 1908, 1941, and 1949; the first *Anglo-American Cataloging Rules* (AACR) in 1967; and the second edition of AACR (AACR2) in 1978. Beginning in the 1970s, the International Federation of Library Associations (IFLA) developed a series of International Standard Bibliographic Description (ISBD) rules to encourage the standardization of cataloging practice internationally.[3] Several ISBD specifications exist, including (but not limited to) ISBD(G): General International Standard Bibliographic Description; ISBD(M): International Standard Bibliographic Description for Monographic Publications; and ISBD(S): International Standard Bibliographic Description for Serials. The current version of the Anglo-American cataloging code, a substantial revision issued in 1988 (AACR2R), was largely based on the ISBDs.

Although some codes are acknowledged to have been less successful than others, it can fairly be said that library cataloging rules have always tried to adhere to fundamental principles, including the principle of user convenience, and have always attempted to facilitate the ultimate objectives of the catalog. Cutter's objects can be seen reflected more than one hundred years later in the first three of the four "user tasks" defined in the IFLA *Functional Requirements for Bibliographic Records*:

to *find* entities that correspond to the user's stated search criteria (i.e., to locate either a single entity or a set of entities in a file or database as the result of a search using an attribute or relationship of the entity);

to *identify* an entity (i.e., to confirm that the entity described corresponds to the entity sought, or to distinguish between two or more entities with similar characteristics);

to *select* an entity that is appropriate to the user's needs (i.e., to choose an entity that meets the user's requirements with respect to content, physical format, etc., or to reject an entity as being inappropriate to the user's needs);

to acquire or *obtain* access to the entity described (i.e., to acquire an entity through purchase, loan, etc., or to access an entity electronically through an online connection to a remote computer).[4]

CATALOGING RULES AND SPECIFICATIONS

Today's cataloger requires a substantial arsenal of rules, manuals, and documentation. The *Anglo-American Cataloguing Rules*, second edition, 1988 revision (AACR2R) is in most cases the primary guide to content creation for descriptive cataloging, including the formulation of access points. However, the Library of Congress's own cataloging practice may differ from the letter of AACR2R. A record of these differences, called the *Library of Congress Rule Interpretations* (LCRIs), is published regularly. Because LC is the largest single source of MARC21 records and because of the value of consistency in shared cataloging, most cataloging departments follow LCRIs, and their use is encouraged for records entered into OCLC.

Additional rulesets, supporting documentation, and authority files are needed for name and subject cataloging. Name headings are created according to AACR2 Part 2 rules and LCRIs. Name headings can be searched in the national Name Authority File (NAF) which is available online through the bibliographic utilities. Libraries can contribute new headings to the NAF through NACO, the name authority component of the Program for Cooperative Cataloging, which has its own set of policies and documentation.[5] Subject cataloging is not addressed in AACR2. Libraries using the Library of Congress Subject Headings scheme (LCSH) will follow LC's subject cataloging manual and assign subject headings from the "red books" and weekly online updates.[6] Other subject schemes have their own sets of documentation, as do the various classification schemes.

AACR2R and the subject cataloging schemes refer only to the content of bibliographic description. Rules for representing this content in MARC are given in the *MARC21 Format for Bibliographic Data*, published and maintained by the Library of Congress. An abbreviated version that contains less description and fewer examples is available on the Web as the *MARC21 Concise Format for Bibliographic Data*.[7] MARC21 has content requirements of its own that are not covered by the cataloging code, such as the encoding of control fields (for example, the 007 and 008), holdings and locations fields, and note fields not addressed in the cataloging rules. The MARC21 documents constitute the authoritative documentation on both content and encoding of these data elements. The MARC21 specifications themselves are supplemented by stand-alone *code lists*—authority lists of coded values required for certain data elements, such as countries, languages, and geographic areas. The Library of Congress also provides stand-alone guidelines for the encoding of certain fields, such as the Electronic Location and Access (856) field.[8]

Most cataloging is created either in one of the national bibliographic utilities (OCLC or RLIN) or created in local systems and uploaded to one or both of the bibliographic utilities. The utilities each have their own input standards and guidelines and their own sets of code lists. The primary cataloging manual for OCLC users is *Bibliographic Formats and Standards*, which is often used in preference to other documentation as it combines both content and encoding guidelines.[9]

Catalogers working with specific types of materials may need additional manuals. For example, serials catalogers participating in the national CONSER (Conversion of Serials) project will follow the *CONSER Editing Guide* and *CONSER Cataloging Manual* in preference to other authorities.[10] The Library of Congress publishes, and many cataloging departments follow, LC's internal rules for cataloging rare books, loose-leaf publications, and other special types of materials where practice differs significantly from AACR2.

Given this complex environment, it is not surprising that substantial training is required to develop competency in traditional library cataloging. An ALA committee that developed an outline of the "essential elements" of a training program for entry-level catalogers noted that the program would probably take from six months to one year to complete.[11] Library cataloging not only requires a high level of skill, but is also costly in staff time. One 1997 study cited the cost of cataloging a monograph and preparing it for the shelf as $48.19, while a 1992 study at Iowa State University found it took the cataloging department an average of 1.97 hours to catalog a serial and 1.32 hours to catalog a monograph.[12] The creation of a single, full cataloging record was estimated to cost the Library of Congress between $50 and $100.[13]

Because of the high cost involved in cataloging a work from scratch (called *original cataloging*), libraries rely heavily on *copy cataloging*. In copy cataloging, some preexisting catalog record for the work (*copy*) is obtained and used as the basis for local modifications. Copy cataloging is more formulaic and is often done by lower-level staff according to detailed written procedures. The OCLC and RLIN databases are prime sources of cataloging copy, but several other sources exist, including procurement services, such as approval plan vendors. Libraries that obtain copy from OCLC make a distinction between *LC copy*—cataloging records created by the Library of Congress—and *contributed copy*—records created by other library members of OCLC. LC copy is generally considered higher quality, and libraries may treat it with more streamlined procedures and less review.

Many involved in metadata initiatives take it as axiomatic that traditional library cataloging is too complex to be performed by nonprofessionals and too expensive to be practically applied to many types of resources. These complaints cannot be dismissed out of hand. Even moderately sized cataloging departments tend to have libraries of documentation, established mechanisms for training, workflow procedures that allow for staff specialization, library management systems with sophisticated cataloging support modules, access to national shared cataloging systems, software tools or vendor services to support authority control—an entire bibliographic apparatus that is lacking outside the library environment.

FUNDAMENTALS OF CATALOGING

It is clearly not possible to give a comprehensive description of library cataloging here. The following is intended only to convey the flavor of this type of resource description. The cataloging code and MARC21 encoding are covered together as they can hardly be separated in today's cataloging environment.

Rules for bibliographic description are covered in Part 1 of AACR2R. Description is divided into eight areas, each of which can contain one or more data elements that may vary according to the type of material being described. These areas correspond to fields or blocks of fields in MARC:

Title and statement of responsibility area

Edition area

Material (or type of publication) specific details area

Publication, distribution, etc., area

Physical description area

Series area

Note area

Standard number and terms of availability area

The first area, "Title and statement of responsibility," contains the title proper along with what is called the general material designation (GMD), parallel titles, other title information, and statements of responsibility. Whenever possible, AACR2R prescribes a chief source of information (from which the content of the data element should be taken) and, if necessary, alternate acceptable sources of information. The chief source of information for the title proper varies according to the type of material; for example, for a printed book or serial, it is the title page, whereas for a music CD, it is the disc itself and any permanently affixed label. Although the title should in most cases be recorded as it appears on the chief source of information, the words of the title should be capitalized according to AACR2R rules of capitalization.

The *GMD* is an optional element indicating the broad type of material, taken from an authority list given in AACR2R. GMDs include such literals as "text," "motion picture," and "sound recording." A *parallel title* is the title proper in another language or script. *Other title information* is most commonly the subtitle. The *statement of responsibility* records the agents responsible for the content. There are rules governing which types of agents associated with the work can be noted, what to do when there are multiple agents, and how to record the names.

Data elements within an area are separated by prescribed punctuation based on the ISBD. For example, the title is separated from other title information by a colon and from a statement of responsibility by a slash. A simple title and statement of responsibility area may look like this:

The book on the bookshelf / by Henry Petroski.

A more complex example might look like this:

Proceedings of the Bicentennial Conference on Bibliographic Control for the New Millennium : confronting the challenges of networked resources and the Web : Washington, D.C., November 15-17, 2000 / sponsored by the Library of Congress Cataloging Directorate ; edited by Ann M. Sandberg-Fox.

Each of the data elements comprising the title and statement of responsibility area is encoded in separate subfields of the MARC21 245 field. MARC itself requires the cataloger to supply additional information about the content. The two indicators of the 245 are used to specify whether an added entry should be created for the title and the number of characters to ignore when sorting on the title. Encoded in MARC21 and displayed in a formatted way, the first example would appear as:

245 14 $a The book on the bookshelf / $c by Henry Petroski.

The first indicator "1" specifies an added entry for the title; the second indicator "4" indicates filing should begin with the word "book," as the initial article and space will be ignored. The title proper appears in subfield a, and the statement of responsibility in subfield c.

The other seven areas are treated similarly. AACR2R specifies the allowable data elements, prescribed sources of information for determining the content, rules for how to represent the content (e.g., abbreviation, capitalization, authority lists of terms), and prescribed punctuation. MARC21 specifies the field tagging, indicators, and subfields used to encode the content. Briefly, the edition area (MARC21 250) can contain data elements relating to edition statements and to statements of responsibility specific to particular editions. The third area, "Material (or type of publication) specific details," (MARC21 254, 255, 256, 362) is unused for some forms of material and has material-specific names for other forms of materials. For cartographic materials, for example, area 3 is called the "mathematical data area" (MARC21 255) and is used for recording scale, projection, and coordinates. The fourth area (MARC21 260) is used for information relating to publication and/or distribution, including the name(s) of the publisher or distributor, the place of publication or distribution, and the date(s) of publication, distribution, and copyright.

The rules for the physical description area (MARC21 300) vary greatly depending on the format of material. Data elements that can be recorded include the number of parts, other physical details (such as the playing speed of a sound recording), the dimensions of the item, and a description of accompanying material. The series area (MARC21 440, 800, 810, 811, 830) is used if the item being described was issued as part of a series. The notes area (MARC21 fields beginning with "5") is used for descriptive information that cannot be given in the other areas. For each type of material, the allowable notes and the order in which they should appear are prescribed, and, in some cases, the actual wording of the note is prescribed. Such information as the contents of the work, the intended audience, other formats in which the work is available, and restrictions on use can be recorded in notes. The final area (MARC21 020, 022, and other fields) is for the recording of standard numbers, such as the International Standard Book Number (ISBN) and the International Standard Serial Number (ISSN).

Part 2 of AACR2R is concerned with the choice and form of access points, or headings by which cataloging records may be retrieved. In the current computer environment, any word in any element of the bibliographic record could conceivably be used for retrieval. Elements treated as access points in the cataloging rules, however, are often searchable in special ways, such as via browse indexes. There are essentially two types of access points: bibliographic and subject.

Bibliographic access points include names of authors and certain other agents associated with a work, names of corporate bodies related to the work in certain ways, names of series, and titles. A key concept is that of *main entry*, or the primary access point of the cataloging record, which is encoded as a 1xx field in MARC21; all other bibliographic access points are *added entries* and are encoded as 4xx, 7xx, or 8xx fields. (The notation "nxx" means any field tag beginning with the digit "n." For example, a 1xx field would be any of 100, 110, 120, or 130.) AACR2R has extensive rules for determining the main entry, which interestingly enough is based on the relatively ambiguous concept of authorship, rather than on something more straightforward like the title. Although the main entry was logistically important in card catalog systems, its necessity in the current environment has been questioned. Some maintain that a primary access point is still useful for certain functions, such as displaying citations and ordering retrieval sets. Others argue that the complexity of ascertaining the main entry outweighs its usefulness.

In any case, although main and added entries are distinguished from each other, the rules for their formulation are the same. Headings for names of persons, geographic names, names of corporate bodies, and a special type of title known as "uniform title" are addressed. For names of persons, there are two issues: the choice of name and the form of name. For choice of name, the general rule is to choose the name by which a person is commonly known (e.g., Jimmy Carter rather than James Earl Carter), but additional rules cover cases in which this is ambiguous, such as authors who have written under one or more pseudonyms, or persons who have changed their name. Once the name itself has been chosen, the form of name must be determined, which includes such considerations as fullness, language, and order of entry for names used as access points. Birth and/or death dates are added to distinguish identical names.

To complete the bibliographic record, two types of resource description not covered in AACR2R must also be performed: subject cataloging and classification. *Subject cataloging* is the assignment of topical access points. Most bibliographic records for nonfiction works contain at least one subject heading taken from a controlled vocabulary. The *Library of Congress Subject Headings* (LCSH) is most commonly used by larger public, academic, and research libraries, while smaller public libraries and school libraries often prefer the *Sears List of Subject Headings*. Special types of libraries may use other controlled vocabularies more suited to their subject matter and user population—for example, the National Library of Medicine's *Medical Subject Headings* (MeSH), or the Getty *Art and Architecture Thesaurus*. Subject terms are encoded as 6xx tags in MARC, distinguished both by the type of subject term (e.g., personal name, topical term, geographic area) and the vocabulary used.

Classification, or the assignment of a notation from a selected classification scheme, serves multiple purposes. As part of a *call number*, or a label used as a shelving location for physical items, the classification number groups materials on similar topics together on the bookshelf. A *shelflist*, a printed or online list in shelf order of all physical items held by a library, is used by many libraries as an inventory control device. Classification can also be used as a form of subject access in retrieval. As with subject headings, different types of organizations prefer to use different classification schemes for their call numbers, with larger and academic libraries tending to use the Library of Congress Classification, other libraries tending to use the Dewey Decimal Classification, and European libraries preferring the Universal Decimal Classification.

Figure 6-1 shows a formatted screen display of a MARC21 bibliographic record. Nearly half the fields are 0xx fields containing various control numbers and processing codes. The 050 field contains the LCC classification, and the 082 contains the DDC classification. The remainder of the record contains simple descriptive data with main entry, title statement, edition statement, imprint, physical description, a bibliography note, and three LCSH subject headings. Figure 6-2 shows the public online catalog display of the same record.

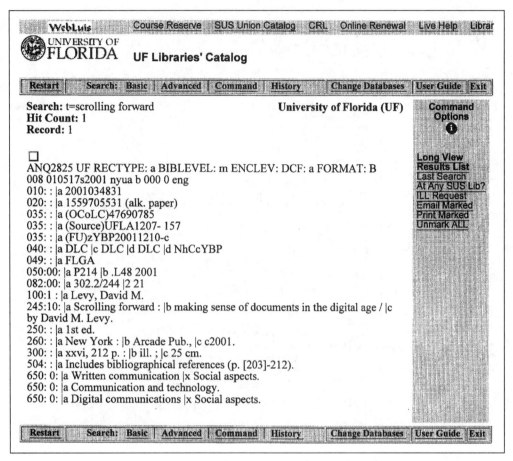

FIGURE 6-1 "Technical Services" (MARC) view of a bibliographic record. From the University of Florida.

CATALOGING ELECTRONIC RESOURCES

Both MARC and the cataloging code have undergone substantial changes to accommodate the description of electronic resources. When AACR was first published in 1978, it contained a chapter on machine-readable data files (chapter 9) that was substantially revised in the 1988 revision as computer files. The USMARC Advisory Committee approved adding a Computer Files format to USMARC in 1981. As the name "computer files" implies, initially both MARC and the cataloging rules focused on data files (such as social science survey data) and physically distributed publications (such as software on floppy disks and encyclopedias on CD-ROM). To a large extent, the history of cataloging in the 1990s can be seen as an attempt to cope with the rapid growth in remotely accessible digital resources—first, files and services accessed through Internet protocols such as FTP and TELNET and, later, the full variety of web-accessible resources.

A seminal development in this respect was the OCLC Internet Resources Project funded by a grant from the U.S. Department of Education and carried out from 1991 to 1993 under the leadership of Martin Dillon. The first part of the project attempted to categorize the types of resources available through the Internet at that time. The second

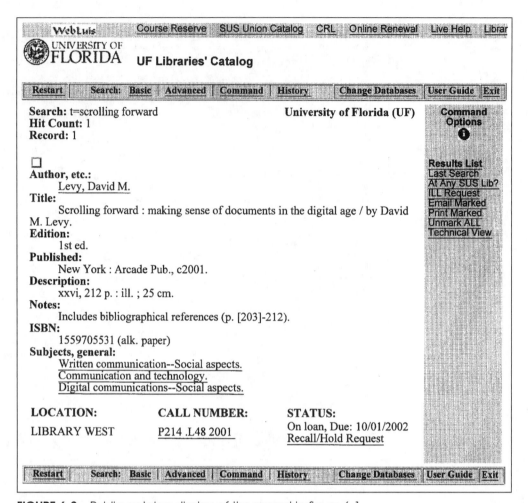

FIGURE 6-2 Public catalog display of the record in figure 6-1.

part was an experiment in applying the existing AACR2 and MARC rules to the cataloging of a sample of those resources, resulting in a documented list of problem areas in USMARC and AACR2. A direct outcome of the project was the issuance of Nancy Olson's *Cataloging Internet Resources: A Manual and Practical Guide*, which was influential in encouraging the cataloging of Internet resources and in shaping early cataloging practice.[14] Another outcome was the addition of the Electronic Location and Access (856) field to USMARC.

The 856 field currently is used most to carry the URLs of web-accessible resources. It should be noted, however, that this MARC field essentially predated the Web, having been proposed in 1992 and approved in 1993, the same year that the Mosaic browser was released. The 856 was originally designed for recording the modes of access most prevalent in the Internet Resources Project study: file transfer, email, and remote login. The subfield u for URI was added as a modification to the 856 six months after its addition to the format.

Other changes to MARC in the early 1990s included adding a set of coded values for the physical description of computer files (007), adding a code for "remote," and adding data fields for describing online systems and services. Changes to the cataloging code were slower to come, partly because of the more complex process of governance for AACR2 and partly because of the inherent conservatism of cataloging leaders. In 1997, ISBD(ER) for electronic resources was released and served as the basis for a complete revision to AACR2 chapter 9, issued in 2001. The title of chapter 9 was changed at this time from "Computer Files" to "Electronic Resources." The revised chapter 9 covers both *direct access* resources (those with physical carriers that are inserted into a computer, like CD-ROMs and tape cartridges) and *remote access* resources (those with no physical carrier connected via a network or directly attached storage devices).

The title (MARC21 field 245) for an electronic resource is taken from the chief source of information, which is any "formally presented evidence" in the resource itself, including such sources as a title screen, home page, main menu, initial display of information, file header, physical carrier, or metadata encoded in HTML or XML <meta> tags. When multiple allowable sources are present, the "fullest" or most complete source should be used. The source from which the title was taken must always be given in a note. The GMD for all electronic resources is "electronic resource."

If the electronic resource contains an edition statement, as indicated by such words as "edition," "issue," "version," or "update," that information should be given in the edition area (MARC21 field 250)—for example, "Version 5.20."

The name of area 3 (MARC21 field 256) for electronic resources is "Type and extent of resource area." For the type of resource, only three terms are allowed: "electronic data," "electronic program(s)," and "electronic data and program(s)." This is regrettable, as it is confusing to users to describe such resources as electronic journals and websites as "electronic data." Library of Congress practice is sensibly to omit this unhelpful information. ISBD(ER) specifies a longer and more useful list, including such terms as "electronic journal," "electronic image data," and "electronic online service." It is possible that future versions of the cataloging code will either incorporate the longer list or, more likely, eliminate area 3 for electronic resources.

Publication and distribution information (MARC field 260) is given for electronic resources in the same fashion as for other types of resources. All remote access resources, even personal home pages, are considered to be published. Physical description (MARC field 300) is allowed only for direct access resources, not for remote access. Allowable notes include the nature and scope of the file (where the type of resource can be described less cryptically than in area 3) and any system (hardware or software) requirements for using the file. A note specifying the "mode of access" for the file, for example, "World Wide Web," is required for remote access resources, as is a note giving the date on which the resource was viewed for cataloging.

Electronic resources, of course, have characteristics in common with other types of materials: they may be maps, manuscripts, sound recordings, or other textual or nontextual materials. The cataloging rules call for describing all aspects of the item, so that, for example, electronic journals are described according to the rules for serials as well as those for electronic resources. Some very common types of digital resources—including websites and online databases—have no nonelectronic analog and are poorly addressed by current cataloging rules. These resources are neither static, like monographs, nor issued successively, like serials, but are continuously updated. In this respect they bear the most similarity to loose-leaf publications, so catalogers usually attempt to describe them using the rules pertaining to loose-leafs. A major update to AACR2R, chapter 12 ("Serials"), is now available (ALA, 2002). The revision recognizes two different types of "continuing resource": *successive* (issued in discrete parts, like serials and series), and *integrating* (continuously updated, like loose-leafs, databases, and websites). This should clarify and simplify cataloging practice for these important resources.

Another major cataloging issue raised by digital resources concerns the treatment of different versions of a work. It is common for digital objects to be electronic versions of artifactual objects (documents, maps, etc.) as well as for the same content to exist in multiple digital formats (e.g., HTML, PDF, MS Word). This situation makes it critical to reexamine how versions are treated in cataloging, both to minimize the work of the cataloger and to maximize the intelligibility of the catalog to the user. Current thinking is focused on the distinction made by the FRBR between works, expressions, manifestations, and items, and how these distinctions might be better integrated into both the catalog code and MARC in the future.

It is commonly said that the only constant in today's digital environment is change. It is fairly certain that both the types of digital information resources available and the methods by which users will access these resources will be changing, and that "traditional" library cataloging will also change to accommodate what is new. Those who are interested should follow the activities of the primary maintenance organizations in this area. MARC21 is maintained by the Library of Congress, with the advice of the MARC Advisory Committee.[15] Changes to the cataloging code are the concern of the Joint Steering Committee for Revision of AACR, an international group to which the main channel of input from the United States is the ALA Committee on Cataloging: Description and Access (commonly known as CC:DA).[16]

NOTES

1. John Metcalfe, *Information Retrieval, British and American, 1876–1976* (Metuchen, N.J.: Scarecrow, 1976), 5.
2. Charles A. Cutter, *Rules for a Dictionary Catalog*, 4th ed. (Washington, D.C.: Government Printing Office, 1904), 6.
3. IFLANET, Family of ISBDs (web page), available at http://www.ifla.org/VI/3/nd1/isbdlist.htm. Accessed 17 June 2002.
4. International Federation of Library Associations and Institutions, *Functional Requirements for Bibliographic Records: Final Report*, UBCIM Publications, new series, vol. 19 (Munich: K. G. Saur, 1998), available at http://www.ifla.org/VII/s13/frbr/frbr.htm. Accessed 17 June 2002.
5. Program for Cooperative Cataloging NACO home page, available at http://www.loc.gov/catdir/pcc/naco.html. Accessed 17 June 2002.
6. Bibliographic and order information for all these publications is available from the Cataloging Distribution Service. Library of Congress, Cataloging Distribution Service, Bibliographic Products and Services (home page), available at http://lcweb.loc.gov/cds/. Accessed 17 June 2002.
7. Library of Congress, Network Development and MARC Standards Office, *MARC21 Concise Format for Bibliographic Data*, 2001 Concise Edition, available at http://lcweb.loc.gov/marc/bibliographic/. Accessed 17 June 2002.
8. Library of Congress, Network Development and MARC Standards Office, *Guidelines for the Use of Field 856*, available at http://www.loc.gov/marc/856guide.html. Accessed 18 June 2002.

9. *Bibliographic Formats and Standards,* 3rd ed. (Dublin, Ohio: OCLC Online Computer Library Center, 2002), available at http://www.oclc.org/oclc/bib/about.htm. Accessed 18 June 2002.
10. *CONSER Editing Guide,* 1994, available at http://www.carl.org/tlc/crs/edit7375.htm. Accessed 18 June 2002; *CONSER Cataloging Manual,* available at http://www.carl.org/tlc/crs/manl1573.htm. Accessed 18 June 2002.
11. Association for Library Collections and Technical Services, *Training Catalogers in the Electronic Era: Essential Elements of a Training Program for Entry-Level Professional Catalogers,* available at http://www.ala.org/alcts/publications/educ/training.html. Accessed 18 June 2002.
12. Scott Bennett, "Just in Time Scholarly Monographs," *Journal of Electronic Publishing* 4, no. 1 (September 1998), available at http://www.press.umich.edu/jep/04-01/bennett.html. Accessed 18 June 2002; Lori L. Osmus and Dilys E. Morris, "Serials Cataloging Time and Costs: Results of an Ongoing Study at Iowa State University," *Serials Librarian* 22, no. 1/2 (1992).
13. *LC21: A Digital Strategy for the Library of Congress* (Washington, D.C.: National Academy Press, 2000), 123, available at http://www7.nationalacademies.org/cstb/pub_lc21.html. Accessed 18 June 2002.
14. Nancy B. Olson, ed., *Cataloging Internet Resources: A Manual and Practical Guide,* 2nd ed., available at http://www.purl.org/oclc/cataloging-internet. Accessed 18 June 2002.
15. See the link to "MARC Development" from the Library of Congress, Network Development and MARC Standards Office, MARC Standards page at http://lcweb.loc.gov/marc/.
16. Joint Steering Committee for Revision of Anglo-American Cataloguing Rules (home page), available at http://www.nlc-bnc.ca/jsc/. Accessed 26 August 2002; Committee on Cataloging: Description and Access (home page), available at http://www.ala.org/alcts/organization/ccs/ccda/ccda.html. Accessed 26 August 2002.

READINGS

Anglo-American Cataloguing Rules. 2nd ed. Prepared by the American Library Association, the British Library, the Canadian Committee on Cataloguing, the Library Association, the Library of Congress. Edited by Michael Gorman and Paul W. Winkler. Chicago: American Library Association, 1978.

>   Although you may not want to read this cover to cover, a careful look at the organization and content of AACR2 will go a long way toward conveying the nature and spirit of library cataloging rules.

International Federation of Library Associations and Institutions. *ISBD(ER): International Standard Bibliographic Description for Electronic Resources.* Available at http://www.ifla.org/VII/s13/pubs/isbd.htm.

Olson, Nancy B., ed. *Cataloging Internet Resources: A Manual and Practical Guide.* 2nd ed. Dublin, Ohio: OCLC, 1997. Available at http://www.purl.org/oclc/cataloging-internet.

>   How to apply AACR2 and ISBD(ER) to Internet-accessible resources, written before the 2001 revision of chapter 9.

Svenonius, Elaine. *The Intellectual Foundation of Information Organization.* Cambridge, Mass.: MIT Press, 2000.

>   A difficult but illuminating work well on its way to becoming a classic, this book gives a conceptual framework for the process of organizing information in the tradition of Anglo-American descriptive and subject cataloging.

7 The TEI Header

The Text Encoding Initiative (TEI) is an international project established in 1987 under the joint sponsorship of the Association for Computers in the Humanities, the Association for Computational Linguistics, and the Association for Literary and Linguistic Computing. The goal of the TEI was to develop guidelines for the consistent SGML encoding of electronic texts and to encourage their use and exchange for humanities scholarship. The *Guidelines for Electronic Text Encoding and Interchange* is available in three main versions. The 1999 version is known as TEI P3 and defines the SGML encoding of texts. It has been superseded by the current 2002 version, TEI P4, which was fully revised to implement XML support while remaining compatible with TEI P3. A third version, TEI Lite, is smaller and easier to use. The examples and discussion that follow are based on TEI P3.

The TEI *Guidelines*, when first published in 1994, ran to 1,300 pages and purportedly weighed seven pounds. TEI is so large because it attempts to deal with the markup of many different kinds of texts for many types of historical, literary, and linguistic analysis. However, the only part of the TEI *Guidelines* concerned with metadata is chapter 5, which defines the TEI Header. As TEI P4 puts it:

> This chapter addresses the problems of describing an encoded work so that the text itself, its source, its encoding, and its revisions are all thoroughly documented. Such documentation is equally necessary for scholars using the texts, for software processing them, and for cataloguers in libraries and archives. Together these descriptions and declarations provide an electronic analogue to the title page attached to a printed work. They also constitute an equivalent for the content of the code books or introductory manuals customarily accompanying electronic data sets.[1]

As the preceding quotation hints, the drafters of the TEI *Guidelines*, as humanities scholars themselves, were heavy library users and well aware of the needs of libraries. In the early days of humanities computing, individual scholars (or their graduate assistants) converted texts to electronic form and marked them up to suit their own research purposes. The authors of TEI assumed that scholars would create TEI-encoded texts and TEI headers, but they also assumed that librarians would use the headers as the basis for cataloging the texts to appear in the library catalog. Therefore, they were careful to design the header in congruence with ISBD, while not requiring adherence to AACR in providing content.

The TEI header contains four sections, which, because the header is defined as an SGML DTD, are named here with their SGML tags:

<fileDesc> contains the bibliographic description of the electronic text;

<encodingDesc> describes the relationship between the electronic text and the source(s) from which it was derived;

<profileDesc> describes the nonbibliographic aspects of the text, specifically the languages used, the situation in which it was produced, and topical and genre descriptors;

<revisionDesc> contains the revision history of the file.

Although the header is only a small subset of the entire TEI specification, it, too, allows some complexity and offers a number of options. Most elements are optional, and there are nearly always alternative ways of representing the same content. For example, the value of almost any element can be represented as a simple text string, as a text string delimited with paragraph and other formatting markers, or as a series of subelements more specifically delimiting the content.

THE FILE DESCRIPTION

The <fileDesc> is the only required section and the one that was explicitly designed to conform to ISBD. It contains seven subsections:

<titleStmt> information about the title and those responsible for the intellectual content;

<editionStmt> information relating to the edition of the text;

<extent> the approximate size of the electronic text;

<publicationStmt> information on the publication or distribution of the electronic text;

<seriesStmt> information about the series to which the text belongs;

<notesStmt> notes providing additional information about the text;

<sourceDesc> a bibliographic description of the source text(s) from which the electronic text was derived.

The correspondence between the first six areas and six of the areas of ISBD/AACR2R description (see chapter 6 of this text) is not accidental.

Within the <titleStmt>, information about the electronic text and the nonelectronic source is intermixed. Subelements include <title>, which contains the title of the work; <author>, which contains the author of the (original) work; <sponsor>, <funder>, and <principal> for the sponsors, funders, and principal researchers responsible for the creation of the electronic version of the text; and <respStmt>. The <respStmt> is a statement of responsibility for the electronic version of the text and can contain the names of persons and organizations responsible for compiling, transcribing, digitizing, marking-up, or otherwise contributing to the creation of the text. Within the <respStmt>, <name> subelements contain the names of the principals, and <resp> subelements contain the relation of the principals to the text.

    <titleStmt>

        <title>Wind and water : poems</title>

        <author>Walters, Winston</author>

        <respStmt>

            <resp>Creation of machine-readable text:</resp>

            <name>Digital Library Center, Midtown University</name>

            <resp>TEI markup</resp>

            <name>John Monroe, Midtown University </name>

        </respStmt>

    </titleStmt>

Like area 2 in AACR2R, the <editionStmt> can contain information relating to a particular edition of the text and a statement of responsibility specifically pertaining to that edition. The <editionStmt> within the <titleStmt> is meant to refer to the electronic edition and is infrequently used, as there is little guidance as to when different electronic versions should be considered different editions.

The <extent> element records the approximate size of the electronic file:

<extent>ca. 9876 kilobytes</extent>

The <publicationStmt> describes publication and distribution details of the electronic file. It can be a textual description in sentences or it can have subelements; if the latter, it must include at least one of the three subelements <publisher>, <distributor>, or <authority>. The <authority> is a person or an organization responsible for making the electronic file available in ways other than publication or distribution. Within any of the three subelements the following may occur: <pubPlace> for place of publication or distribution, <address> for the address of the publisher or distributor, <idno> for any number used to identify the item, <availability> for terms of availability such as restrictions on use, and <date>.

```
<publicationStmt>

    <publisher>Midtown University Electronic Texts Project</publisher>

    <address>

        <addrLine>Box 570</addrLine>

        <addrLine>Midtown University</addrLine>

        <addrLine>Midtown, OH</addrLine>

    </address>

    <date>1999</date>

    <idno type="MUETP">99-182</idno>

</publicationStmt>
```

The <seriesStmt> element records the series in which the electronic publication was issued, if any. It can contain <title>, <idno> and <respStmt> elements. The <idno> element would be used for numbers identifying the series, such as an ISSN.

The <notesStmt> element can contain any relevant information about the electronic text that doesn't fit into other defined elements. Each individual note is contained within a <note> subelement.

Finally, the <sourceDesc> is a required element describing the source(s) from which the electronic file was derived. It may contain a simple prose description, a loosely structured citation in the <bibl> subelement, or a fully structured description in the <biblFull> subelement. All the subelements allowed within a <fileDesc> are allowed within the <biblFull>.

```
<sourceDesc>

    <biblFull>

        <titleStmt>

            <title>The Unmaking of a Mayor</title>

            <author>William F. Buckley, Jr.</author>

        </titleStmt>

        <publicationStmt>

            <publisher>The Viking Press, Inc.</publisher>

            <pubPlace>New York</pubPlace>

            <date>1966</date>

            <idno type="LCCN">66-20339</idno>

        </publicationStmt>

    </biblFull>

</sourceDesc>
```

THE PROFILE DESCRIPTION

If the <fileDesc> section is analogous to descriptive cataloging, the <profileDesc> section is roughly analogous to subject cataloging, at least in the content of the optional <textClass> element. The <textClass> element can contain one or more of the following elements:

<keywords> keywords or phrases identifying the topic or nature of the text;

<classCode> a classification code for the text;

<catRef> categories within some taxonomy.

The <keywords> and <classCode> tags take the attribute "scheme" to designate the controlled vocabulary or classification scheme used.

<textClass>

    <keywords scheme="LCSH">

        <term>Written communication—Social aspects</term>

        <term>Communication and technology</term>

        <term>Digital communications—Social aspects</term>

    </keywords>

</textClass>

If the "scheme" attribute is omitted, the use of uncontrolled keywords is assumed. If the scheme is given, the value of the attribute should be predefined in the <encodingDesc> section <classDecl> element, as noted in the following section.

In addition to <textClass>, the <profileDesc> section can contain the elements <creation> for information about the creation of the text, and <langUsage> for information about the languages and dialects used within the text.

THE ENCODING DESCRIPTION

Although the TEI header was intended to provide the same categories of bibliographic and subject description that library catalogers would use for a work, it was also intended to fulfill some nonbibliographic functions. The <encodingDesc> section details the methods used in creating and marking up the electronic text, and as such serves some of the same purposes as the "code books and introductory manuals customarily accompanying electronic data sets."

The <encodingDesc> may contain the following elements:

<projectDesc> describes the project creating the electronic file, including the purpose for which the file was created and the process by which it was created;

<samplingDesc> describes the rationale and methods used in sampling texts in the creation of a corpus or collection;

<editorialDecl> describes the editorial principles and practices applied;

<tagsDecl> lists each of the tags used in the markup of the text, with usage information;

<refsDecl> specifies how references are constructed;

<classDecl> names the taxonomies used for classification or subject terms or both.

For scholars using a text, two of the most important elements are <editorialDecl> and <tagsDecl>. The <editorialDecl> element can be used to indicate any changes and editorial decisions made to a text: whether end-of-line hyphens were removed, whether spelling or punctuation was normalized, what types of markup were applied, whether markup was done manually or by program, whether and how the text was checked for errors, and so on.

The <tagsDecl> element supplies detailed information about the markup used and how it should be displayed or rendered. If the element is used at all, every tag used in markup should be listed within it. Within <tagsDecl>, the <tagUsage> subelement indicates the name of the tag in a "gi" attribute and the number of occurrences of the element in the text in an "occurs" attribute:

<tagsDecl>

    <tagUsage gi="p" occurs="101">

</tagsDecl>

The <rendition> subelement indicates how the content should be treated and is related to named elements via the "render" attribute:

<tagsDecl>

    <rendition id="rend.p">break indent</rendition>

    <tagUsage gi="p" occurs="101" render="rend.p"</rendition>

</tagsDecl>

The <classDecl> element defines any classification schemes or controlled vocabularies used in the profile description section of the header. A taxonomy can be defined by a reference to some externally defined scheme, or it can be described directly within the <classDecl> using <category> and <catDesc> subelements. In either case, the <bibl> subelement can contain an unstructured bibliographic citation to the name of the scheme.

<classDecl>

    <taxonomy id="DDC">

        <bibl>Dewey Decimal System</bibl>

    </taxonomy>

</classDecl>

```
<classDecl>

    <taxonomy id="MT">

        <bibl>Midtown Local Classification Scheme</bibl>

        <category id="MT.100"

            <catDesc>University Administration</catDesc>

        </category>

        <category id="MT.105"

            <catDesc>Office of the President</catDesc>

        </category>

        <category id="MT.110"

            <catDesc>Office of the Provost</catDesc>

        </category>

        . . .

    </taxonomy>

</classDecl>
```

THE REVISION DESCRIPTION

Finally, the <revisionDesc> section contains the history of revisions made to the electronic text. Notations can be made in unstructured text within the <change> element or may be structured using subelements for dates, names, statements of responsibility, and changes made:

```
<revisionDesc>

    <change>

        <date>August 1998</date>

        <respStmt>

            <name>Emily Hart</name>

            <resp>ed.</resp>

        </respStmt>

        <item>Corrected tagging of proper names</item>

        <item>Completed taxonomy description in header</item>

    </change>

</revisionDesc>
```

THE TEI HEADER AND LIBRARY CATALOGING

Although the drafters of the TEI header specification expected most headers would be created by humanities scholars, in practice most TEI-encoded texts are created in libraries or in electronic text centers associated with libraries. As noted by Brad Eden,

> It is not at all uncommon for the header not to be created for, but to be created by, a cataloger, nor for a draft header to be translated into MARC and fed directly into the local cataloging system, where final adjustments are made and it is translated from MARC back to SGML and re-embedded in the document.[2]

In some projects, the MARC record for the print version of a work is used as the basis of the TEI header. Whatever the workflow, it is common for both traditional library cataloging and TEI headers to exist for the same work. The TEI header, because it is encoded in SGML like the text it describes, can be searched and displayed from the same full-text systems used to deliver the TEI texts. Libraries, however, like to have bibliographic records for all their holdings displayed in their online catalogs, requiring the creation of a stand-alone MARC record that can be integrated into the catalog system. As a result, both the cataloging and TEI communities are interested in examining the relationship between the two metadata schemes.

On the cataloging side, a CC:DA task force evaluated the TEI header as a source of metadata for cataloging records. The Task Force on Metadata and the Cataloging Rules was established to address the use of nontraditional metadata schemes, or records derived from them, in library catalogs. Its final report, based primarily on examination of the TEI header and the Dublin Core, concluded that metadata could not be integrated into library catalogs unless it was created according to AACR2 and subject vocabularies such as LCSH.[3]

A more detailed subreport on the TEI header noted that the header fulfilled more functions than those of bibliographic description, and, therefore, the TEI header and the traditional cataloging record are not substitutes for each other. The report then noted the inadequacies of TEI content in AACR2 terms: the creator of the header is probably ignorant of AACR2, AACR2-prescribed sources of information are not followed, rules for capitalization and punctuation are not followed, and authoritative AACR2 forms of name are not used. In sum, the wholly unsurprising conclusion was that if metadata creators do not follow AACR2 cataloging rules for content, the metadata they create is unlikely to adhere to AACR2 cataloging rules.

At the same time that the CC:DA task force was active, a conference was held at the Library of Congress on "TEI and XML in Digital Libraries." One of the breakout groups that held discussions at the meeting focused on "Descriptive Metadata: MARC, AACR2 and the TEI Header." Group members agreed there needed to be good "convertibility" between the header and MARC, and they made several recommendations to facilitate mapping between the two. They also made the following recommendation concerning content:

> Establish consensus for best practices and develop toolkit for [the TEI header], to include:
>
> guidelines for descriptive data—AACRlite(?), Authority lists
>
> tagging guidelines

minimal descriptive data element specifications

text selection, etc., guidelines[4]

As a follow-up effort, representatives from major text encoding initiatives at the University of Michigan and the University of Virginia met to review the relationship between the TEI header and MARC and to recommend best practices for creating TEI headers to encourage "compatible content." Their report prescribed a set of chief sources of information to be used for various types of electronic texts and gave guidelines for the content of various tags. For example, guidelines for use of the <author> element within the <fileDesc> area include this advice:

> Use discrete tags with <author> tag for "last name," "first name," "middle name," "date," "position title" to allow future flexibility in display, indexing and in transferring to MARC. Whenever possible, establish or use nationally established forms of names. The name should be inverted and entered in the established form.[5]

Most of the guidelines are useful even outside the context of mapping to library cataloging. The TEI header, like the TEI *Guidelines* overall, are designed to allow the encoder a great deal of flexibility in what data are recorded and how they are tagged in SGML. Although this can encourage wide implementation, such leeway can also make it difficult to exchange, share, or search across headers created by different projects. Guidelines can facilitate this by encouraging consistency in content creation and encoding. For example, the guidelines clarify which elements should be used to describe the original source and which should be used to describe the electronic text; they suggest standard formats for some elements, such as <extent> and <date> element; and they clarify the relationship between tags.

The TEI header has become a widely used metadata scheme and has lent itself to adaptation for a wide range of SGML- and XML-encoded textual materials far beyond scholarly humanities texts, including journal articles, newspaper articles, and electronic theses. Because the header can be embedded in the document it describes, it is particularly suited for applications that search both data and metadata and for those requiring self-documenting objects. Regardless of whether or not the bibliographic portions of the header evolve into closer conformity with AACR2/MARC, the usefulness of the TEI header in documenting nonbibliographic aspects of a text, including details of its markup and revision, guarantee that it will remain the dominant standard for description of electronic texts. In addition, the TEI header has served as a model for the bibliographic description component of several other SGML/XML-based metadata schemes, including the EAD and the DDI.

NOTES

1. C. M. Sperberg-McQueen and L. Burnard, eds., *TEI P4: Guidelines for Electronic Text Encoding and Interchange*, Text Encoding Initiative Consortium, XML Version (Oxford, Providence, Charlottesville, Bergen: 2002), available at http://www.teic.org/Guidelines2/index.html. Accessed 19 June 2002.
2. Brad Eden, "Metadata, TEI, and the Academic Library Community: An Update," in *<TEI 10>: Text Encoding Initiative Tenth Anniversary User Conference*, available at http://www.stg.brown.edu/conferences/tei10/tei10.papers/eden.html. Accessed 19 June 2002.
3. Committee on Cataloging: Description and Access, Task Force on Metadata and the Cataloging Rules, Final Report (August 21, 1998), available at http://www.ala.org/alcts/organization/ccs/ccda/tf-tei2.html. Accessed 19 June 2002.

4. TEI and XML in Digital Libraries, June 30–July 1, 1998, Washington, D.C., Working Group 1: Descriptive Metadata: MARC, AACR2, and the TEI Header Discussion Summary and Recommendations, available at http://www.umdl.umich.edu/workshops/teidlf/ teigrp1.html. Accessed 19 June 2002.
5. TEI/MARC "Best Practices" (June 16, 2001), available at http://www.lib.umich.edu/staff/ ocu/teiguide.html. Accessed 19 June 2002.

READINGS

Committee on Cataloging: Description and Access, Task Force on Metadata and the Cataloging Rules. Final Report (August 21, 1998). Available at http://www.ala.org/alcts/organization/ ccs/ccda/tf-tei2.html.

> Includes a chapter analyzing the TEI header for its usability in library systems.

Seaman, David. *The Electronic Text Center Introduction to TEI and Guide to Document Preparation.* Available at http://etext.lib.virginia.edu/tei/uvatei.html.

> The University of Virginia's internal guidelines for marking up documents according to TEI. Includes a chapter on the TEI header and examples of completed headers for various types of materials.

TEI and XML in Digital Libraries. Available at http://www.umdl.umich.edu/workshops/teidlf/.

> Notes from a meeting at the Library of Congress, held June 30–July 1, 1998; includes consideration of compatibility between MARC/AACR2 and TEI.

Text Encoding Initiative (home page). Available at http://www.tei-c.org/. Accessed 20 June 2002.

> Information about the TEI consortium, history, projects, and *Guidelines*.

8 The Dublin Core

The Dublin Core Metadata Element Set is a general-purpose scheme for resource description originally intended to facilitate discovery of information objects on the Web.

THE ELEMENT SET

The origin of the Dublin Core is by now nearly legendary. In the fall of 1994, the Second International World Wide Web Conference was held in Chicago with the theme "Mosaic and the Web." Although most of the conference tracks addressed the potential of the infant Web for transforming the way knowledge is presented, many of the participants were concerned with how all this newly available content would be found. Three of the attendees—Stu Weibel of OCLC, Joseph Hardin of NCSA, and the late Yuri Rubinski of Softquad—took the initiative to convene a multidisciplinary workshop in March 1995 to address which descriptive data elements were essential for discovery of networked information resources. A stated goal of the meeting was "to achieve consensus on a core set of data elements for document analogs and explore elements for other network-specific object types." Because the workshop was held at OCLC headquarters in Dublin, Ohio, the core set of data elements proposed there became known as the Dublin Core, and the workshop itself was retrospectively dubbed "DC1," the first of an ongoing series of Dublin Core metadata workshops.

The development of official specifications related to the Dublin Core is managed by the Dublin Core Metadata Initiative (DCMI), which consists of a small, paid directorate advised by a board of trustees, and a large number of loosely organized volunteers. Over time the DCMI has developed a governance structure and formal procedures for the approval of new specifications and the adoption of new terms. Most of the business of the DCMI is carried out in working groups, which provide a forum for discussion of specific issues and may draft requirements or specifications documents. Specifications follow a progression of statuses similar to that used by the World Wide Web Consortium (W3C), from "Working Draft," through "Proposed Recommendation" to "Recommendation." The status of Recommendation is equivalent to a standard; the specification is considered stable and supported for adoption by implementers. The approval of new metadata terms (elements or qualifiers) is the responsibility of a small, high-level committee called the Usage Board.

The Dublin Core Metadata Element Set (Dublin Core) itself consists of fifteen data elements. Identifiers and definitions of the elements are excerpted here from the reference definition of the Dublin Core:[1]

Identifier: Title
Definition: A name given to the resource.

Identifier: Creator
Definition: An entity primarily responsible for making the content of the resource.

Identifier: Subject
Definition: The topic of the content of the resource.

Identifier: Description
Definition: An account of the content of the resource.

Identifier: Publisher
Definition: An entity responsible for making the resource available.

Identifier: Contributor
Definition: An entity responsible for making contributions to the content of the resource.

Identifier: Date
Definition: A date associated with an event in the life cycle of the resource.

Identifier: Type
Definition: The nature or genre of the content of the resource.

Identifier: Format
Definition: The physical or digital manifestation of the resource.

Identifier: Identifier
Definition: An unambiguous reference to the resource within a given context.

Identifier: Source
Definition: A reference to a resource from which the present resource is derived.

Identifier: Language
Definition: A language of the intellectual content of the resource.

Identifier: Relation
Definition: A reference to a related resource.

Identifier: Coverage
Definition: The extent or scope of the content of the resource.

Identifier: Rights
Definition: Information about rights held in and over the resource.

All elements are optional, and all elements are repeatable. The scheme itself is format-independent, meaning that it is not tied to any single data representation the way, for example, the TEI header is tied to SGML/XML. The scheme is also not tied to any particular set of content rules, although recommended best practice is noted in the comments attribute for some elements, and additional recommendations are given in an official usage guide.[2] Following these documents for recommended best practice, a simple Dublin Core description could look like this:

Title="The Electronic Text Center Introduction to TEI and Guide to Document Preparation"

Creator="Seaman, David"

Subject="Text Encoding Initiative"

Subject="SGML markup rules"

Description="Guidelines written by the University of Virginia Electronic Text Center for marking up electronic texts using the TEILITE.DTD, a subset of the TEI tagset."

Date="1995"

Type="text"

Language="en"

Identifier="http://etext.lib.virginia.edu/tei/uvatei.html"

Dublin Core Qualifiers is a companion specification to the Dublin Core Metadata Element Set.[3] A *qualifier* either identifies the encoding scheme used in representing a Dublin Core element or refines the meaning of an element. An *encoding scheme* qualifier indicates the scheme or authority list used in representing the value of an element. An *element refinement* qualifier can narrow the meaning of an element but may not extend or change it. An important characteristic of element refinement qualifiers is that they can be ignored and the meaning of the value of the element will still make sense. This requirement, also known as the "dumb down principle," is based on the realization that not all applications processing Dublin Core metadata will necessarily recognize all qualifiers, so it must be possible to "dumb down" to the basic, unqualified meaning of the element.

Qualifiers are specific to individual elements. The element Date, for example, has five approved element refinement qualifiers (Created, Valid, Available, Issued, Modified) and two approved encoding scheme qualifiers (DCMI period, and W3C-DTF). The element Title has one element refinement qualifier (Alternative) and no encoding scheme qualifiers. Qualifiers have their own definitions that may reference other specifications or authority lists.

Despite the simplicity of the Dublin Core scheme, certain problems have arisen repeatedly in applications. One issue concerns the overlap in meaning in the definition of some elements. Creator can be seen as a particular type of Contributor, and Source is a particular type of Relation. This has led to confusion among implementers about when it is appropriate to use one element rather than another. At one point, a proposal to combine the elements Creator, Contributor, and Publisher into a single element called "agent" was considered and rejected. It has also been suggested that use of Source be deprecated in favor of Relation. However, the reasons for including Creator and Source in the original specification remain valid to many implementers. The bibliographic community has always accorded authorship special status, as reflected in the AACR2 concept of main entry. Distinguishing the special role of Creator from other contributors can make logical or practical sense in some applications. Along the same line, an important use of Dublin Core is to describe electronic versions of resources created by retrospective conversion projects. A special element for recording the nondigital source of the electronic resource can be justified in this context.

A second persistent issue concerns the nature of description when multiple versions exist. For example, the name of the photographer will generally be recorded as the creator of a photograph. However, if the photograph has been digitized and exists as a JPEG image, it can be argued that the person who scanned the photo is the creator of the image. Some Dublin Core implementers feel that the scanning technician is intellectually meaningless and should be recorded, if at all, as a contributor. Others believe that a Dublin Core record should accurately describe the resource in hand, which implies that for the JPEG image, the scanner is the creator and the photographer is at best a contributor. This principle, known as "one-to-one," prescribes that if multiple versions of a resource exist, each should be separately and accurately described.

SYNTAXES FOR DUBLIN CORE

Although the two Recommendations defining the Dublin Core and the Dublin Core Qualifiers are meant to convey semantics only, for a metadata scheme to be usable in practice it must have one or more generally accepted syntactical representations. The first encoding specification to reach Recommendation status was for HTML.[4] This specification makes use of <meta> "name" and "content" attributes, in the generic format:

<meta name = "PREFIX.Element_name"

content = "element_value">

The prefix is arbitrary and used to link to the Dublin Core specification. This is represented in HTML by a set of attributes to the <link> element:

<link rel="schema.PREFIX"

href="http://purl.org/dc/elements/1.1/"

title="Dublin Core Metadata Element Set, Version 1.1">

The HTML Recommendation specifies using the capitalized "DC" as the prefix. A portion of the Seaman document description shown above could be represented in the following HTML:

```
<link rel="schema.DC"

      href="http://purl.org/dc/elements/1.1/"

      title="Dublin Core Metadata Element Set, Version 1.1">

<meta name="DC.Title"

      content="The Electronic Text Center Introduction to TEI and Guide to
      Document Preparation">

<meta name="DC.Creator"

      content="Seaman, David">

<meta name="DC.Identifier"

      content="http://etext.lib.virginia.edu/tei/uvatei.html">
```

Encoding scheme qualification is represented by use of the <meta> "scheme" attribute:

```
<meta name="DC.Type"

      scheme="DCMIType"

      content="text">
```

Element refinement qualification is represented in "dot" notation:

```
<meta name="DC.Date.created"

      content="1995">
```

Representing Dublin Core semantics in HTML is fairly straightforward and works particularly well in environments where web pages are spidered and indexed by search engines configured to take advantage of <meta> tags. There are, however, some limitations and drawbacks. For applications that require metadata records, as opposed to metadata embedded in documents, XML tends to be the preferred exchange syntax. Also, HTML cannot represent more complex constructions—for example, where sets of repeated elements need to be grouped to be meaningful.

Dublin Core can also be represented in XML. Several XML schemas have been developed for particular applications of Dublin Core, including one approved for use with Open Archives Initiative metadata harvesting applications. The DCMI home page links to a list of schemas that are supported by the Dublin Core community. In addition, general guidelines for representing both qualified and unqualified Dublin Core in XML have been issued by UKOLN.[5] UKOLN recommends that implementers make use of the XML namespace facility to uniquely identify Dublin Core elements, which should be represented as XML elements. The Seaman document represented in simple Dublin Core according to the UKOLN specification might look like this:

```
<?xml version="1.0"?>

<metadata

      xmlns="http://myorg.org/myapp/"
```

```
  xmlns:xsi="http://www.w3.org/2001/XMLSchema-instance"

  xsi:schemaLocation="http://myorg.org/myapp/ http://myorg.org/myapp/
  schema.xsd"

  xmlns:dc="http://purl.org/dc/elements/1.1/">

  <dc:title> The Electronic Text Center Introduction to TEI and Guide to
  Document Preparation </dc:title>

  <dc:creator> Seaman, David </dc:creator>

  <dc:identifier> http://etext.lib.virginia.edu/tei/uvatei.html </dc:identifier>

</metadata>
```

In this example, the XML schema used is a (fictitious) schema referenced by the URI "http://myorg.org/myapp/schema.xsd." The XML namespace for the Dublin Core metadata element set itself is referenced with the namespace statement that begins "xmlns:dc=" indicating that Dublin Core element names will be prefaced by "dc:" and that the definition of DC elements will be found in the document at http://purl.org/dc/elements/1.1/. The UKOLN specification recommends representing Dublin Core element names (property names) in lowercase (that is "dc:title" rather than "dc:Title").

To encode qualified Dublin Core, a namespace statement for the reference definition of the Dublin Core Qualifiers must be added, shown in the following example as "xmlns:dcterms=." UKOLN recommends representing element refinement qualifiers as elements rather than as attributes, so that, for example, the Date qualifier "Created" would be represented as:

```
  <dcterms:created>2002</dcterms:created>
```

rather than

```
  <dc:date type="created">2002</dc:date>.
```

In contrast, encoding scheme qualifiers should be represented using a "scheme" attribute, and the language of a value should be represented using the XML "lang" attribute.

```
  <?xml version="1.0"?>

  <metadata

    xmlns="http://myorg.org/myapp/"

    xmlns:xsi="http://www.w3.org/2001/XMLSchema-instance"

    xsi:schemaLocation="http://myorg.org/myapp/ http://myorg.org/myapp/
    schema.xsd"

    xmlns:dc="http://purl.org/dc/elements/1.1/"

    xmlns:dcterms="http://purl.org/dc/terms/">
```

```
<dc:title xml:lang="en"> The Electronic Text Center Introduction to TEI
and Guide to Document Preparation </dc:title>

<dc:creator> Seaman, David </dc:creator>

<dcterms:created> 1995 </dcterms:created>

<dc:identifier scheme="URI"> http://etext.lib.virginia.edu/tei/uvatei.html
</dc:identifier>
```

```
</metadata>
```

Dublin Core can also be represented in XML according to the rules of the Resource Description Framework (RDF). The Recommendation, "Expressing Simple Dublin Core in RDF/XML," was approved by the DCMI in October 2002 (http://www.dublin core.org/documents/2002/07/31/dcmes-xml/). According to the Recommendation, the use of RDF must be declared with an <rdf:RDF> tag. A single RDF encoding can be used to represent multiple resources, as long as each resource to be described is encapsulated within a separate <rdf:Description> element. No qualifiers or locally defined elements can be used, and the resulting RDF/XML cannot be embedded in web pages.

The actual encoding of the Dublin Core elements is quite straightforward, as the example below shows.

```
<?xml version="1.0"?>

<!DOCTYPE rdf:RDF PUBLIC "-//DUBLIN CORE//DCMES DTD
2002/07/31//EN" "http://dublincore.org/documents/2002/07/31/dcmes-
xml/dcmes-xml-dtd.dtd">

<rdf:RDF xmlns:rdf="http://www.w3.org/1999/02/22-rdf-syntax-ns#"

    xmlns:dc="http://purl.org/dc/elements/1.1/">

    <rdf:Description rdf:about="http://etext.lib.virginia.edu/tei/uvatei.html">

        <dc:title>The Electronic Text Center Introduction to TEI and Guide
        to Document Preparation</dc:title>

        <dc:creator>Seaman, David</dc:creator>

        <dc:date>2002-07-31</dc:date>

    </rdf:Description>

</rdf:RDF>
```

Note that if the resource has a single URI, it is encoded as the value of the rdf:about attribute, rather than as the value of a <dc:identifier> element. If the resource has multiple URIs, the additional URI(s) may be given in <dc:identifier>.

There is no approved Recommendation for expressing qualified Dublin Core in RDF/XML, but a proposed Recommendation is working its way through the approval process.[6] According to this document, the Dublin Core elements and element refinement qualifiers correspond to RDF properties and subproperties. Encoding scheme qualifiers, on the other hand, correspond to RDF "classes" or "types." In the following example, which follows the proposed Recommendation, two assertions are made. First, the value of the element refinement qualifier "created" is stated to be 1995. Second, "created" itself is noted to be a subproperty of the Dublin Core element Date.

```
<rdf:Description>

    <dcq:created>1995</dcq:created>

</rdf:Description>

<rdf:Description about="http://purl.org/dc/terms/created">

    <rdfs:subPropertyOF

        rdf:resource="http://purl.org/dc/elements/1.1/date"/>

</rdf:Description>
```

Another syntactical requirement, beyond the ability to represent simple and qualified Dublin Core, is some mechanism for combining elements from Dublin Core and other defined metadata element sets. From the beginning, implementers realized that the Dublin Core would have to be augmented by additional elements to be useful in specific application areas or domains. The element prefix serves this function by indicating the scheme from which an element was taken.

A good example of this is provided by a project called BIBLINK, funded by the European Commission. BIBLINK was designed to encourage publishers to contribute standard descriptive metadata for electronic documents to national bibliographic services that would in turn send enhanced metadata back to the publishers. BIBLINK defined a metadata element set with nineteen elements.[7] Twelve of these were taken from the Dublin Core, and seven were defined specifically for BIBLINK, including a checksum, place of publication, frequency, and price. A BIBLINK-compliant description in HTML uses prefixes to distinguish standard Dublin Core from BIBLINK-specific elements:

```
<meta name="BIBLINK.Checksum"

content="fd66e37fb693491e84e184b092121265">

<meta name="DC.Title" content="Taylor-Schechter Unit Home Page">
```

The use of the namespace facility provides a more formal mechanism for extensibility in XML and RDF. (Note, however, that XML DTDs do not explicitly support namespaces, so use of XML schema is preferred for document definition.) The following example, taken from the UKOLN "Guidelines for Implementing Dublin Core in XML," shows a record that includes both Dublin Core elements and the IEEE Learning Object Model (LOM) element "TypicalLearningTime."

```
<?xml version="1.0"?>

<record

    xmlns="http://myorg.org/learningapp/"

    xmlns:xsi="http://www.w3.org/2001/XMLSchema-instance"
```

```
xsi:schemaLocation="http://myorg.org/learningapp/ http://myorg.org/
learningapp/schema.xsd"

xmlns:dc="http://purl.org/dc/elements/1.1/"

xmlns:ims="http://www.imsglobal.org/xsd/imsmd_v1p2">

<dc:title> Frog maths </dc:title>

<dc:identifier> http://somewhere.com/frogmaths/ </dc:identifier>

<dc:description> Simple math games for 5-7 year olds. </dc:description>

<ims:typicallearningtime>

     <ims:datetime> 0000-00-00T00:15 </ims:datetime>

</ims:typicallearningtime>

</record>
```

APPLICATION PROFILES

As demonstrated by the preceding BIBLINK example, when the Dublin Core is used to describe resources for a particular project or application, it is not uncommon for implementers to supplement it with additional elements or qualifiers needed by that application. Implementers may also feel the need for stricter limitations on usage (for example, to define some required elements) or more specific guidelines on content than appear in the Dublin Core itself.

Application profiles are one way to formalize the definition of metadata schemes based on Dublin Core. Formally, an application profile is a scheme designed for a particular application that consists of data elements from one or more previously defined schemes. It can refine the meaning of existing elements, but it cannot expand the meaning of elements or introduce new elements. It can also specify limits on the use of elements, such as mandating conditions of use (e.g., mandatory, nonrepeatable) or specifying permitted or required data representations or controlled vocabularies.

Application profiles are best implemented as XML schema, as namespaces are supported, and XML schemas support local usage constraints, such as authority lists of values, required elements, and limitations on repeatability. Application profiles can also be implemented in RDF with slightly less flexibility. However, conceptually, application profiles can be established as written implementers' agreements and encoded in any syntax, so long as machine-understandability and technical enforcement are not required. In some communities, the idea of the application profile is being expanded to include the type of information that would commonly appear in a user guide, including more guidelines for choice and form of content than even XML schema language can enforce.

The BIBLINK scheme mentioned earlier is an example of an application profile and has been represented as an XML schema for this purpose.[8] Some application profiles are being developed under the auspices of the DCMI, such as the Libraries application profile being developed by the Libraries Working Group. This profile is being developed to support library applications of the Dublin Core, such as use as an interchange format between systems using different metadata standards; use in metadata harvesting applications, such as those following the Open Archives Initiative Metadata Harvesting Protocol; and use in creation of simple library catalog records with Dublin Core semantics. Other application profiles are under development within the DCMI for government, education, and environmental domains.

USES AND ISSUES

With or without the addition of domain-specific terms, the Dublin Core has proven useful in several library contexts. It is often used in subject gateways or portals, where the description of a resource appearing in the web gateway is generated from a database of brief Dublin Core information. It is also popular for describing electronic texts and images created in retrospective digitization projects, particularly those involving large numbers of items and in which full library cataloging may not be affordable or warranted. Also, for certain types of materials, such as photographs or newspaper articles, the application of AACR2 rules may be problematic, discouraging the integration of these items into the main library catalog. Here, use of Dublin Core–based schemes allows the advantage of some standardization while giving project designers the leeway to identify data elements and guidelines that are meaningful to them. For example, a project could decide to use AACR2 rules and associated authority files only for name headings in the Creator and Contributor fields, and not for formulating titles or for other aspects of bibliographic description.

Another common situation occurs when metadata is stored in the local database according to some richer scheme, but is converted to Dublin Core for use in a union catalog, Internet search engine index, or other external database containing contributions from multiple sources. The Dublin Core serves as a least common denominator to which more complex schemes can be mapped, so that searching can take place over a consistent set of data elements. The prime example of this is the Open Archives Initiative protocol for metadata harvesting, which requires that, at a minimum, all participating sites have the ability to export unqualified Dublin Core.

It should be noted that the long-term significance of the Dublin Core may lie less in its utility as a resource description scheme than in the role of the DCMI in bringing together so many disparate communities of interest. The DCMI has created an organization that is truly international in scope and participation, and it has brought to the fore issues related to language and multilingual representation of both metadata and metadata schemes. DCMI workshops have created a venue for libraries, museums, and other cultural heritage institutions to exchange information with governmental organizations, scientific agencies, web developers, computer scientists, educators, and others, enriching all these communities.

The DCMI has also played an important role in making the library community aware of interoperability issues beyond the closed MARC environment. From developing an early theoretical architecture for combining metadata from diverse schema (the "Warwick Framework") to current use of XML and RDF namespaces, researchers associated with the Dublin Core have always acknowledged the real-world need to integrate descriptive and administrative metadata originating from different sources at different times. Crosswalks to Dublin Core have been developed from nearly all important descriptive metadata schemes. Various prototypes developed for the DCMI registry effort have attempted to incorporate terms from application profiles and related domain-specific schemes as well as from the official Dublin Core namespaces. The heavy involvement of some members of the DCMI in the development of RDF and the Semantic Web has helped to promote awareness of these initiatives within the library community. The DCMI itself has deliberately broadened its mission in recent years, seeking to become a general forum for issues related to cross-domain discovery and frameworks for interoperability.

At the same time, the DCMI has been criticized for taking too long to produce basic guidance for Dublin Core implementers. There are still no approved Recommendations for syntactical representation of qualified Dublin Core in XML and RDF. Guidelines for representing citations to journal articles in Dublin Core have been under development since 1998 and are still unfinished. Element refinement qualifiers for the Creator, Contributor, and Publisher elements were omitted from the Dublin Core Qualifiers because of lack of consensus within the Usage Board, and currently are still pending, despite a great need for these among implementers. It remains to be seen whether the needs of implementers will be satisfied more or less well as the interests of the DCMI focus increasingly on theoretical and practical issues of interoperability.

NOTES

1. *Dublin Core Metadata Element Set, Version 1.1: Reference Description,* available at http://dublincore.org/documents/dces/. Accessed 21 June 2002.
2. Diane Hillmann, *Using Dublin Core,* available at http://dublincore.org/documents/2001/04/12/usageguide/. Accessed 21 June 2002.
3. *Dublin Core Qualifiers,* available at http://dublincore.org/documents/dcmes-qualifiers/. Accessed 21 June 2002.
4. John Kunze, *Encoding Dublin Core in HTML* (IETF RFC2731), available at http://www.ietf.org/rfc/rfc2731.txt. Accessed 21 June 2002.
5. Andy Powell and Pete Johnson, "Guidelines for Implementing Dublin Core in XML," 12 March 2002, available at http://www.ukoln.ac.uk/metadata/dcmi/dc-xml-guidelines/. Accessed 21 June 2002.
6. Stefan Kokkelink and Roland Schwänzl, "Expressing Qualified Dublin Core in RDF/XML," 29 August 2001, available at http://www.dublincore.org/documents/2001/08/29/dcq-rdf-xml/. Accessed 24 June 2002.
7. "BIBLINK Core Field Semantics," available at http://hosted.ukoln.ac.uk/biblink/wp8/fs/bc-semantics.html. Accessed 24 June 2002.
8. Jane Hunter, *An XML Schema Approach to Application Profiles,* 3 October 2000, available at http://archive.dstc.edu.au/maenad/appln_profiles.html. Accessed 24 June 2002.

READINGS

Dekkers, Makx, and Stuart L. Weibel. "Dublin Core Metadata Initiative Progress Report and Workplan for 2002." *D-Lib Magazine* 8, no. 2 (February 2002). Available at http://www.dlib.org/dlib/february02/weibel/02weibel.html.

> A "state of Dublin Core" report from 2002. *D-Lib Magazine* has published numerous articles on Dublin Core, including reports from most of the Dublin Core workshops. These reports, read in order, constitute a history of the evolution of the DCMI.

Dublin Core Metadata Initiative (home page). Available at http://www.dublincore.org/.

> Many relevant documents are linked to from the Dublin Core home page, including the current reference description of the Dublin Core specification itself (http://www.dublincore.org/documents/dces/) and the Dublin Core qualifiers (http::www.dublincore.org/documents/dcmes-qualifiers/). Approved DCMI Recommendations and proposed Recommendations are listed under the link "Documents." The "Resources" link includes a bibliography of writings related to Dublin Core.

Guenther, Rebecca, and Priscilla Caplan. "Metadata for Internet Resources: The Dublin Core Metadata Elements Set and Its Mapping to USMARC." *Cataloging and Classification Quarterly* 22, no. 3/4 (1996).

> A discussion of some of the issues raised in attempting to map from Dublin Core to MARC. The Library of Congress maintains an official crosswalk from MARC to Dublin Core at http://lcweb.loc.gov/marc/marc2dc.html and between Dublin Core, MARC21, and GILS at http://www.loc.gov/marc/dccross.html.

9

Archival Description and the EAD

An archival collection (or *archives*) has been defined as "an organized collection of the noncurrent records of an institution, government, organization, or corporate body, or the personal papers of an individual or family, preserved in a repository for their historical value."[1] A wide range of agencies may be responsible for archives, including government bodies, units within businesses or non-profit organizations, and special collections and manuscript departments within libraries.

PRINCIPLES OF ARCHIVAL DESCRIPTION

As noted in chapter 6, librarianship has a long tradition of bibliographic description, currently embodied in AACR2R and associated rulesets. Archivists also have a tradition of archival description, which differs from bibliographic description in a number of important ways. While bibliographic description is centered on the single publication, archival description centers on aggregations called a *record group* when referring to the papers of an organization or an *archival collection* when referring to the papers of an individual. (Both types of aggregation are called *fonds* in Anglo-Canadian archives.) These materials are related by *provenance*, or the history of creation and ownership of the materials. Because the basic unit of archival description is an aggregation, description of the physical characteristics of items within the collection is far less important than description of the intellectual characteristics and organization of the collection itself.

Two tenets of archival documentation are *respect des fonds* and the principle of original order. *Respect des fonds*, also known as the principle of provenance, mandates that materials with the same origin must be kept together and not mixed with other materials. *Original order* mandates that the order of creation must be preserved. In the case of institutional records, there may also be legal requirements pertaining to the retention, integrity, and authenticity of the records. The implication for archival description is that the documentation of both provenance and original order is of the highest importance. Archival description usually begins by describing the record group or collection as a whole and proceeds to documenting the various series and subseries within it in a hierarchical manner. Description may go to the level of individual items or may terminate at some higher level.

When AACR2 was published in 1978, it contained a chapter on manuscript cataloging that was universally felt by archivists to be unusable for archives and manuscript collections because it did not take cognizance of long-standing principles of archival description. It focused on the description of individual items instead of aggregations and on physical description as opposed to the documentation of provenance. As a result, Steven Hensen at the Library of Congress drafted *Archives, Personal Papers, and Manuscripts* (APPM), which immediately upon publication in 1983 became the standard for cataloging archives and manuscripts.[2]

In roughly the same period, the National Information Systems Task Force, a group formed by the Society of American Archivists (SAA) with funding from the National Endowment for the Humanities, helped to develop the *USMARC Format for Archives and Manuscripts Control* (AMC). Archivists and manuscripts curators used APPM as the content standard for creating AMC records. RLIN, the catalog and cataloging system of the Research Libraries Group, became the main de facto online union catalog of archives and manuscripts collections in the United States.

AMC cataloging gave an unprecedented level of access to important archival collections. However, because of limitations on the length and structure of MARC records, such cataloging cannot substitute for the more detailed guides, called *finding aids*, traditionally used by archival repositories. The finding aid, which may be in the form of an inventory, a register, or a calendar, is the primary tool for establishing administrative and intellectual control over archives and manuscript collections. Until recently there have been no formal content standards for finding aids, so the form and content of a finding aid can vary widely from one repository to another and, indeed, from one collection to another. However, following the principles of archival description, finding aids generally begin with some kind of high-level description of provenance, which may include a biographical sketch, a corporate history, or an organizational profile as appropriate. The scope and content of the body of materials might then be described, followed by description of individual groupings of materials (e.g., series and subseries), followed by description of files (containers) and, in some cases, even individual items. Figure 9-1 shows a relatively short finding aid.

EAD STRUCTURE AND ELEMENTS

The Encoded Archival Description (EAD) was developed in the 1990s as a way of encoding traditional paper finding aids in machine-readable form. Because, as noted, there was no universally followed standard for creating finding aids, the originators of the EAD gathered sample finding aids from a number of repositories and tried to

Summary Information

Title: W. May Walker Papers
Inclusive Dates: 1901-1974
Bulk Dates: 1925-1974
Call No.: MSS 76-12
Creator: Pansy Walker
Extent: 12.75 Linear/Cubic Feet; 33 Boxes
Repository:
    Special Collections, Florida State University Libraries

Storage: Box 889-921 shelved at Claude Pepper Library, Florida State University. For current information on the location of materials, please consult the Special Collections Department's home page.
Abstract:
    The collection includes correspondence, committee papers, legislative papers, and legal papers such as rulings, opinions, and papers concerning particular cases. Judge Walker served as County Judge of Leon County and on the bench of the 2nd Judicial Circuit. The great majority of the papers in the collection cover the time period from the 1940s until the time of his death, September 16, 1974. Also included among his papers are papers belonging to his father, Nat R. Walker, who was one of the most colorful and significant characters in the history of Florida.

Administrative Information

Acquisition Information:

The W. May Walker Papers were donated to the Special Collections Department, Florida State University Libraries, by Pansy Walker of Tallahassee, Florida, in 1976.

Access:

Collection is open for research.

Usage Restrictions:

Copyright has not been assigned to the Florida State University Libraries. All requests for permission to publish or quote from manuscripts must be submitted in writing to the Director of University Libraries. Permission for publication is given on behalf of Florida State University Libraries as the owner of the physical items and is not intended to include or imply permission of the copyright holder, which must also be obtained by the researcher.

Processing History:

The majority of this collection was processed in August 1976 by staff members of the Special Collections Department. The final two boxes, comprised of the Personal Business Papers series, was only partially processed and remained in that state until February 2002 when it was processed and the finding aid updated accordingly.

FIGURE 9-1 Finding aid. This relatively short finding aid is shown in its entirety up to the container list.

Preferred Citation:

[Identification of item], W. May Walker Papers, Special Collections, Florida State University Libraries, Tallahassee, Florida.

Biography

The Honorable W. May Walker was born in Crawfordville, Wakulla County, Florida on May 2, 1905, the son of Nat R. Walker and Alice (Tully) Walker, both of Crawfordville. After attending public schools in Leon County he received his Bachelor of Laws degree from Cumberland University, Lebanon, Tennessee, in 1927. That same year, after passing the Florida Bar exam, he began the practice of Law in Tallahassee.

Judge Walker then served as County Judge of Leon County from 1932 to 1940 when he took over the Circuit Court Judgeship after the death of J. B. Johnson. He served on the bench of the 2nd Judicial Circuit until the time of his death, September 16, 1974.

He married Pansy Crosby daughter of Joseph and Nora Horton Crosby in 1937 and they have two sons, W. May Walker, Jr. and Joseph Stanley Walker. During his lengthy career judge Walker has presided over many important and sensational cases and was one of the most hard-working and distinguished jurists of the State.

Collection Scope and Content Note

The papers of Judge W. May Walker cover all aspects of his legal career including correspondence, committee papers, legislative papers, rulings and opinions, as well as papers concerning particular cases. Judge Walker served as County Judge of Leon County and on the bench of the 2nd Judicial Circuit. The great majority of the papers in the collection cover the time period from the 1940s until the time of his death, September 16, 1974. Also included among his papers are papers belonging to his father, Nat R. Walker, who was one of the most colorful and significant characters in the history of Florida. A brief biography of Nat Walker is filed with his papers.

Controlled Access Terms

Note:

The following terms have been used to index the description of this collection in the Library's online catalog:

Subject Terms:

- Walker, W. May, 1905-1974
- Walker, Nat R.
- Judges -- Florida

Contents List

Container / Location   **Title**

Series: Series A: Correspondence

accommodate the range of practice found among them. SGML was chosen as an encoding scheme because of its ability to handle lengthy narrative text and multiple levels of hierarchy. Originally implemented as an SGML DTD, the EAD now has an XML DTD as well. The EAD DTD contains three main sections:

<eadheader> contains information about the EAD itself;

<frontmatter> gives a formatted description of the finding aid for publication;

<archdesc> describes the archives or manuscripts collection.

The <eadheader> contains <filedesc>, <profiledesc>, and <revisiondesc> sections very similar to the comparable sections in the TEI header. The <filedesc> includes elements related to the title and publication of the finding aid ; <profiledesc> describes the creation date and language of the finding aid; and <revisiondesc> records changes made to the finding aid over time.

The <frontmatter> section contains information similar to that contained in the <filedesc> section of the <eadheader>, formatted to serve as a printed title page for the finding aid. It is rarely used.

The heart of the EAD is the <archdesc>, which describes the archival collection or record group itself rather than the finding aid. The same descriptive data elements that apply at the highest (collection) level can be repeated for each subunit within it and for subunits within subunits, making the <archdesc> both hierarchical and recursive. A conceptual overview of the high-level subelements within the <archdesc> follows:

<did> descriptive identification

<admininfo> administrative information

<bioghist> biography or history

<scopecontent> scope and content

<organization> organization

<arrangement> arrangement

<note> note

<dao> digital archival object

<daogroup> digital archival object group

<controlaccess> controlled access headings

<add> adjunct descriptive data

<odd> other descriptive data

<dsc> description of subordinate components

    <c01> component (1st level)

        <did>

        <admininfo>

<bioghist>

<scopecontent>

<organization>

<arrangement>

<note>

<dao>

<daogroup>

<controlaccess>

<add>

<odd>

<c02> component (2nd level)

   <did>

    . . .

The <did> (Descriptive Identification) element contains the basic description of materials at any level. Subelements that can occur within the <did> include:

<repository> the name of the holding repository;

<origination> the provenance of the materials;

<unittitle> the title of the unit being described;

<unitdate> the dates of the materials included;

<physdesc> physical description of the materials;

brief summary description of materials;

<unitid> an identifier for the unit;

<physloc> the physical location of the unit.

Although each of these elements may occur at any level of description, some (such as the name of the repository) are more likely to be used at the collection level, while others (such as the physical location of the unit) are more appropriate at lower levels.

Within most of these major subelements of the <did>, data can be entered directly or with further markup into subelements and attributes. Figures 9-2 and 9-3 show simple and more detailed markup for the same collection.

The <admininfo> element contains information relating to the administration of the collection or subunit, such as acquisitions and processing information, custodial history, restrictions on access and/or use, and the form preferred for citation. The <bioghist> element can contain a biographical sketch or agency history in narrative or chronological format. The <scopecontent> element is used to summarize the topical coverage of the collection or subunit. The <arrangement> and <organization> subele-

```
<did>
    <repository>Harry Ransom Humanities Research Center</repository>
    <origination>Stoppard, Tom</origination>
    <unittitle>Tom Stoppard Papers</unittitle>
    <unitdate>1944-1995</unitdate>
    <physdesc>68 boxes (28 linear feet)</physdesc>
    <abstract>The papers of British playwright Tom Stoppard (b.
    1937) encompass his entire career and consist of multiple
    drafts of his plays, from the well-known
    <title render="italic">Rosencrantz and Guildenstern Are
    Dead</title> to several that were never produced,
    correspondence, photographs, and posters, as well as
    materials from stage, screen, and radio productions from
    around the world.</abstract>
</did>
```

FIGURE 9-2   Portion of an EAD showing a collection marked up with minimal detail.
From the *Encoded Archival Description Application Guidelines, version 1.0.* Reprinted
by permission of the Society of American Archivists.

```
<did>
    <head>Summary Description of the Tom Stoppard Papers</head>
    <repository>
        <corpname>The University of Texas at Austin
        <subarea>Harry Ransom Humanities Research Center</subarea>
        </corpname>
    </repository>
    <origination>
        <persname source="lcnaf" encodinganalog="100">Stoppard,
        Tom</persname>
    </origination>
    <unittitle encodinganalog="245">Tom Stoppard Papers, </unittitle>
    <unitdate type="inclusive">1944-1995</unitdate>
    <physdesc encodinganalog="300">
        <extent>68 boxes (28 linear feet)</extent>
    </physdesc>
    <unitid type="accession">R4635</unitid>
    <physloc audience="internal">14E:SW:6-8</physloc>
    <abstract>The papers of British playwright Tom Stoppard (b.
    1937) encompass his entire career and consist of multiple
    drafts of his plays, from the well-known
    <title render="italic">Rosencrantz and Guildenstern Are
    Dead</title> to several that were never produced,
    correspondence, photographs, and posters, as well as
    materials from stage, screen, and radio productions from
    around the world.</abstract>
</did>
```

FIGURE 9-3   Collection shown in fig. 9-1, marked up with more detail. From the *Encoded
Archival Description Application Guidelines, version 1.0.* Reprinted by permission of the
Society of American Archivists.

ments may be used within <scopecontent> to delimit this information or can be external to <scopecontent> at the same level of description.

The <controlaccess> tag is a wrapper element for encoding controlled forms of names and subjects intended for use as access points. Subelements include types of names (<corpname>, <famname>, <persname>), places (<geogname>), subjects

(<subject>), and genre (<genreform>). In all these subelements, the authority file used should be specified by the attribute "source."

<controlaccess>

<head>Subjects</head>

<subject source="lcsh">Civil War — Florida</subject>

<subject source="lcsh">Railroads — Florida</subject>

</controlaccess>

The description of subordinate components <dsc> element serves as a wrapper for the description of component parts. The component parts themselves are encoded within a container element that can be represented with or without numbering—that is, either as repeated <c> elements, or as <c01> <c02> . . . <c0n>. If numbering is used, it increments only when component parts are nested within one another, to indicate the level of nesting.

<c01 level="series"><did><unittitle>Series one</unittitle></did>

<c02 level="subseries"><did><unittitle>Subseries one</unittitle></did>

<c02 level="subseries"><did><unittitle>Subseriestwo</unittitle></did>
</c02>

</c01>

<c01 level="series"><did><unittitle>Series two</did></unittitle></c01>

The <container> element can indicate the logical designation of boxes, folders, and other physical containers at any level. Because most archival materials are not available on open shelves for end users to retrieve, physical location is often omitted.

<c01 level="series">

<did>

<container type="box">1-14</container>

<unittitle>Campaign materials</unittitle>

. . .

Archival finding aids vary in how they present information to the users. Some finding aids group summary information about major subunits, such as series, together and then itemize the contents of specific containers at the end. Others follow the description of each subunit with an inventory of the containers in the subunit. The "type" attribute of the <dsc> wrapper indicates which structure is followed in the EAD, with the value "analyticoverview" indicating the first format and "combined" indicating the second.

The EAD also supports both internal linking from one part of the finding aid to another, and external linking to other files. Some EAD linking elements were developed to support the XML XLink and XPointer specifications in anticipation of widespread support for these features, but simpler HTML-like linking is also supported. All defined elements support an "id" attribute, which can be used to designate the element as the target of an internal link. External links may be established to related documents, such as other finding aids, or to digital representations of objects described by the finding aid. In the latter case, the special element <dao> (digital archival object) is used. If multiple representations of the same object exist (for example, a thumbnail and a JPEG), links to different versions are grouped within the <daogroup> wrapper.

<c03 level="item"><did>

<unittitle>Letter to Dorothea Huxley</unittitle>

<unitdate>May 4, 1929</unitdate>

<dao href="http://www.server.edu/letter124.jpg"></dao></did></c03>

It is assumed that the encoded EAD will be used with stylesheets to create printed or online displays of the finding aid, and the DTD contains many elements to facilitate display. The <did> and most other elements within the <archdesc> allow the subelement <head>, for entering a section header, and most elements also allow a "label" attribute. For example, the encoding

<did>

<repository label="Repository">The Chester A. Mann Archives</repository>

. . .

</did>

can generate various displays depending on the stylesheet used, such as

Repository: The Chester A. Mann Archives

or

Repository. The Chester A. Mann Archives

Because printed finding aids often give container listings for boxes, folders, microform reels, and so on in tabular form, there are also special elements to facilitate tabular display.

The EAD was designed to support mapping between metadata in the EAD and MARC. Most elements allow the attribute "encodinganalog," which takes the value of a MARC tag:

<subject source="lcsh" encodinganalog="650">Civil War — Florida</subject>

In theory, an EAD can be converted by program into a MARC record by making use of the "encodinganalog" attributes, although content designation within MARC fields (indicator values and subfielding) would still be problematic. Conversely, an existing MARC record for a collection could be used to populate certain elements within the EAD. Although such conversions appear to be rarely implemented in practice, it is common to link between a MARC collection-level cataloging record and the EAD for the same collection. The EAD is converted and stored in an HTML version, and a URI for the EAD is entered in the MARC 856 field.

856 42 $3 Finding aid for this collection
$u http://www.server.edu/archives/fa1234.htm

Although EAD defines the semantics of the finding aid, until recently there have been no corresponding content standards for finding aids. The most general framework for archival description is provided by the General International Standard Archival Description (ISAD(G)) developed by the International Council on Archives Committee on Descriptive Standards.[3] ISAD(G) provides a high-level description of twenty-six elements for use in both collection-level cataloging records and finding aids, but relies on other standards to provide content rules. In Canada, *Rules for Archival Description* (RAD), first published in 1990, has been widely implemented as a guide to the formulation of content for finding aids.[4] In the United States in particular, the development of the EAD has provided incentive for the archival community to examine the practice of creating finding aids and to work toward the continued development of content standards for them. The Society of American Archivists and the Canadian Council on Archives have been working on the U.S./Canadian Standards Reconciliation Project, informally known as CUSTARD. CUSTARD will attempt to produce an international version of RAD that harmonizes U.S. and Canadian practice and unifies content guidelines for cataloging and finding aid creation.

The EAD has been most widely implemented in special collections departments in academic libraries. There are significant collections of EADs at Harvard University (http://findingaids.harvard.edu/), the University of Virginia Library (http://www.lib.virginia.edu/speccol/guides/), Duke University (http://odyssey.lib.duke.edu/findaid/), and many other U. S. universities. Some states, including Kentucky and New Mexico, have established union databases of finding aids, including contributions from academic institutions, historical societies, and state libraries. One of the largest collections is the Online Archive of California, which aggregates EAD-encoded finding aids from archives, museums, and libraries throughout the state of California (http://www.oac.cdlib.org/).

For the most part, however, state and federal agencies, historical societies, and corporations have been slower to adopt the EAD than have archives associated with academic institutions. Some argue that the EAD is not well-suited to describing these other types of collections, although others have found no substantial difference in archival description despite the nature of the parent organization. Certainly the EAD is one of the more difficult metadata standards to implement, requiring expertise in archival description and some knowledge of a rather complex SGML/XML DTD. Implementing the EAD requires editing tools and software for search and display of SGML/XML-encoded text that many smaller institutions might find difficult to support. This was particularly burdensome when the EAD was SGML-based, and few software applications were designed to support SGML-encoded text. It seems likely that with the popularity of XML, there will be a higher level of general familiarity with XML encoding and a larger selection of tools to support the creation, retrieval, and display of XML-based metadata, trends that could help the EAD become established in a wider range of archives.

NOTES

1. *ODLIS: Online Dictionary of Library and Information Science*, available at http://vax.wcsu.edu/library/odlis.html. Accessed 24 June 2002.
2. Steven L. Hensen, *Archives, Personal Papers, and Manuscripts: A Cataloging Manual for Archival Repositories, Historical Societies, and Manuscript Libraries,* 2nd ed. (Washington, D.C.: Society of American Archivists, [1983], 1989).

3. International Council on Archives, "ISAD(G): General International Standard Archival Description: adopted by the Committee on Descriptive Standards, Stockholm, Sweden, 19–22 September 1999," 2nd ed., available at http://www.ica.org/biblio/com/cds/isad_g_2e.pdf. Accessed 24 June 2002.

4. Canadian Committee on Archival Description, *Rules for Archival Description*, available at http://www.cdncouncilarchives.ca/archdesrules.html. Accessed 26 August 2002.

READINGS

The EAD is extremely well documented. The SAA publishes the tag library and a very useful manual of application guidelines, both of which are available in print and on the Web:

Encoded Archival Description (EAD) Official Web Site. Accessed 26 August 2002. Available at http://www.loc.gov/ead.

> The Library of Congress is the official maintenance agency for EAD documentation. Their EAD website contains background information and pointers to official versions of the DTDs and documentation.

Society of American Archivists, EAD Round Table. "EAD Help Pages." Accessed 24 June 2002. Available at http://www.iath.virginia.edu/ead/.

> A compilation of links to additional EAD documentation and tools. A particularly useful set of tools, including data entry templates for various SGML/XML authoring software and stylesheets for displaying EAD, is available in the EAD Cookbook.

Society of American Archivists. *Encoded Archival Description: Application Guidelines. Version 1.0.* Chicago: SAA, 1999. Available at http://lcweb.loc.gov/ead/ag/aghome.html. Accessed 24 June 2002.

Society of American Archivists. *Encoded Archival Description: Tag Library. Version 1.0.* Chicago: SAA, 1998. Available at http://lcweb.loc.gov/ead/tglib/tlhome.html. Accessed 24 June 2002.

A wealth of articles has been published about all aspects of EAD development and implementation. *American Archivist* 60 (fall 1997) is a special issue devoted to the EAD. Articles of particular interest from this and other sources include:

Fox, Michael. "Implementing Encoded Archival Description: An Overview of Administrative and Technical Considerations."

> The practical details of software and systems to support EAD.

Kiesling, Kris. "EAD as an Archival Descriptive Standard."

> Describes the EAD in context of other standards efforts.

Meissner, Dennis. "First Things First: Reengineering Finding Aids for Implementation of EAD."

> How the EAD has caused archivists to reevaluate the form and function of finding aids.

Pitti, Daniel. "Access to Digital Representations of Archival Materials: The Berkeley Finding Aid Project." RLG Digital Image Access Project: Proceedings from an RLG Symposium (Palo Alto: The Research Libraries Group, 1995), 73–81. Available at http://sunsite.berkeley.edu/FindingAids/EAD/diap.html.

> The early development of the EAD.

Smith, MacKenzie. "DFAS: The Distributed Finding Aid Search System." *D-Lib Magazine* 6, no. 1 (January 2000). Available at http://www.dlib.org/dlib/january00/01smith.html.

> A project to implement broadcast search across distributed repositories of EADs.

Metadata for Art and Architecture

10

The description of works of art and architecture, as well as of other visual materials, has been a focus of interest for the Getty Information Institute, the Visual Resources Association (VRA), and other individuals and organizations involved in art scholarship. This chapter looks at traditional MARC cataloging, the categories for the Description of Works of Art, and the VRA Core Categories.

CATALOGING VISUAL MATERIALS

Visual materials (art objects, photographs, graphic images) can be cataloged according to traditional library cataloging rules. A MARC format for visual materials (VIM) was developed in the 1980s and, although the stand-alone MARC formats were eliminated through format integration in the 1990s, data elements specific to visual materials remain. Chapter 8 of AACR2R addresses graphic materials, including opaque objects, such as two-dimensional art originals and reproductions; projected materials, such as slides; and collections of graphic materials. AACR2R chapter 10, "Three-Dimensional Artefacts and Realia," provides rules for sculptures and other three-dimensional artworks. Rules in chapter 4, dealing with unpublished materials, and rules for cataloging archival collections are also often applicable. The Library of Congress has issued a manual, *Graphic Materials—Rules for Describing Original Items and Historical Collections,* for describing graphic materials within the AACR2 framework, supplementing and departing from the rules where necessary.[1]

Many projects successfully use AACR2/MARC cataloging for visual materials, but there are special challenges in applying both MARC and the content rules. Art originals are often held in museums and galleries that do not have the bibliographic apparatus or staff expertise required to create MARC records efficiently. Similarly, reproductions (such as slides and images) may be held in academic departments or specialized libraries without traditional cataloging expertise. Although use of AACR2 presupposes that the basic principles of description hold for both textual documents and visual materials, there are significant differences between books, which are published in runs of identical copies each with an authoritative title page, and art objects, the originals of which are unique, which may or may not be "in hand," and which may or may not have documentary information. The application of AACR2 is problematic in several respects, including the need to describe both originals and reproductions or surrogates, and the lack of traditional sources of information. For example, AACR2R chapter 8 gives no guidance on how to construct titles for items that lack them apart from two examples, one of which, "[Photograph of Alice Liddell]," would be of little use to someone attempting to catalog a collection of photographs, unless it were desirable for all titles to file under "photograph of."

The issue of how to describe depictions of works of art or architecture is complex. Even the matter of what to call them is not straightforward. The term *surrogate* implies that the secondary object is meant to substitute for the original, which is not always the case. *Reproduction* implies a mechanical adherence to the original that would not apply to many photographs; *art reproduction* is defined in the appendix to AACR2R in even more limited terms, as "a mechanically reproduced copy of a work of art, generally as one of a commercial edition." The Visual Resources Association (VRA) initially preferred the term *visual document* and later *visual image* or just *image*. Here, we will use the term *visual representation* or simply *representation*.

Regardless of what representations are called, their treatment dominates any attempt to describe collections of art and architecture. Even museums and galleries that own original works will also commonly hold an array of representations of these works, from photographs to X-ray imagery. Visual resources collections used for teaching may hold no original works at all, but rather sets of photos, slides, and/or digital images. Regardless of the intent of the cataloging code, MARC records for visual representations typically combine information pertaining to the work of art and information pertaining to the representation in nonstandard ways.

Whether it is because of the difficulty of applying cataloging rules to visual resources, the lack of examples and guidelines, or other reasons, catalogers have been inconsistent in their use of MARC for these materials. The *ArtMARC Sourcebook* compared the use of MARC in twenty-three different projects describing art originals and/or representations and found enormous variation in practice. Although there was inconsistency in the use of nearly all the MARC fields, some areas appeared to be particularly problematic, including where to put information pertaining to the visual representation, which note fields to use for information not specifically defined in MARC, and use of subject fields. In some cases, there appeared to be cultural differences between librarians and curators of visual resources:

> [L]ibrarians who catalog drawings and photographs of structures consider building names to be subjects or names or corporate bodies; they are cataloging the representation rather than the building. Visual resources catalogers, on the other hand, are generally cataloging the work, in this case a building, rather than the slide, photograph or architectural drawing, and thus the title is the name of the building.[2]

Another problem area in the cataloging of visual resources is the use of appropriate controlled vocabularies for describing works of art and architecture. General-purpose subject vocabularies, such as LCSH, were felt to be inapplicable, and many visual resources collections were described using local vocabularies or no authority at all. In the 1980s, the Getty Information Institute took a proactive approach in this area and sponsored the development of the *Art and Architecture Thesaurus* (AAT), the *Union List of Artist Names* (ULAN), and the *Getty Thesaurus of Geographic Names* (TGN), all of which have become fundamental tools for resource description. Other resources include the *Thesaurus for Graphic Materials I: Subject Terms* published by the Library of Congress, which is intended specifically for subject indexing of "historical images which are found in many libraries, historical societies, archives, and museums," and ICON-CLASS, an international subject classification system for art images. Metadata schemes intended for the description of works of art and architecture encourage the application of these vocabulary control tools.

CATEGORIES FOR THE DESCRIPTION OF WORKS OF ART (CDWA)

The *Categories for the Description of Works of Art* (CDWA) was developed in the early 1990s by the Art Information Task Force (AITF), a project of the College Art Association of America and the Getty Art History Information Program, later known as the Getty Information Institute. The AITF brought together art historians, museum curators and registrars, and visual resources specialists with the goal of achieving cross-community consensus on basic elements for the description for works of art.

The initial scope included "movable" objects typically collected by museums, representations of such objects, and performance art (architecture was added later). At the time the AITF was working, museum collection management systems primarily provided inventory control and were little used by scholars in support of research. Thus, an explicit focus of the task force was to encourage the recording of information in such a way that it would be useful for scholarly art historical research. The first version of the CDWA, released in 1994, was superseded in 2000 by the current version 2.0, which is available from the Getty website.[3]

The CDWA defines semantic categories and some content rules, but prescribes no syntax. There is an assumption that data will be represented in tables in relational databases, but no assumption or requirement that local databases will implement the categories exactly as they are specified. According to the introduction,

> The Categories describe the content of art databases by articulating a conceptual framework for describing and accessing information about objects and images. They identify vocabulary resources and descriptive practices that will make information residing in diverse systems both more compatible and more accessible. They also provide a framework to which existing art information systems can be mapped and upon which new systems can be developed.

The CDWA defines twenty-seven main categories, each with a number of subcategories, resulting in a total of nearly three hundred elements. Of these, roughly two dozen are designated as the "core," the minimum set of elements needed to uniquely and unambiguously identify a work of art. In a major change between versions, categories in

2.0 are divided into two sets, "Object, Architecture or Group" and "Authorities/ Vocabulary Control." The first set of categories describes the work itself (or its representation, or the metadata record describing it), while the second set describes "extrinsic information about persons, places, and concepts related to the work," with the rationale that these data are better stored in authority records.

Categories are defined in terms of five attributes: "Definition," "Discussion," "Relationships," "Uses," and "Access." Subcategories may also have the attributes "Examples" and "Terminology/format." Figure 10-1 shows the definition of the subcategory Measurements—Shape. The choice and definition of these attributes emphasize the focus on use by the art historian and scholar. "Discussion" is a narrative explanation of how the category should be used, including the art historical importance of the data. "Uses" indicates how the data might be used by a researcher; for example, for the element Title or Names—Text it is noted, "In some cases, the title assigned to a work by the artist provides essential insight into the meaning of the work." "Access" indicates how a category could be used in retrieval, specifically noting when the data provide a primary access point.

One characteristic of the CDWA is its explicit recognition of the pervasive uncertainty and subjectivity of art historical information. The ability to record variant names for persons, places, and topics is central. In addition, nearly every category allows the subcategories Remarks, which can be used for scholarly notes similar to footnotes, and Citations, which is encouraged for documenting the source of all information in the metadata. These subcategories assist the researcher in evaluating the quality and authenticity of the information provided.

The online version of the CDWA includes examples of resource description for several different types of objects, including prints, drawings, photographs, sculpture, needlepoint, artifacts, and buildings. Figure 10-2 shows a cataloging example for a painting. Because of its complexity and comprehensiveness, the CDWA is rarely implemented in its entirety. However, as a framework, it has been used as the basis of a number of museum databases, and it has influenced the development of metadata specifications for many projects and applications, including access points for CIMI's CHIO (Cultural Heritage Information Online) project in the mid-1990s and the Museum Loan Network Directory. The web version of the CDWA lists standards that the CDWA either maps to or forms the basis of, including the Foundation for Documents of Architecture/ Architectural Drawings Advisory Group's *Guide to the Description of Architectural Drawings* data categories, the Art Museum Image Consortium (AMICO) data dictionary, the CIMI Access Points, CIDOC's *International Guidelines for Museum Object Information*, the Museum Documentation Association (MDA) Spectrum, and the VRA Core Categories.

THE VRA CORE

The VRA Core Categories specification was developed by the Visual Resources Association Data Standards Committee. When the committee began developing the VRA Core, the CDWA was circulating for review and committee members were familiar with it. However, catalogers of visual resources had a focus different from that of the art historians and museum curators who developed the CDWA and who were primarily

Measurements - Shape

DEFINITION

The outline, form, or characteristic configuration of a work or part of a work, including its contours.

EXAMPLES

> *square*
> *rectangular*
> *round*
> *oval*
> *triangular*
> *cylindrical*
> *hexagonal*

DISCUSSION

Recording the shape of a work provides context for its measurements and physical appearance. Objects may change shape over time, as when a rectangular panel painting has been cut down to an oval shape. Also, various shapes may be associated with multiple occurrences of MEASUREMENTS - DIMENSIONS - EXTENT, as when a round drawing is mounted on a square secondary support. Each shape will have corresponding dimensions and dates.

The extent of detail indicated about shape will depend on the object being described and the policy of the holding institution. Shape may be indicated when it is a distinguishing characteristic. In the context of a painting collection, for example, round or oval would seem more important to record than rectangular, because most paintings in a typical museum of Western art are rectangular.

USES

Shape is important to some lines of inquiry. For example, a scholar may wish to examine the composition of round paintings of the Northern Baroque.

ACCESS

The information in this subcategory makes it possible to identify and group together similar objects.

TERMINOLOGY/FORMAT

The use of a controlled vocabulary is recommended, such as the AAT Attributes and Properties hierarchy.

This subcategory may be linked to an authority, such as GENERIC CONCEPT IDENTIFICATION, which can be populated with terminology from the controlled vocabularies named above.

FIGURE 10-1   Definition of the subcategory Measurements—Shape from the *Categories for the Description of Works of Art.* Source: Murtha Baca and Patricia Harpring, eds., *Categories for the Description of Works of Art,* The J. Paul Getty Trust and College Art Association, Inc., c2000. Available at http://www.getty.edu/research/institute/standards/cdwa/.

CDWA Fielded Example: Oil Painting 1

Example with Image
Next Fielded Example >>

1.3	Object/Work -Type	painting
2.1	Classification -Term	Paintings
4.1	Title or Name -Text	Irises
7.1	Measurements - Dimensions	71 x 93 cm (28 x 36 5/8 in.)
7.1.2	Measurements - Dimensions - Type	height
7.1.3	Measurements - Dimensions - Value	71
7.1.4	Measurements - Dimensions - Unit	cm
7.1.2	Measurements - Dimensions - Type	width
7.1.3	Measurements - Dimensions - Value	93
7.1.4	Measurements - Dimensions - Unit	cm
8.1	Materials and Techniques - Description	oil on canvas, applied with brush and palette knife
8.3.1	Materials and Techniques - Materials - Name	impasto
8.3.2	Materials and Techniques - Processes - Imple.	brush
8.3.2	Materials and Techniques - Processes - Imple.	palette knife
8.4.2	Materials and Techniques - Materials - Name	oil paint
8.4.2	Materials and Techniques - Materials - Name	canvas
14.1	Creation - Creator	Vincent van Gogh
14.1.3	Creation - Creator - Identity	Gogh, Vincent van (Dutch painter, 1853-1890)
14.1.4	Creation - Creator - Role	painter
14.2	Creation - Date	1889
14.2.1	Creation - Date - Earliest Date	1889
14.2.2	Creation - Date - Latest Date	1889
18.1.1	Subject Matter - Description - Indexing Terms	irises
18.1.1	Subject Matter - Description - Indexing Terms	Iridaceae
18.1.1	Subject Matter - Description - Indexing Terms	soil
18.1.1	Subject Matter - Description - Indexing Terms	nature
18.2.1	Subject Matter - Identification - Indexing Terms	Irises
18.3.1	Subject Matter - Interpretation - Indexing Terms	regeneration
19.1	Context - Historical/Cultural	exhibited at Salon des Indépendants, September 1889
19.1.2	Context - Historical/Cultural - Event Name	Salon des Indépendants
19.1.3	Context - Historical/Cultural - Date	September 1889
26.1	Current Location - Repository Name	J. Paul Getty Museum
26.2	Current Location - Geographic Location	Los Angeles (California, USA)
26.3	Current Location - Repository Numbers	90.AP.20
27.1	Descriptive Note - Text	This work was painted when the artist was recuperating from a severe attack of mental illness, and it depicts the garden at the asylum at Saint-Rmy. It is influenced by the work of Gauguin and Hokusai, and is remarkable for the contrasts of color . . .
28.1	Creator Identification - Name	Gogh, Vincent van
28.2	Creator Identification - Variant Names	Gogh, Vincent Willem van
28.2	Creator Identification - Variant Names	van Gogh, Vincent
28.2	Creator Identification - Variant Names	Vincent van Gogh
28.3	Creator Identification - Dates/Locations	1853-1890, active in Holland
28.3.1	Creator Identification - Birth Date	1853
28.3.2	Creator Identification - Death Date	1890
28.3.7	Creator Identification - Places of Activity	Holland
28.3.7	Creator Identification - Places of Activity	Netherlands, the
28.4.1	Creator Identification - Nationality/Citizenship	Dutch
28.6	Creator Identification - Life Roles	painter

Copyright ©2000 The J. Paul Getty Trust & College Art Association, Inc.

FIGURE 10-2 Cataloging example from the web version of the *Categories for the Description of Works of Art.* Source: Murtha Baca and Patricia Harpring, eds., *Categories for the Description of Works of Art,* The J. Paul Getty Trust and College Art Association, Inc., c2000. Available at http://www.getty.edu/research/institute/standards/cdwa/.

interested in describing original artworks for scholarly use. The typical visual resources curator worked in an academic department or a special library and was responsible for a collection of slides or other surrogates depicting works of art and architecture for classroom use. These materials were often described in local files or databases not included in the library's online catalog, either because the collections were managed outside the library or because of problems in applying AACR2.

The curators of visual resources were acutely aware that they had to describe at least two versions of each resource: the original work of art or architecture (which was unlikely to be in the local collection) and the slide or other surrogate for it. (Of course, in most cases, even more versions would be involved, as slides were usually created from photographs, and digital images in various formats increasingly supplemented slides.) Curators wanted, at a minimum, to be able to share records describing original works, because it didn't make sense for every curator of every collection to catalog the same artworks from scratch. They also wanted a metadata scheme that allowed both the original work and representations of it to be fully described, and that made it clear which elements of description pertained to the original and which pertained to the representation.

The VRA Core was deliberately modeled on the Dublin Core in the sense that it was intended to function as a core set of elements that all implementations could share, supplemented by additional elements at the local level. Like the Dublin Core, there is no prescribed syntax, and elements are assumed to be (although not explicitly stated to be) optional and repeatable. The first version of the VRA Core contained twenty-one categories in three groups that described the original work (then called the "object"), the creator, and the representation (then called the "surrogate"). This was dramatically revised in version 2.0, which contained only two sets of categories: nineteen for the work and nine for the representation (now called the "visual document"). The creator's name and role were added to the set of Work categories, and the remaining creator elements from version 1.0 were eliminated with the realization that they should not be repeated for every work, but rather belonged in a separate authority file. (Interestingly, in version 2.0, no creator information was allowed for describing the visual document.)

The current version of the VRA Core, version 3.0, no longer divides categories into separate element sets for work and representation (now called "image"), but has a single set of seventeen categories that can be applied to either. The intention is that separate records (sets of metadata elements) will be created for each work and representation. A new category, Record Type, recognizes each record as pertaining to either "work" or "image." The other categories are Type (for the genre type of work or image taken from AAT), Title, Measurements, Material, Technique, Creator, Date, Location, ID Number, Style/Period, Culture, Subject, Relation, Description, Source, and Rights.

It should be noted that the VRA Core defines "work" quite differently than the IFLA FRBR, in which a work is an abstract intellectual or artistic creation, realized in an expression and embodied in a manifestation. In the VRA Core, a work is "a physical entity that exists, has existed at some time in the past, or that could exist in the future. It might be an artistic creation such as a painting or a sculpture; it might be a performance, composition, or literary work; it might be a building or other construction in the built environment; or it might be an object of material culture."[4] A work in this sense conflates the IFLA entities from work through manifestation and, in most cases (because artworks and buildings are one of a kind), through the item level as well.

Conceptually, it stands in opposition to the image, which is defined in the VRA Core as a visual representation of a work and is meant to categorize slides, photographs, and digital files. It should be noted that an image could also be a work in its own right, as, for example, a picture of a building taken by a noted photographer.

Each element in the VRA Core 3.0 is described by its name, a definition, defined qualifiers, recommended authority lists or controlled vocabularies for the content of the element, and mappings to the VRA Core 2.0, the CDWA, and Dublin Core. Figure 10-3 shows the definition of the Title category from the VRA Core 3.0 specification. Although implementers are urged to indicate the authority used for content, the scheme contains no semantic device for indicating the authority used.

TITLE
Qualifiers:
    Title.Variant
    Title.Translation
    Title.Series
    Title.Larger Entity
Definition: The title or identifying phrase given to a Work or an Image. For complex works or series the title may refer to a discrete unit within the larger entity (a print from a series, a panel from a fresco cycle, a building within a temple complex) or may identify only the larger entity itself. A record for a part of a larger unit should include both the title for the part and the title for the larger entity. For an Image record this category describes the specific view of the depicted Work.
Data Values: formulated according to data content rules for titles of works of art
VRA Core 2.0: W2 Title; V7 Visual Document View Description
CDWA: Titles or Names-Text; Related Visual Documentation-View; Related Visual Documentation-View- Indexing Terms
Dublin Core: TITLE

FIGURE 10-3 Title category as defined in the VRA Core. From VRA Core Categories, version 3.0, with permission from the Visual Resources Association.

The idea of element qualifiers and the "dot" notation for representing them were adopted from the Dublin Core. For the most part, these function as element refinement qualifiers and narrow the meaning of the category. The category Date, for example, has the qualifiers:

Date.Creation

Date.Design

Date.Beginning

Date.Completion

Date.Alteration

Date.Restoration

However, the data model for qualification is less rigorous than that for the Dublin Core, allowing such constructions as

Creator.Role

Creator.Attribution

Creator.Personal name

Creator.Corporate name

Both Role and Attribution would fail the "dumb-down" test, and the treatment of role as an element (Creator.Role) rather than a true qualifier (e.g., Creator.Artist) means that creator names and roles must always be paired, despite the lack of mechanisms for linking related data elements within a record.

The mechanism for linking between VRA Core records is also considered to be a local implementation issue outside the scope of the descriptive metadata scheme itself. However, it is assumed that mechanisms for linking do exist and that records for works and images will be linked to each other. Users of the VRA Core are supposed to honor the 1:1 principle and describe only a single entity in a single record. If a drawing were scanned to create a JPEG image, the drawing would be fully described on one record and the JPEG on another. The two records would clearly differ in Creator as well as physical details, such as Measurements and Medium, although they might or might not differ in Title, Subject, and Culture categories.

The changes in the VRA Core from versions 1.0 to 3.0 show an evolving awareness of the complexity of the number and types of relationships that must be expressed. An art object may have several representations in different media (slide, photograph, image) and different formats (TIFF, JPEG, GIF). Representations may depict the entire object, parts of the object, or views of the object. Representations may have aspects that do not exist for the object itself, such as lighting features. Works are also related to other works in many ways, including group:item, whole:part, and derivative relationships.

In the VRA Core 3.0, any number of image records can be created, linked to the records for the works they most closely represent. Although works and images can be related technically only by some database implementation, related works can be linked semantically in two ways. For whole:part relationships, the name of the part is supposed to be given in the element Title.Larger Entity. Other types of relationships should be described using the Relation category. Relation is described in the version 3.0 specification as paired elements:

Relation.Identity

Relation.Type

However, it is illustrated in the examples as a single qualified element:

Relation.derived from = Drawing by Georg Pencz in the Staatsarchiv, Nuremberg, Germany

The VRA Core 2.0 and 3.0 specifications have the feel of a work in process, with typographical errors, scanty definitions, and inconsistent examples. However, both versions of the scheme were rapidly and widely accepted. The number of categories, even with qualification, is more manageable than in the CDWA, and the data elements are well attuned to visual resources collections. The VRA is in the process of drafting a manual, "Cataloguing Cultural Objects," which is expected to clarify practice and resolve some of the problems related to lack of documentation. Although it has been noted that the VRA Core has been used by a number of libraries "mostly as inspiration," this is in keeping with the premise of a core element set to encourage consistency and interoperability among implementations.[5] Some notable implementations of the VRA Core include Harvard University's VIA catalog, the Academic Image Cooperative, and the Visual Arts Data Service Catalog.

Harvard University used the VRA Core version 2.0 with some modifications as the basic metadata scheme for its Visual Information Access (VIA) Catalog.[6] This catalog, which gives union access to visual materials from ten different repositories at Harvard, contains linked records for "groups" (sets of related materials), "works" (individual artworks), and "surrogates" (individual representations).

The VRA Core version 3.0 was implemented by the Visual Arts Data Service (VADS), a part of the U.K.'s Arts and Humanities Data Service established to provide digital archiving and advisory services.[7] The VADS catalog contains descriptions and thumbnail images of visual materials from ten different collections ranging from textiles to architecture. VADS chose the VRA Core partly for its prominence, partly for its promotion of vocabulary control, and partly for its mapping to the CDWA and Dublin Core.[8]

The Academic Image Cooperative (AIC) was a planning and prototyping project of the Digital Library Federation (DLF) with funding from the Mellon Foundation.[9] The goal of the AIC was to develop a database of art images to support the teaching of art history survey courses. The AIC developed a metadata model conforming to the VRA Core 3.0 for full-level description of the included images. The AIC database was later incorporated into the broader ArtSTOR initiative.

NOTES

1. Elisabeth Betz Parker, *Graphic Materials—Rules for Describing Original Items and Historical Collections,* 1982 with 1996 updates, available at http://www.tlcdelivers.com/tlc/crs/grph0199.htm. Accessed 25 June 2002. See http://www.loc.gov/rr/print/gm/graphmat.html for other editions.
2. Linda McRae and Lynda S. White, eds., *ArtMARC Sourcebook* (Chicago: American Library Association, 1998), 10.
3. *Categories for the Description of Works of Art,* edited by Murtha Baca and Patricia Harpring, available at http://www.getty.edu/research/institute/standards/cdwa. Accessed 25 June 2002.
4. VRA Core Categories, version 3.0, Introduction, available at http://www.vraweb.org/vracore3.htm. Accessed 25 June 2002.
5. Committee on Cataloging: Description and Access, Task Force on VRA Core Categories, *Summary Report,* 2001, available at http://www.ala.org/alcts/organization/ccs/ccda/tf-vra1.html#report. Accessed 25 June 2002.
6. Harvard University Library, Visual Information Access, available at http://via.harvard.edu:748/html/VIA.html. Accessed 25 June 2002.
7. Visual Arts Data Service (home page), available at http://vads.ahds.ac.uk/index.html. Accessed 25 June 2002.
8. Phil Purdy, "Digital Image Archiving and Advice: In Tandem with the Visual Arts Data Service (VADS)," *Cultivate Interactive* 4 (May 2001), available at http://www.cultivate-int.org/issue4/vads. Accessed 25 June 2002.
9. Digital Library Federation, Academic Image Cooperative, available at http://www.diglib.org/collections/aic.htm. Accessed 25 June 2002.

READINGS

The CDWA and the VRA Core specification are available online:

Baca, Murtha. "A Picture Is Worth a Thousand Words: Metadata for Art Objects and Their Visual Surrogates." In Wayne Jones et al., eds., *Cataloging the Web: Metadata, AACR, and MARC21.* Lanham, Md.: Scarecrow, 2001.

Baca, Murtha, and Patricia Harpring, eds. *Categories for the Description of Works of Art.* The J. Paul Getty Trust and College Art Association, 2000. Available at http://www.getty.edu/research/institute/standards/cdwa/.

Visual Resources Association, Data Standards Committee. Core Categories for Visual Resources, version 3.0. Available at http://www.vraweb.org/vracore3.htm.

Visual Materials: Processing and Cataloging Bibliography. Prints and Photographs Division, Library of Congress, Washington, D.C. Available at http://www.loc.gov/rr/print/vmbib.html.

Special issues of two journals focus on the CDWA and the VRA Core, respectively:

Baca, Murtha, and Patricia Harpring, eds. "Art Information Task Force Categories for the Description of Works of Art." *Visual Resources* 11, no. 3/4 (1996), special issue.

"The VRA Core Categories." *VRA Bulletin* 25, no. 4 (winter 1998), special issue.

Museum Information Standards (web page). Available at http://www.diffuse.org/museums.html. Accessed 26 August 2002.

> The European Commission's Diffuse Project (http://www.diffuse.org) documents standards and specifications facilitating information exchange. Their web pages include a comprehensive list of museum information standards.

11

GILS and Government Information

The acronym GILS stands for many things. Most narrowly, the Government Information Locator Service is a federal initiative applying only to departments and agencies within the executive branch. The technical specifications for implementing GILS, which include a core set of metadata elements, are referred to as the GILS Profile and informally as GILS. More broadly, any implementations using the GILS Profile are known as GILS, so there are many state GILS initiatives. Even more broadly, adoption of the GILS Profile outside the United States and for nongovernmental information has led to the coining of the term Global Information Locator Service to embrace these wider uses.

The federal GILS program has its roots in the information policy of the Clinton administration and the National Information Infrastructure (NII) initiative. It was officially mandated in the 1994 OMB Bulletin 95-01, "Establishment of a Government Information Locator Service" (Office of Management and Budget, 1994). The original GILS vision was for a federation of interoperable agency-based locator services giving public access to agency-produced resources. The Bulletin delineates agency responsibilities for implementing GILS and outlines the high-level goals of identifying public information resources, describing the information available in those resources, providing assistance in obtaining that information, and improving agency electronic records management. GILS therefore had two purposes—the public one of improving access to information and the internal one of improving records management within agencies. Technical specifications are laid out in Federal Information Processing Standard Publication (FIPS Pub.) No. 192: Application Profile for the Government Information Locator Service (National Institute for Standards and Technology, 1994).

Most metadata schemes are defined independently of any search service used to access them. The GILS Profile, however, is written as an application profile of the Z39.50

protocol. In addition to specifying a core set of elements, the GILS Profile requires a GILS server to be a Z39.50 server and specifies precisely the attribute set, diagnostic set, and other features of Z39.50 that must be supported in order to be GILS-compliant.

GILS Core Elements are defined in Annex E of the Profile. Attributes specified include the name of the element, whether or not it is repeatable, and a definition. All elements are optional. The specification does not include content rules, although for some elements, the definition requires that values be recorded using a particular format or controlled vocabulary. Figure 11-1 shows the first several core elements defined in Annex E.

GILS metadata records, called *locator records*, are intended to describe the full range of agency resources. These include not only individual publications, but also databases, catalogs, directories, online services, websites, and even nonbibliographic resources, such as joblines and programs. Consequently, while the basic elements of bibliographic description are present (Title, Originator, Contributor, Date of Publication, Place of Publication, Language of Resource, Abstract), the definitions are worded broadly in order to apply to a wide range of resource types. There is also a strong focus on non-

---

Title (Not Repeatable) This element conveys the most significant aspects of the referenced resource and is intended for initial presentation to users independently of other elements. It should provide sufficient information to allow users to make an initial decision on likely relevance. It should convey the most significant information available, including the general topic area, as well as a specific reference to the subject.

Originator (Repeatable) This element identifies the information resource originator.

Contributor (Repeatable) This element is used if there are names associated with the resource in addition to the Orginator, such as personal author, corporate author, co-author, or a conference or meeting name.

Date Of Publication (Not Repeatable) The discrete creation date in which the described resource was published or updated, though not for use on resources that are published continuously such as dynamic databases. Date of Publication Textual may also provide additional information such as when the resource was originally published. This element may be expressed in one of two forms:

- **Date Of Publication Structured** Date described using the ISO 8601 prescribed structure (fixed 8 characters, YYYYMMDD).
- **Date Of Publication Textual** Date described textually.

Place of Publication (Not Repeatable) The city or town where the described resource was published. May also include country if location of city is not well known.

Language of Resource (Repeatable) This element indicates the language(s) of the described resource as represented by the MARC three character alpha code. If a resource is multilingual, repeat this element for each applicable language.

Abstract (Not Repeatable) This element presents a narrative description of the information resource. This narrative should provide enough general information to allow the user to determine if the information resource has sufficient potential to warrant contacting the provider for further information.

FIGURE 11-1   First seven elements defined in the GILS Core. From Application Profile for the Government Information Locator Service (GILS), version 2, Annex E, available at http://www.gils.net/prof_v2.html.

bibliographic aspects that facilitate use, with such elements as Availability, Access Constraints, Use Constraints, and Points of Contact, all of which have many subelements encouraging detail and granularity of description. Two elements, Purpose and Program, are used to describe the reason for the creation or availability of the information resource and what agency program(s) it supports. In this respect, the GILS Core has some resemblance to the MARC21 Community Information format, which is designed to describe nonbibliographic resources, such as organizations, programs, and services that benefit a community.

A repeatable Cross Reference element is used to group subelements that identify other GILS locator records or information resources that are related to the resource being described. Other elements within the GILS Core describe the geographic and temporal coverage of the resource. Subelements within the Spatial Domain element are defined for the latitude and longitude of north, south, east, and west bounding coordinates, while the Place subelement can record geographic names. Place, like the Controlled Subject Index, is defined with a subelement for the thesaurus in addition to subelements for the term(s):

> Place (Repeatable) This subelement identifies geographic locations characterized by the data set or information resource through two associate constructs:
>
> Place Keyword Thesaurus (Not Repeatable) The name of a formally registered thesaurus or similar authoritative source of Place Keywords. Each keyword is provided in the subordinate repeating field:
>
> Place Keyword (Repeatable) The geographic name of a location covered by a data set or information resource.

GILS itself has no content rules for the GILS Core, apart from the minimal instructions given in the definitions of some elements. However, use of external content rules is encouraged. One of the most widely applied sets of content rules is the *Guidelines for the Preparation of GILS Core Entries* produced by the National Archives and Records Administration (NARA).[1] The guidelines provide additional direction in the formulation of element values, indicate whether an element should be considered optional or mandatory, and give examples of the appropriate use of most elements. They emphasize the importance of using controlled vocabularies for names and index terms, and they specify that agency names be recorded as listed in the *U.S. Government Manual* where possible. They also recommend use of the Cross Reference element for providing links to any online thesauri cited in the Thesaurus subelement of the Controlled Vocabulary element. Examples of good practice for core entries describing various types of entities are given in an appendix. An example of a model GILS Core record is shown in figure 11-2.

In 1997, an evaluation of the first two years of the federal GILS program, commissioned by the GILS Board by request of the Archivist of the United States, was issued. The report concluded that although the vision of assisting users in locating publicly available government information remained valid, the goal of a government-wide locator service had not yet been achieved. Instead, the report found uneven, inconsistent, and stand-alone implementations of GILS by individual agencies as well as increasing confusion about the relative roles of GILS and agency websites. The report recommended refocusing the federal GILS program on identifying and linking to electronically available government information only, abandoning the records management

Automated Information System Example

Title: Retained Records Database

    Acronym: RET

Originator:

    Department/Agency Name: National Archives and Records Administration
    Name of Unit: Office of Records Administration

Local Subject Index:

    Local Subject Term: US Federal GILS

Abstract: The Retained Records Database (RET) contains descriptions of unscheduled records as well as scheduled records that other Federal agencies have not transferred to the National Archives. Information contained in the database also includes the conditions under which the records are maintained, where they are located, the contact person, a tickler date indicating when the records should be re- evaluated, and scheduling data. The History File contains records previously listed in RET that have now been transferred to the National Archives or a Federal Records Center. The Oral History File contains descriptions of oral history projects through 1992. Routine updates and additions to the system occur semi- annually.

Begin Date: 1990

Purpose: The Retained Records Database was created to provide a centralized source of information about older series of permanent or potentially permanent records maintained in agency custody so that these records can be tracked and eventually transferred to the National Archives.

Agency Program: 44 U.S.C. 29 authorizes the Archivist of the United States to undertake certain records management functions.

Time Period of Content: 1755 -

Availability:

    Distributor:
        Name: Office of Records Administration
        Organization: National Archives and Records Administration
        Street Address: 8601 Adelphi Road
        City: College Park
        State: MD
        ZIP Code: 20740
        Country: USA
        Telephone: 301- 713- 6677
        Fax: 301- 713- 6850
    Order Process: Currently, there is no on- line access to the system outside of the Office of Records Administration. Printouts from the system may be requested by calling or writing the Office. The first 100 pages are free; additional pages cost $.20 per page. Fees may be paid in cash, by check or money order payable to the National Archives Trust Fund and must be paid in advance.
    Technical Prerequisites: Connection to ICASS, IBM- PC compatible microcomputer

FIGURE 11-2 Beginning of a sample GILS core record taken from the NARA Guidelines. From National Archives and Records Administration, *Guidelines for the Preparation of GILS Core Entries,* published online by the Defense Technical Information Center, available at http://www.dtic.mil/gils/documents/naradoc/.

function, and emphasizing the need to be government-wide. It is unclear what a current evaluation would conclude. However, some consolidation of GILS searching has occurred; the Government Information Locator Service run by the Government Printing Office aggregates the databases of thirty-five different federal agencies, including the GPO itself, and offers federated searching of two other aggregated GILS sites.[2]

Several states have adopted GILS for access to state government information. In Find-it! programs in Illinois, Washington, and other states, state agencies are encouraged to embed GILS Core metadata in their web pages for public electronic documents. State-run spiders then gather the metadata and make it accessible through central search services. Some states provide GILS tutorials and training while others provide simple web forms for metadata entry that hide the details of the GILS Core element set. A few state GILS initiatives have chosen to implement other metadata element sets, such as the Dublin Core, in preference to the GILS Core. Because guidelines and practices can differ from state to state, some effort has been made to promote interoperability between states' GILS implementations. A common subject authority list, called the GILS Topic Tree, was consortially developed to improve cross-state searching by providing a consistent subject vocabulary. To get around the problem of different element sets, the states of Washington, Utah, and Minnesota tested cross-state searching using *Z tokens*, numeric identifiers that relate each metadata element to an attribute in the Z39.50 Bib-1 attribute set.[3] For example, Dublin Core Creator and GILS Originator elements might both be mapped to the Z token 1003 "Author-name," which could then be used for cross-state searching.

The GILS Core is not universally used for describing government information. The Australian Government Locator Service (AGLS) has chosen to implement a core element set based on the Dublin Core with a few extensions, including Function, for the business function of the agency; Availability, for how the resource may be obtained or contacted; Audience, for the target audience of the resource; and Mandate, for the legal instrument that requires the resource to be created or provided.[4] Similarly, the Dublin Core has been used as the basis for metadata schemes for government information in Canada, Denmark, Finland, Ireland, New Zealand, and the United Kingdom.[5] A report by a working group established by the Canadian Chief Information Officer Branch compared GILS and Dublin Core as the basis for a metadata standard for government information and recommended implementation of Dublin Core.[6] Among the criteria evaluated, the report cited the comparative complexity of GILS, the low level of adoption of GILS within the United States, and the low potential for user involvement in the GILS governance structure. The Government Working Group of the Dublin Core Metadata Initiative has drafted an application profile for use of Dublin Core in a government context that is currently out for review.[7] A statement by the Working Group clarifying the relationship between GILS and Dublin Core is pending.

NOTES

1. National Archives and Records Administration, *Guidelines for the Preparation of GILS Core Entries*, published online by the Defense Technical Information Center, available at http://www.dtic.mil/gils/documents/naradoc/. Accessed 26 June 2002.
2. U.S. Government Printing Office, Superintendent of Documents, Government Information Locator Service (GILS) (home page), available at http://www.access.gpo.gov/su_docs/ gils/index.html. Accessed 26 June 2002.

3. Philip Coombs, *White Paper on the Use of Numeric Tokens in Resource Descriptions*, 20 September 1999, available at http://www.statelib.wa.gov/projects/imls/tokens.htm. Accessed 27 June 2002.

4. Australian Government Locator Service (home page), available at http://www.govonline. gov.au/projects/standards/agls.htm. Accessed 27 June 2002. See also the AGLS User Manual at http://www.naa.gov.au/recordkeeping/gov_online/agls/user_manual/intro.html.

5. Dublin Core Metadata Initiative, "Adoption of Dublin Core by Governments," available at http://dublincore.org/news/adoption/. Accessed 27 June 2002.

6. Government On-Line Ad hoc Interdepartmental Metadata Working Group, "Selecting and Implementing a Metadata Standard for the Government of Canada," 22 March 2001, available at http://www.cio-dpi.gc.ca/im-gi/references/meta-standard/meta-standard00_e.asp. Accessed 27 June 2002.

7. Dublin Core Metadata Initiative, DCMI Government Working Group (web page), available at http://dublincore.org/groups/government/. Accessed 27 June 2002.

READINGS

Global Information Locator Service (GILS) (home page). Accessed 27 June 2002. Available at http://www.gils.net/.

> The federal GILS home page, with links to information about GILS initiatives, implementations, policy background, tools, and the GILS profile. The GILS Topic Tree is available on the official GILS site at http://www.gils.net/trees.html. Information on the history and development of the topic tree is collected at http://www.fidocat. com/gils/.

Moen, William E., and Charles R. McClure. *An Evaluation of the Federal Government's Implementation of the Government Information Locator Service, Final Report.* 30 June 1997. Available at http://www.access.gpo.gov/su_docs/gils/gils-eval.

> The evaluation of federal GILS implementations gives a thorough history of the GILS movement from a legislative and policy perspective, as well as describing the evaluation itself and its conclusions and recommendations.

12

Metadata for Education

Recent years have seen a great deal of activity in the development of specialized metadata schemes for describing educational materials. This chapter highlights MARC21 fields for curriculum information, the GEM metadata element set for lesson plans and similar curriculum resources, and the IEEE LOM scheme for learning resources.

AACR2/MARC

Some materials used in instruction are, of course, books, videos, software, and other items held by libraries. Standard AACR2/MARC cataloging can be used to integrate these materials into the library catalog. In 1993, several changes were made to USMARC at the request of the Northwest Ohio Education Technology Foundation and its partners to enhance the recording of curriculum-related information. Fields of particular relevance to education include the Summary Note (520), Target Audience Note (521), Study Program Information (526), and Index Term—Curriculum Objective (658). MARC records containing these fields are sometimes called CEMARC, or "Curriculum-Enhanced MARC," and are of particular interest to educators in K–12.

The 520 field (Summary, Abstract, Annotation, Scope, etc., Note) can be used with first indicator "1" to record the entire text of a review of the book, software, or other resource being cataloged. Although rarely entered by school library media center staff, reviews are often included in records purchased from vendors.

The 521 field (Target Audience Note) can be used to record general information about the target audience: for example, "Program designed for geographers, planners, geologists, meteorologists, and others who have a professional interest in analyzing spatial data." (This and all other examples in this section are taken from the *MARC21*

Concise Format for Bibliographic Data.) Field 521 can also be used for specific information about reading grade level, interest age level, interest grade level, special audience characteristics, and motivation interest level. Subfield a records the target audience and subfield b indicates the organization that determined the target audience. The note

> 521 2#$a7 & up.

indicates that the interest grade level (designated by first indicator value "2") is grades 7 and above.

Field 526 (Study Program Information) is used to indicate whether the material is a component of any particular study program. For example, the Accelerated Reader program is popular in elementary and middle schools. Books in the program are assigned points according to their length and level of difficulty; students select and read books within given point ranges and take computerized tests to indicate their comprehension. The 526 field can be used to indicate a title is part of Accelerated Reader:

> 526 0#$aAccelerated Reader/Advanced Learning Systems$b5.0$c4.0$d75

Subfield a records the name of the program, subfields b and c give the interest and reading levels, and subfield d records the point value.

The 658 field (Index Term—Curriculum Objective) is used to record which state, national, or special curriculum objectives are addressed by the material. This is particularly important today when standardized testing tied to formal achievement specifications is the norm. It is also somewhat problematic to supply in practical terms, in that the same item might satisfy several dozen curriculum objectives in different states. Subfield a is defined for the main objective, subfield b for the sub-objective, subfield c for a coded representation of the objective, and subfield d for the strength of the correlation with the objective. Subfield 2 records the curriculum standard in which the objective appears. Coded values for a small number of curriculum standards are given in the MARC Code List for Relators, Sources, Description Conventions. In the following example, "ohco" represents the Ohio state curriculum objectives.

> 658 ##$aReading objective 1 (fictional)$bunderstanding language, elements of plots, themes, motives, characters, setting by responding to the multiple-meaning word$cNRPO2-1991$dhighly correlated.$2ohco

Data values for these CEMARC fields are not governed by AACR2; their content is fully described in MARC21 and the MARC Code List. As the vast majority of school library media centers purchase their cataloging records, use of these fields depends largely on their implementation by vendors. The Follett Corporation, for example, supplies reading level, interest level, and review sources, and puts information about the Accelerated Reader and Reading Counts programs in the 526 field.

GEM

Many educational resources, such as lesson plans, unit plans, and activities, are not traditionally included in library catalogs. There is, however, great interest in sharing these materials regionally and nationally. As a result, a number of government and industry initiatives have launched major projects to catalog educational materials. One of these is the Gateway to Educational Materials (GEM), a project of the U.S. Department of Education and the ERIC Clearinghouse on Information and Technology at Syracuse University. The project's goal is to "provide 'one-stop, any-stop' access to the substantial, but uncataloged, collections of Internet-based educational materials available on various federal, state, university, non-profit, and commercial Internet sites."[1]

To this end, GEM has developed a central site for searching educational resources, a metadata element set (currently GEM 2.0), software tools, and documentation and training aids to help participants create metadata both for their own local indexes and for the central GEM repository. Metadata can be embedded in the resource itself using <meta> tags or written to stand-alone HTML files; in either case, it is harvested by the GEM harvester.

The GEM initiative has worked closely with the Dublin Core Metadata Initiative in developing the GEM element set, known simply as "GEM." GEM 2.0 consists of the fifteen Dublin Core elements and their qualifiers extended with a set of GEM-specific elements and qualifiers that are described briefly here.

The Audience element is defined as "a class of entity for whom the resource is intended" and is somewhat equivalent to the MARC 521 note. The qualifiers Beneficiary and Mediator are intended to distinguish between the target student learner and the teacher, trainer, or other entity that mediates access to the resource. Other qualifiers are Level for the grade or other level of the material, Age for the age or age range of the target audience, and Prerequisites. It is interesting to note that the Audience element and its qualifier Mediator were brought before the DCMI Usage Board by the Dublin Core Education Working Group and approved as two of the first domain-specific Dublin Core terms. A *domain-specific* term is one for which a general cross-domain need has not been demonstrated, but the need within a specific community has been established. The DCMI still needs to clarify how DCMI-approved domain-specific terms differ from other domain-specific extensions used in Dublin Core–based schemes and how these terms will be represented in registries and in exchange syntaxes.

Other GEM-specific elements are Cataloging, Duration, Essential Resources, Pedagogy, and Standard. The Cataloging element does not pertain to the resource but rather to the metadata record itself; it contains "information about the individual and/or agency that created the GEM catalog record" and has the qualifier Role to indicate that entity's role in cataloging.

The Duration element describes the time or number of sessions needed to use the resource. The Essential Resources element is a listing of other resources needed to successfully use the resource being described, such as background reading or art supplies (rulers, colored pencils, construction paper).

The Pedagogy element identifies pedagogical methods and procedures and has the qualifiers Grouping, TeachingMethod, and Assessment, the values for all of which should be selected from a registered controlled vocabulary. The qualifier Grouping gives the context in which instruction should take place, from individualized through small group to large homogeneous and large heterogeneous groups. The GEM-registered controlled vocabulary for TeachingMethod includes such values as "Lab procedures," "Demonstration," and "Hands-on learning." The Assessment qualifier records the preferred method of student assessment, such as "Standardized testing," "Testing," or "Self-evaluation."

The element Standard, like the MARC 658 field, relates the resource to state and/or national educational standards. Unlike the 658, it is not intended as an index term, but can be entered as unstructured free text or as a structured value including the name of the curriculum standard, the authority for the standard, and the major and sub-objectives. The single qualifier, Correlator, identifies the individual or organization that correlated the resource to the standard.

The GEM profile also extends the Dublin Core with element refinement qualifiers for Dublin Core elements. It adds a Role qualifier to Creator, Contributor, and Publisher elements; PlacedOnline and RecordCreated qualifiers to the Date element; PriceCode to the Rights element; and computing Platform to the Format element. It adds three qualifiers to Identifier to distinguish between public standard identifiers (PublicID), the unique GEM system identifier (SID), and the unique local system identifier used by the contributing institution (SDN). It also adds more than a dozen qualifiers to the Relation element to identify such related external materials as content ratings, various types of reviews, quality scores, and order information. One of these qualifiers, conformsTo, was accepted by the DCMI Usage Board as a domain-specific element refinement qualifier. It is meant to be used for "a reference to an established standard to which the resource conforms."

Three levels of cataloging are defined by the GEM initiative: GEM Profile, Level One, and Level Two. The GEM Profile is the minimal level acceptable and consists of mandatory elements Cataloging, Format, Audience.Level, Online Provider (a role value of Publisher), Type, Title, GEM Subject, Date.RecordCreated, Rights, and Description. Level One cataloging, which is recommended, consists of the GEM Profile plus the elements Keywords and Audience. Level Two cataloging is anything exceeding Level One. Figure 12-1 shows an example of Level Two cataloging from the GEM Training Manual. In this example of record display, "Your own classroom court" is a hotlink to the resource itself.

GEM is not associated with any specific body of content rules. The GEM website offers a number of tools to help in the creation of GEM metadata, including a free cataloging module available in Java and web-based versions, a training manual, and data entry templates (called "style sheets") developed by participating organizations. The GEM project also has developed authority lists for several elements, including most of the education-specific elements and the element Subject. Where an authority list is available, its use is required. GEM also allows local projects to develop their own controlled vocabularies. Apart from the required use of controlled vocabularies, however, available guidelines offer minimal guidance on how to represent data values. The AskERIC stylesheet, for example, instructs the user to enter author names as they appear on the document, but neither the training manual nor the other stylesheets address the question.

In the abstract, the GEM element set is syntax-independent, and GEM semantics, like Dublin Core semantics, can be represented in a variety of formats. In practice, however, records meant for inclusion in the GEM Gateway must be created in a format the GEM project can accept. If an existing local database is being converted to GEM, the batch output can be in XML, in a local GEM-defined syntax called "syntax-1," or in HTML. If the GEM cataloging module is being used to create individual records, the output is HTML. An example of HTML created by the cataloging client is shown in figure 12-2.

Level Two (Documentation) Cataloging Example

Title: Your own Classroom Court

GEM Subject: **Level One:** Social Studies
Level Two: United States Government

Keyword: Constitutional law, Courts, Equal protection, Trial by jury

Description: To allow students the opportunity to further their knowledge of the law and its legal proceedings. To experience "trial by a jury of your peers" in simple matters. To give each student a job in the courtroom and to vary these positions throughout the year.

Creator: Rita Irene Esparza

Resource Type: Lesson Plan

Grade Levels: 9-12

Audience: **A tool for whom?** Teachers
Who is the ultimate beneficiary? Students

Pedagogy: **Grouping:** Large group instruction
Teaching Methods: Hands-on learning, Role Playing

Identifier: **SID:** AskERIC
SDN: AELP-GOV0053

Date: Generated by GEMCat.

Format: Text/HTML

Cataloging Agency: **Application:** GEMCat (This information is generated by GEMCat.)
Version: 3.21 (This information is generated by GEMCat.)
Name: GEM
Email: geminfo@geminfo.org
URL: http://www.geminfo.org

Online Provider: **Organization/Person Name:** AskERIC
Email: askeric@askeric.org
URL: http://www.askeric.org

Language: English

FIGURE 12-1 Example of GEM Level Two cataloging. From the *GEMCat Training Manual*, prepared November 1, 2000, by the Gateway to Educational Materials Project, Syracuse University. GEM is sponsored by the United States Department of Education.

Level Two (Documentation) Cataloging Metadata

```
<meta name="DC.package.begin" content="1">
<meta name="DC.title" content="(lang=en)Your own Classroom Court">
<meta name="DC.format" content="(scheme=IMT)(type=contentType)text/HTML">
<meta name="GroupStart" content="1">
<meta name="DC.publisher" content="(type=role)onlineProvider">
<meta name="DC.publisher" content="(type=name)AskERIC">
<meta name="DC.publisher" content="(type=email)askeric@askeric.org">
<meta name="DC.publisher" content="(type=homePage)http://www.askeric.org">
<meta name="GroupEnd" content="1">
<meta name="DC.type" content="(scheme=GEM)Lesson plan">
<meta name="GroupStart" content="2">
<meta name="DC.subject" content="(scheme=GEM)(type=levelOne)Social studies">
<meta name="DC.subject" content="(scheme=GEM)(type=levelTwo)United States government">
<meta name="GroupEnd" content="2">
<meta name="GroupStart" content="3">
<meta name="DC.creator" content="(type=namePersonal)Rita Irene Esparza">
<meta name="GroupEnd" content="3">
<meta name="DC.date" content="(scheme=ISO8601:1988)(type=recordCreated)1999-04-01T13:48:53-
5:00">
<meta name="DC.description" content="The goal of this lesson is to allow students the opportunity to
further their knowledge of the law and its legal proceedings. To experience trial by a jury of your peers in
simple matters. To give each student a job in the courtroom and to vary these positions throughout the
year.">
<meta name="GroupStart" content="4">
<meta name="DC.identifier" content="(scheme=GEM)(type=SID)AskERIC">
<meta name="DC.identifier" content="(type=SDN)AELP-GOV0053">
<meta name="GroupEnd" content="4">
<meta name="DC.subject" content="(type=keywords)Constitutional law,Courts ,Equal protection,Trial by
jury">
<meta name="DC.language" content="(scheme=Z39.53)(type=text)English,">
<meta name="GroupStart" content="5">
<meta name="DC.rights" content="(type=priceCode)0">
<meta name="GroupEnd" content="5">
<meta name="DC.package.end" content="1">
<meta name="GEM.package.begin" content="1">
<meta name="GroupStart" content="6">
<meta name="GEM.cataloging" content="(type=application)GEMCat">
<meta name="GEM.cataloging" content="(type=version)3.21">
<meta name="GEM.cataloging" content="(type=name)GEM">
<meta name="GEM.cataloging" content="(type=email)geminfo@geminfo.org">
<meta name="GEM.cataloging" content="(type=homePage)http://www.geminfo.org">
<meta name="GroupEnd" content="6">
<meta name="GEM.grade" content="(scheme=GEM)(type=grade)9,10,11,12">
<meta name="GroupStart" content="7">
<meta name="GEM.audience" content="(scheme=GEM)(type=toolFor)Teachers">
<meta name="GEM.audience" content="(scheme=GEM)(type=beneficiary)Students">
<meta name="GroupEnd" content="7">
<meta name="GEM.pedagogy" content="(scheme=GEM)(type=grouping)Large group instruction">
<meta name="GEM.pedagogy" content="(scheme=GEM)(type=teachingMethods)Hands-on learning,Role
playing">
<meta name="GEM.package.end" content="1">
```

FIGURE 12-2   HTML metadata created by the GEM cataloging module. From the *GEMCat Training Manual,* prepared November 1, 2000, by the Gateway to Educational Materials Project, Syracuse University. GEM is sponsored by the United States Department of Education.

IEEE/LOM AND ADL/SCORM

While GEM is primarily concerned with lesson plans, curriculum units, and similar materials, a number of other initiatives focus on systems for managing and describing learning objects. These include the Institute of Electrical and Electronics Engineers (IEEE) Learning Technology Standards Committee (LTSC), the IMS Global Learning Consortium (IMS), the British ARIADNE (Alliance of Remote Instructional Authoring and Distribution Networks for Europe) project, and the U.S. Department of Defense's Advanced Distributed Learning (ADL) initiative. Learning objects have been variously defined but are widely perceived as small units of instructional content that can be reused in different contexts. The IEEE LTSC defines learning objects to include nondigital as well as digital content, but most definitions include digital content only. In any case, it is generally agreed that learning objects should be self-contained units that are capable of being reused for different purposes and capable of being combined with other learning objects to produce new instructional aggregations.

The initiatives just mentioned have focused a great deal of effort on the development of effective metadata schemes for learning objects. (In fact, one educational theorist laments that so many more resources have been spent on developing metadata standards than on developing instructional theories that "we will find ourselves with digital libraries full of easy-to-find learning objects we don't know how to use."[2]) This activity has been necessary for at least two reasons. First, learning objects are not exclusively or even primarily text, but can be any (digital) medium or multimedia, so external metadata is crucial for discovery. Second, learning objects as atomic units of content must be described at a level of granularity that traditional library cataloging cannot accommodate.[3] Applicable metadata schemes must not only describe these small units but do it in such a way that they can be sequenced with other units to achieve meaningful programs of instruction.

The schemes promoted by these three initiatives are historically related and can be considered variants or profiles of one another. The IEEE Draft Standard for Learning Object Metadata (LOM) was initially based on early specifications from ARIADNE and was developed with significant input from IMS. ARIADNE subsequently modified its own specification to be a compatible profile of IEEE LOM. The IMS Learning Resource Meta Data Specification consists of the IEEE LOM plus IMS modifications, which may subsequently be incorporated into the IEEE draft. ADL's Sharable Content Object Reference Model (SCORM) has three metadata element sets for raw media, content, and courses, which are each profiles of the IMS Learning Resource Meta Data. It should also be noted that in 2001 the IEEE LTSC and the DCMI published a memorandum of understanding expressing their joint commitment to collaboration on the development of interoperable metadata for learning, education, and training. The remainder of this chapter will focus on the IEEE Draft Standard for Learning Object Metadata (LOM), but much of this applies to the other schemes as well.

LOM consists of several dozen metadata elements grouped in nine categories. The "General" category consists of elements describing the learning object as a whole, including such aspects as title, description, and topical keywords. The "Lifecycle" category is defined as describing "the history and current state of this learning object and those entities that have effected this learning object during its evolution." In addition to version and status information, Lifecycle includes names and roles of contributors,

AMERICAN LIBRARY ASSOC
50 E HURON ST
CHICAGO, IL 60611
DATE 05/26/04
TIME 12:48 PM
SALE
MASTERCARD
TOTAL $39.41
CUSTOMER COPY

...uding the creator. This breaks with library bibliographic practice, which would treat authorship as a general characteristic, and moves toward an event-based characterization as described by Carl Lagoze.[4] Other categories are "Meta-Metadata," for information describing the cataloging rather than the learning object; "Technical," for technical characteristics of the learning object; "Educational," for educational or pedagogic characteristics; "Rights," for intellectual property rights and conditions of use; "Relation," for relationships with other learning objects; "Annotation," for documenting comments; "Classification," for categorizing the object within systems of classification, including pedagogical classifications, such as reading level.

Each metadata element is described in terms of seven attributes: "name," "explanation," "size," "order," "example," "value space," and "datatype." The "size" attribute specifies... allowed for the element; for nonrepeatable elements, the size... repeatable elements, size specifies the smallest number a compliant... to support. "Order" indicates whether there is meaning to the order of repeatable elements, for example, from general to more specific. "Value space" is used to specify allowable values, either by reference to an authority list within the LOM or by reference to an external scheme. When a controlled vocabulary is used, the element value must be given as a "source, value" pair, with "source" indicating the vocabulary, for example,

> "LOMv1.0", "Questionnaire"

"Datatype" indicates the nature of the values, which may be "LangString," "DateTime," "Duration," "Vocabulary," "CharacterString," or "Undefined." Most string values are defined as "LangString," a datatype consisting of a language code in quotation marks followed by a comma and the string value in quotation marks, for example,

> "en", "16th century France"

LOM elements are defined as parts of aggregates, or structures, that begin with the category and may include intermediate levels. For example, in the "General" category, the aggregate Identifier includes the two elements Catalog ("The name or designator of the identification or cataloging scheme for this entry") and Entry ("The value of the identifier within the identification or cataloging scheme that designates or identifies this learning object"). Figure 12-3 shows a page from the draft IEEE LOM specification, defining the first several elements in the "Lifecycle" category.

Not surprisingly, the LOM specification focuses heavily on educational metadata, with eleven of the fifty-eight defined elements falling in the "Educational" category. Two elements address interactivity: Interactivity Type, with the prescribed values "active," "expositive," and "mixed," and Interactivity Level, with values ranging from "very low" to "very high." The element Learning Resource Type is similar to the GEM Resource Type but uses a different authority list. The Semantic Density element attempts to rate the conciseness of the learning object, with values from "very low" to "very high." The element Intended End User Role indicates whether the learning object was designed for teachers, authors, learners, or managers. The element Context indicates whether the intended learning environment is school, higher education, training, or other. Other elements in the "Educational" category are fairly self-explanatory, including Typical Age Range, Difficulty, Typical Learning Time, Description, and Language. Educational/pedagogical metadata can also be carried in the "Classification" category, if the value can be

Nr	Name	Explanation	Size	Order	Value Space	Datatype	Example
2	Life Cycle	This category describes the history and current state of this learning object and those entities that have affected this learning object during its evolution.	1	unspecified	-	-	-
2.1	Version	The edition of this learning object.	1	unspecified	-	LangString (smallest permitted maximum: 50 char)	("en", "1.2.alpha"), ("nl", "voorlopige versie")
2.2	Status	The completion status or condition of this learning object	1	unspecified	draft final revised unavailable NOTE: When the status is "unavailable" it means that the learning object itself is not available.	Vocabulary (State)	-
2.3	Contribute	Those entities (i.e., people, organizations) that have contributed to the state of this learning object during its life cycle (e.g., creation, edits, publication). NOTE 1: This data element is different from 3.3:Meta-Metadata.Contribute. NOTE 2: Contributions should be considered in a very broad sense here, as all actions that affect the state of the learning object	smallest permitted maximum: 30 items	ordered	-	-	-

Nr=Number

Figure 12-3 Page from the draft IEEE LOM specification. From IEEE Std. 1484.12.1. Copyright © 2002 IEEE. All rights reserved.

measured on a standardized scale. For example, reading age schemes, reading level schemes, IQ schemes, skills the user is intended to master, and tasks the user must be able to accomplish could all be represented as elements within "Classification."

Although the LOM specification does not have associated content rules, it does place high value on use of controlled vocabularies. More than half the elements reference some authority, and seventeen authority lists are defined in the specification itself. LOM allows the use of other, nonconflicting vocabularies, but specifies that in order to maximize interoperability, if a non-LOM vocabulary is used, and the value taken from that vocabulary is also defined in LOM, the value should be designated as coming from LOM.

In contrast to the emphasis on controlled vocabularies for subject, classification, and educational elements, LOM, like GEM, has no required name authority for authors and contributors. LOM specifies that contributor values be entered according to the vCard specification, which prescribes the structure of name and contact information but not the choice or form of the values.[5] This may reflect a perception that authorship is less important a property of curriculum materials and learning objects than it is of scholarly and research works.

Although the LOM itself is syntax independent, IMS has published XML schema definitions and DTDs for Learning Resource Meta Data, and ADL has published XML schema definitions for SCORM extensions to the IMS schema. Figure 12-4 shows the beginning of an example metadata record in XML, taken from the IMS site.

Several projects are experimenting with use of LOM or related schemes for learning object metadata. These are relatively complex schemes, and records to be useful must be relatively lengthy: IMS has defined a core of nineteen recommended (though not required) data elements. Therefore, the time and level of skill required to create compliant metadata are an issue. This is exacerbated by the philosophical and practical premise that learning objects should be as atomic as possible, leading to the need to create a relatively large number of metadata records describing many small units. The creation of educational metadata is being facilitated by the development of automated tools and by central support from projects, many of which receive state or federal grant support. Much of it also takes place in the for-profit environment by companies marketing to academic and business training sectors. The degree of coordination in the development of metadata schemes between large educational initiatives, such as IMS, IEEE LTSC, ARIADNE, and ADL SCORM, has been impressive.

However, interoperable metadata description is only a small piece of the overall problem of making learning objects reusable and interoperable on a wide scale. Other challenges include consistent terminologies and design principles in development of the learning objects themselves, and appropriate overarching architectures and theories of instructional design. We can expect to see continued heavy investment in all these areas throughout the decade as the potential of learning objects technology to transform education is pursued.

```xml
<?xml version="1.0" encoding="UTF-8"?>
<!-- edited with XML Spy v3.5 (http://www.xmlspy.com) by Boyd W Nielsen
(NETg) -->
<lom xmlns="http://www.imsglobal.org/xsd/imsmd_v1p2"
     xmlns:xsi="http://www.w3.org/2001/XMLSchema-instance"
     xsi:schemaLocation="http://www.imsglobal.org/xsd/imsmd_v1p2
imsmd_v1p2p2.xsd">
     <general>
          <identifier>x-ims-plirid-v0.DUNS.05-107-
9929.nloid.en_US_72475</identifier>
          <title>
               <langstring xml:lang="en-US">Microsoft SQL Server 7.0:
Implementing a Database - Part 1</langstring>
          </title>
          <catalogentry>
               <catalog>http://www.netg.com/catalog1.html</catalog>
               <entry>
                    <langstring xml:lang="en-US">72475</langstring>
               </entry>
          </catalogentry>
          <language>en</language>
          <description>
               <langstring xml:lang="en-US">This is the first course
in a five part series that will provide students with the knowledge to
implement a database solution with Microsoft SQL Server
7.0.</langstring>
          </description>
          <keyword>
               <langstring xml:lang="en-US">Windows NT</langstring>
          </keyword>
          <keyword>
               <langstring xml:lang="en-US">Microsoft</langstring>
          </keyword>
          <keyword>
               <langstring xml:lang="en-US">Database</langstring>
          </keyword>
          <keyword>
               <langstring xml:lang="en-US">SQL Server
7.0</langstring>
          </keyword>
          <keyword>
               <langstring xml:lang="en-US">Microsoft
BackOffice</langstring>
          </keyword>
          <structure>
               <source>
                    <langstring xml:lang="x-
none">LOMv1.0</langstring>
               </source>
               <value>
                    <langstring xml:lang="x-
none">Collection</langstring>
               </value>
          </structure>
          <aggregationlevel>
               <source>
                    <langstring xml:lang="x-
none">LOMv1.0</langstring>
               </source>
               <value>
                    <langstring xml:lang="x-none">3</langstring>
```

FIGURE 12-4 Beginning of a sample metadata record, taken from the IMS site. Reprinted by permission of the IMS Global Learning Consortium, Inc.

NOTES

1. GEM Project Site (home page), available at http://www.geminfo.org/. Accessed 1 July 2002.
2. David A. Wiley, untitled (web document), available at http://wiley.ed.usu.edu/docs/encyc.pdf. Accessed 1 July 2002.
3. Joseph B. South and David W. Monson, "A University-wide System for Creating, Capturing, and Delivering Learning Objects," in D. A. Wiley, ed., *The Instructional Use of Learning Objects,* online version, available at http://www.reusability.org/read. Accessed 1 July 2002.
4. Carl Lagoze, "Business Unusual: How 'Event-Awareness' May Breathe Life into the Catalog," in *Proceedings of the Bicentennial Conference on Bibliographic Control for the New Millennium,* Library of Congress, November 15–17, 2000, available at http://lcweb.loc.gov/catdir/bibcontrol/lagoze_paper.html. Accessed 1 July 2002.
5. T. Howes, M. Smith, and F. Dawson, "A MIME Content-Type for Directory Information," RFC 2425, available at http://www.imc.org/rfc2425. See also F. Dawson and T. Howes, "vCard MIME Directory Profile," RFC 2426, available at http://www.imc.org/rfc2426. Accessed 1 July 2002.

READINGS

Specifications discussed in this chapter are cited here, followed by the parent website. The websites should be consulted for current versions of the specifications, some of which are updated fairly frequently, and for related specifications, tools, and documentation.

ARIADNE Educational Metadata Recommendation, version 3.0, available at http://ariadne.unil.ch/Metadata/. The ARIADNE home page is available at http://www.ariadne-eu.org/. The ARIADNE project was discontinued in 2000, but the work is being carried on by the ARIADNE Foundation.

GEM 2.0, available at http://www.geminfo.org/Workbench/gem2.html. The home page of the GEM Project Site for project participants is available at http://www.geminfo.org/. The Gateway to Educational Materials, the GEM search interface, is available at http://www.thegateway.org/welcome.html.

Greenberg, Jane, ed. *Metadata and Organizing Educational Resources on the Internet.* New York: Haworth Press, 2000. Simultaneously published as *Journal of Internet Cataloging* 3, nos. 1 and 2/3 (2000).

> A collection of essays covering several different metadata schemes, projects, and applications.

IEEE Draft Standard for Learning Object Metadata (IEEE P1484.12.1/D6.4), available at http://ltsc.ieee.org/doc/wg12/LOM3_00.pdf. The home page of the IEEE Learning Object Standards Committee, IEEE P1484.12 Learning Object Metadata Working Group is available at http://ltsc.ieee.org/wg12/.

IMS Learning Resource Meta Data Information Model, version 1.2 Final Specification, available at http://www.imsproject.org/metadata/imsmdv1p2p1/imsmd_infov1p2p1.html. The home page of the IMS Global Learning Consortium is available at http://www.imsproject.org/.

Sharable Content Object Reference Model (SCORM) 1.2 Content Aggregation Model, available at http://www.adlnet.org/ADLDOCS/Document/SCORM_1.2_CAM.doc. The home page of the Advanced Distributed Learning Network is available at http://www.adlnet.org/.

Wiley, David A., ed. *The Instructional Use of Learning Objects.* Association for Instructional Technology, 2001. Online version available at http://www.reusability.org/read/.

> A collection of essays that together constitute a primer on the theory of learning objects and the practice of implementing them. Although this is not the focus, some of the essays touch on metadata standards and issues. The entire book is available online, with the ability to comment on and submit corrections to the text.

ONIX International

13

ONIX (Guidelines for ONline Information eXchange) is a scheme initially developed by publishers for exchanging trade information in electronic form with e-tailers, retailers, wholesalers, distributors, and other parties in the book supply chain. In fact, two metadata schemes with a similar purpose were developed roughly coterminously on different sides of the Atlantic. The EDItEUR Product Information Communication Standards (EPICS) were drafted under the auspices of EDItEUR, an international organization for promoting electronic commerce in the book and serials sectors. The initial version of ONIX was developed by the Association of American Publishers (AAP). Version 1.0 of ONIX and the EPICS Data Dictionary version 3.02 were both released in January 2000.

Work immediately began to unite the two efforts. A new version of ONIX, more consistent with EPICS and intended for both U.S. and European implementation, was released in May 2000 under the name ONIX International 1.01. EPICS was redefined as a more comprehensive data dictionary of which ONIX could be seen as a subset. Both schemes are maintained by EDItEUR under the direction of a single international steering committee. The last public release of EPICS remains 3.2, while ONIX is being actively expanded and strongly promoted. The base specification, now called the ONIX Product Record, was updated in version 2.0 to include data for e-books. ONIX for Serials, which consists of three sets of metadata elements for title, item, and subscription package records, is under development.

The initial impetus for both EPICS and ONIX was the rapid rise of electronic bookselling in the latter half of the 1990s. Most large e-tailers (electronic retailers) had established preferred formats for accepting publisher data, but these formats differed from one another, causing a publisher to have to separately format several different feeds. At the same time, e-tailers and other distributors were in fact receiving quantities of data in nonpreferred message formats and saw immediate advantage to having a single format adopted by all publishers. Publishers realized some standardization was necessary to get their market information to online booksellers rapidly and accurately. They also realized that web e-tailing had to compensate for lack of the physical, browsable book by providing surrogates in the form of images and content information. The introduction to the first published edition of ONIX noted that in online bookstores, books with cover images, reviews, and additional online information outsold books without that information eight to one.

As a result of the multiple purposes the ONIX record was designed to serve, the information carried in an ONIX product record can be seen as a liberal superset of the information in a traditional library bibliographic record. In addition to descriptive metadata to allow a reader to find and identify a title, the ONIX product record contains promotional information to encourage a reader to purchase a title, and also trade information for use by the bookseller or distributor.

ONIX is specified in terms of an XML DTD that defines each element with two tag names—a pneumonic textual name (e.g., <PublisherName>) and a short, coded version (e.g., <b081>). The first is called the *reference name* and the latter the *short tag*. The ONIX 2.0 specification defines each element in terms of five attributes—an unlabeled description, Format, Code list, Reference name, and Short tag. "Format" includes both data type and length, for example, "fixed length, two numeric digits" or "variable length text, suggested maximum 200 characters." "Code list" refers to authority lists of coded values, which may be external or defined within ONIX. Each element is also illustrated by an example. Figure 13-1 shows the element definition for the Record Source Type Code from the ONIX Product Information Guidelines, Release 2.0.

The ONIX scheme is characterized by a heavy emphasis on coded values, use of *composites* (sets of data elements that must occur together), and multiple options for representing the same data. The treatment of key numbers illustrates all three characteristics. Separate metadata elements are defined for the ISBN, EAN-13, UPC, and a few other product numbers. Alternatively, a three-element composite may be used. In the composite, the first element, Product Identifier Type Code, holds a coded value for the

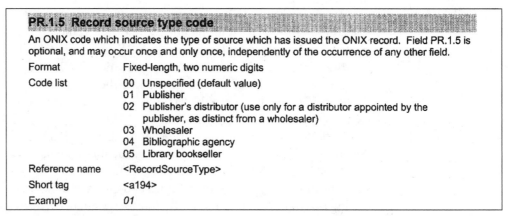

PR.1.5 Record source type code

An ONIX code which indicates the type of source which has issued the ONIX record. Field PR.1.5 is optional, and may occur once and only once, independently of the occurrence of any other field.

Format	Fixed-length, two numeric digits
Code list	00 Unspecified (default value)
	01 Publisher
	02 Publisher's distributor (use only for a distributor appointed by the publisher, as distinct from a wholesaler)
	03 Wholesaler
	04 Bibliographic agency
	05 Library bookseller
Reference name	<RecordSourceType>
Short tag	<a194>
Example	*01*

FIGURE 13-1   ONIX element definition. From ONIX Product Information Guidelines, Release 2.0 <Product Record>. Copyright 2001, EDItEUR Limited. Reprinted with permission of EDItEUR Limited.

type of identifier to follow (e.g., "02" means ISBN). The second element, Identifier Type Name, is a textual string used only when the type code identifies a nonstandard, proprietary scheme. The third element, Identifier Value, contains the actual key number. The composite can be repeated to represent as many key numbers as needed.

The pairing of a code for the type of identifier with an element for the identifier value itself is typical ONIX structure. Another common pattern is to pair coded values with elements for equivalent textual values, with the former required and use of the latter either optional or limited to special cases. For example, two elements in the specification are defined for coded values describing the form of material: Product Form and Book Form Detail. A third element, Product Form Description, may contain a textual description of the form of material but should only be used when the coded values in the other two elements are inadequate to describe the item.

Treatment of title data gives another example of the range of options available in ONIX. A title can be represented simply using the Distinctive Title of Product element:

<DistinctiveTitle>The genetics of the dog</Distinctive Title>

Alternatively, a composite can be used that includes an element for coded type of title (here the value "01" indicates a distinctive title) and another element for the title text:

<TitleType>01</TitleType>

<TitleText>The genetics of the dog</TitleText>

If there is a need to indicate nonsorting characters, another form can be used:

<TitlePrefix>The</TitlePrefix>

<TitleWithoutPrefix>genetics of the dog</TitleWithoutPrefix>

In all cases, the method of capitalization used can optionally be indicated via the Text Case Flag element, which includes values for sentence case, title case, and all capitals.

<TitleType>01</TitleType>

<TextCaseFlag>02</TextCaseFlag>

<TitleText>The Genetics of the Dog</TitleText>

This illustrates another general characteristic of the ONIX scheme. Apart from required use of coded values, ONIX avoids prescribing rules for choice or form of content. Rather, it allows data to be represented in various ways, providing elements to explicitly indicate which representation was used.

As noted, ONIX contains many elements similar to those used in library cataloging, including key numbers, names of authors and other contributors, edition information, imprint information, physical description, audience, and subject. However, many of these entities are treated quite differently than in library cataloging. Authorship, for example, is represented by use of the Contributor composite, which must include a contributor role code. Elements are defined for representing personal names in unstructured normal order, in unstructured inverted order, and in structured form separately delimiting parts of the name, such as prefixes and titles. A person's name can be given in one, two, or all three forms within the same composite. A single unstructured element is defined for names of corporate contributors. Conferences cannot be entered as contributors, although there are elements for representing the names of conferences associated with the publication. There are no guidelines for formulating personal or corporate names and no name authority referenced within the standard.

Subject terms are categorized as main subjects or additional subjects. For main subject, only subject schemes recognized as book trade standards in particular countries or regions can be used. The two dominant subject vocabularies used in the book trade are the BASIC (Book And Serial Industry Communications) list used primarily in the United States and the BIC (Book Industry Communication) list used in the United Kingdom. In typical ONIX fashion, separate sets of main subject elements are defined specifically for BASIC and BIC terms, while for terms from other schemes, a Main Subject composite can be used pairing codes for the subject vocabulary with the subject term itself. Only one main subject can be assigned, and its use is strongly encouraged, although not required. The Additional Subjects composite can be used to give additional subject terms or to record subjects from other vocabularies, including LC Classification, LCSH, Dewey, and Abridged Dewey.

Promotional information is mainly accommodated in two sets of elements, one for textual descriptions and one for links to images, audio, and video. Textual descriptions can be entered in the Annotation or Main Description elements and/or in an Other Text composite. The composite includes an element for the text itself, a coded value indicating the nature of the text (table of contents, review, etc.), a coded value indicating the format of the text (ASCII, HTML, etc.), an element for the author and title of the source text, and elements for linking to external textual descriptions. All sorts of text are allowed, from flap and back cover copy to descriptions for various audiences (salespeople, press, teachers, bookstore, library) to the full text of the first chapter or even the entire work. There are also elements for explicit sales promotion information, such as descriptions of advertising campaigns, and book club adoption information. Composites for linking include elements for the type of target (software demo, front cover image, etc.), the format and resolution of the target, the type of link, the link itself, and information associated with downloading, including captions, credits, copyright, and terms.

Trade information in the ONIX product record includes sets of elements for the description of rights and comprehensive supplier, price, and availability information. The latter can include such information as returns policies, availability dates, batch bonuses, and tax rates for European countries.

Figure 13-2 shows a sample ONIX record, using reference names, from the ONIX Product Information Guidelines, Release 2.0.

Other ONIX specifications include the Main Series Record and Subseries Record (two guidelines developed for the German ONIX user group and not implemented elsewhere) and ONIX for Serials, which is currently in draft form. ONIX for Serials defines three record formats. The Serial Title record provides bibliographic information for serial titles consistent with the ONIX Product record, with additional elements for contacts, publishing history, and price and supply information. The specification states that if a serial is published in print and electronic versions, separate records should be created for each. It does not address whether or when different versions or formats of an electronic publication warrant separate records, but there may be an assumption that any publication with a unique ISSN would require a separate ONIX record. It appears that title changes will be addressed in future versions of the specification by an expan-

```
<Product>
    <RecordReference>1234567890</RecordReference>
    <NotificationType>03</NotificationType>
    <ISBN>0816016356</ISBN>
    <ProductForm>BB</ProductForm>
    <DistinctiveTitle>British English, A to Zed</DistinctiveTitle>
    <Contributor>
        <ContributorRole>A01</ContributorRole>
        <PersonNameInverted>Schur, Norman W</PersonNameInverted>
        <BiographicalNote>A Harvard graduate in Latin and Italian literature, Norman
        Schur attended the University of Rome and the Sorbonne before returning to the
        United States to study law at Harvard and Columbia Law Schools.  Now retired
        from legal practice, Mr Schur is a fluent speaker and writer of both British and
        American English</BiographicalNote>
    </Contributor>
    <EditionTypeCode>REV</EditionTypeCode>
    <EditionNumber>3</EditionNumber>
    <LanguageOfText>eng</LanguageOfText>
    <NumberOfPages>493</NumberOfPages>
    <BASICMainSubject>REF008000</BASICMainSubject>
    <AudienceCode>01</AudienceCode>
    <ImprintName>Facts on File Publications</ImprintName>
    <PublisherName>Facts on File Inc</PublisherName>
    <PublicationDate>1987</PublicationDate>
    <Height>9.25</Height>
    <Width>6.25</Width>
    <Thickness>1.2</Thickness>
        <MainDescription>BRITISH ENGLISH, A TO ZED is the thoroughly updated,
        revised, and expanded third edition of Norman Schur's highly acclaimed
        transatlantic dictionary for English speakers.  First published as BRITISH SELF-
        TAUGHT and then as ENGLISH ENGLISH, this collection of Briticisms for
        Americans, and Americanisms for the British, is a scholarly yet witty lexicon,
        combining definitions with commentary on the most frequently used and some
        lesser known words and phrases. Highly readable, it's a snip of a book, and one
        that sorts out – through comments in American – the "Queen's English" –
        confounding as it may seem.</MainDescription>
        <ReviewQuote>Norman Schur is without doubt the outstanding authority on the
        similarities and differences between British and American English.  BRITISH
        ENGLISH, A TO ZED attests not only to his expertise, but also to his undiminished
        powers to inform, amuse and entertain. – Laurence Urdang, Editor, VERBATIM,
        The Language Quarterly, Spring 1988 </ReviewQuote>
    <SupplyDetail>
        <SupplierSAN>1234567</SupplierSAN>
        <AvailabilityCode>IP</AvailabilityCode>
    <Price>
        <PriceTypeCode>01</PriceTypeCode>
        <PriceAmount>35.00</PriceAmount>
    </Price>
    </SupplyDetail>
</Product>
```

FIGURE 13-2   Sample ONIX record using reference names. From ONIX Product Information Guidelines, Release 2.0 <Product Record>. Copyright 2001, EDItEUR Limited. Reprinted with permission of EDItEUR Limited.

sion of the publishing history composite, the assumption being that information about earlier publishers and titles will be accumulated in the record for the current serial title.

The ONIX Serial Item record is designed to communicate information about "discrete parts" of serial publications, which would ordinarily be issues but might in some cases be articles or other units. Potential uses include current awareness services and library check-in. The Serial Item record contains an identifier for the item being described and information about the containing serial title, but the bulk of the information is given in Journal Issue and Content Item composites. The Journal Issue composite contains composites and elements that identify the issue in terms of enumeration and cover date, title, type of issue, and inclusive pages. If the issue contains papers from a conference, conference information can also be given. The Journal Issue composite is repeatable and can be used to identify the last previous issue as well as the current issue, a feature that should be useful for library check-in. The Content Item composite can be used for fairly detailed description of items within the issue, such as articles, editorials, and reviews. It contains such composites and elements as pagination, title and contributor, subjects, associated dates, and associated conference information.

The Subscription Package record can communicate information about combined subscriptions, in which two or more serial publications are offered together for a single price. The record contains two sets of elements applying to the package as a whole: information identifying the subscription package by an identification number and title (probably local to a publisher or an agent), and pricing and supply information. Individual titles offered within the package are described by elements within the Title Package composite, which is repeated for each title. The Title Package composite identifies the title by key number and title. Within the Title Package composite, a Journal Issue composite identifies the starting and ending dates of coverage of that title within the package.

ONIX for Serials, having been drafted more recently than the ONIX Product Record, illustrates some of the directions in which the ONIX specifications are moving. ONIX for Serials relies more heavily on generalized composites in preference to defining specific elements for particular types of values. For example, ONIX for Serials has no element defined specifically for the ISSN; the only way to represent an ISSN is through the Serial Title Identifier composite, which contains a coded value for type of identifier paired with a value for the identifier itself. ONIX for Serials also introduces the use of XML attributes for types of values that were defined as XML tags in earlier specifications, such as the Text Case Flag:

<TitleText textcase="02">Title in Title Case</TitleText>

The ONIX Product Record was developed by publishers primarily to serve their need to communicate product information to online booksellers and other distributors. However, libraries have been quick to see potential uses of ONIX data as well. Library systems vendors have added to their online catalogs the ability to display tables of contents, reviews, artwork, and other enriched content, and publishers' ONIX records are seen as a possible source of such content. The Library of Congress has explored several uses of ONIX, such as integrating ONIX feeds into the Cataloging In Publication (CIP) processing stream and linking from catalog records to tables of contents extracted from ONIX.[1] Bibliographic information in the ONIX product record can be mapped to MARC21, although the resultant record cannot be used in library catalogs without substantial editing, primarily because of the lack of name authority in ONIX and the use of different authorities for a number of other data elements. For example, ONIX uses an ONIX-defined "Contributor Role Code List" for the values of the Contributor role element, while MARC21 uses MARC relator codes. It is also difficult to infer the AACR2 distinction between main and added entry from the information in ONIX Contributor and role elements and to apply appropriate MARC21 subfielding to undifferentiated ONIX heading strings.

ONIX was immediately welcomed by publishers and booksellers as a standard that addressed a clear and obvious need. It was also welcomed by libraries as a potential source of earlier and richer data for catalogs and other systems. It is fairly certain that ONIX usage will increase rapidly and that the family of specifications will continue to grow and be maintained. It should be noted, however, that ONIX is still an immature scheme with only a short history of use in production environments. It is likely the specifications will undergo modification as they are exercised by the exchange of greater quantities of ONIX data in business situations. It also seems likely that we will soon see the development of ONIX "profiles," as groups of implementers agree to use only certain sets of ONIX options to improve interoperability.

NOTE

1. *LC Cataloging Newsline: Online Newsletter of the Cataloging Directorate Library of Congress* 9, no. 12 (November 2001), available at http://www.loc.gov/catdir/lccn/lccn0912. html. Accessed 3 July 2002.

READINGS

Association for Library Collections and Technical Services. Committee on Cataloging: Description and Access. Task Force on ONIX International. Final Report. Available at http://www.ala.org/alcts/organization/ccs/ccda/tf-onix3.html.

> The CC:DA Task Force on ONIX International issued this report on ONIX in December 2001. Although based on ONIX International 1.2.1, the report is an excellent study of ONIX characteristics, implementations, and library application.

Barnes&Noble.com (home page). Available at http://www.bn.com. Accessed 27 August 2002.

> It is interesting to study the way some booksellers have implemented ONIX. Barnes and Noble provides documentation to help publishers contribute their ONIX-formatted data in a way that the bookseller can accept. This documentation is available on the "help desk" portion of the Barnes and Noble website at http://www. barnesandnoble.com/help/pub_submit_onix1.asp.

EDItEUR (home page). Available at http://www.editeur.org. Accessed 27 August 2002.

> This website links to guidelines and XML DTDs for the ONIX family of specifications.

Library of Congress, Network Development and MARC Standards Office. *ONIX to MARC21 Mapping* (December 2000). Available at http://lcweb.loc.gov/marc/onix2marc.html.

14

Metadata for Geospatial and Environmental Resources

A surprisingly wide variety of information resources have some geographical component. Books and articles are written about topics rooted in place, such as the history of Belarus or piano bars in New York. Newspapers tend to have regional coverage, and photographs often portray identifiable locations. Social science data sets and scientific research data commonly have geographical limitations. Accordingly, most metadata schemes for describing information resources have some element(s) for recording geographic information.

This chapter begins with a standard designed specifically for describing digital geospatial resources, and continues with some metadata schemes for biological and species information which often have geospatial components.

THE FGDC CSDGM

One of the earliest specifications to call itself a metadata standard is the Content Standard for Digital Geospatial Metadata (CSDGM) issued by the Federal Geographic Data Committee (FGDC). The FGDC began work on the standard in 1992 and issued the first version in 1994. Executive Order 12906, "Coordinating Geographic Data Acquisition and Access: The National Spatial Data Infrastructure," signed in 1994 by President Clinton, mandated that federal agencies collecting or producing new geospatial data must use the CSDGM to describe that data and must make the metadata accessible to a National Geospatial Data Clearinghouse. The clearinghouse, coordinated by the FGDC, provides federated searching of CSDGM metadata from distributed metadata repositories via Z39.50, in a manner similar to the way GPO Access provides searching of GILS metadata.

Digital spatial data may be anything from a satellite photograph to a Geographic Information Systems (GIS) dataset. According to the CSDGM, digital geospatial metadata is intended to serve four functions: (1) to determine that data exist for a geographic location, (2) to help ascertain if the data meet a specific need (fitness for use), (3) to allow the user to acquire an identified set of data, and (4) to facilitate processing and use of a dataset.

The current version of the CSDGM standard was issued in June 1998 and is available from the FGDC website (http://www.fgdc.gov/metadata/contstan.html). It defines data elements and *compound elements*, which are comprised of groups of data elements and/or other compound elements. Data elements are described in terms of six attributes: a name, a definition, "Type," "Domain," and "Short name." "Type" indicates the data type of the value, such as integer, real number, text, date, or time. "Domain" specifies the values that can be supplied for an element, either as a list of values, as a reference to an external authority list, or as a set of restrictions on the range of values that can be assigned. "Short name" is a name of eight characters or fewer that can be used for convenience in implementing the standard; the short name for the element Maintenance and Update Frequency is "update." Compound elements are defined in terms of their name, "Type" (always "compound"), and "Short name," and may also be described by a set of "production rules" that indicate the combination of elements and compounds comprising them. Figure 14-1 shows a page of the CSDGM standard defining the Spatial Domain compound.

Organization of the CSDGM Standard

The standard is organized into ten sections:

1. Identification Information
2. Data Quality Information
3. Spatial Data Organization Information
4. Spatial Reference Information
5. Entity and Attribute Information
6. Distribution Information
7. Metadata Reference Information
8. Citation Information
9. Time Period Information
10. Contact Information

The first seven sections actually constitute the metadata record, while the last three sections define common information structures used in two or more of the preceding metadata sections. Within the metadata record, the Identification Information and Metadata Reference Information are mandatory, and the other sections are mandatory if applicable.

The Identification Information section includes a required compound element for citation information, which is defined in the Citation Information section of the standard. Citation information can contain bibliographic information, such as title, creator (called "originator"), edition, publication place, publisher, publication date, and series.

Federal Geographic Data Committee
Content Standard for Digital Geospatial Metadata

FGDC-STD-001-1998

1.5   Spatial Domain - the geographic areal domain of the data set.
       Type: compound
       Short Name: spdom

1.5.1   Bounding Coordinates - the limits of coverage of a data set expressed by latitude and longitude values in the order western-most, eastern-most, northern-most, and southern-most. For data sets that include a complete band of latitude around the earth, the West Bounding Coordinate shall be assigned the value -180.0, and the East Bounding Coordinate shall be assigned the value 180.0
         Type: compound
         Short Name: bounding

1.5.1.1   West Bounding Coordinate -- western-most coordinate of the limit of coverage expressed in longitude.
             Type: real
             Domain: -180.0 <= West Bounding Coordinate < 180.0
             Short Name: westbc

1.5.1.2   East Bounding Coordinate -- eastern-most coordinate of the limit of coverage expressed in longitude.
             Type: real
             Domain: -180.0 <= East Bounding Coordinate <= 180.0
             Short Name: eastbc

1.5.1.3   North Bounding Coordinate -- northern-most coordinate of the limit of coverage expressed in latitude.
             Type: real
             Domain: -90.0 <= North Bounding Coordinate <= 90.0;
                 North Bounding Coordinate >= South Bounding Coordinate
             Short Name: northbc

1.5.1.4   South Bounding Coordinate -- southern-most coordinate of the limit of coverage expressed in latitude.
             Type: real
             Domain: -90.0 <= South Bounding Coordinate <= 90.0;
                 South Bounding Coordinate <= North Bounding Coordinate
             Short Name: southbc

1.5.2   Data Set G-Polygon -- coordinates defining the outline of an area covered by a data set.
         Type: compound
         Short Name: dsgpoly

1.5.2.1   Data Set G-Polygon Outer G-Ring -- the closed nonintersecting boundary of an interior area.
             Type: compound
             Short Name: dsgpolyo

1.5.2.1.1   G-Ring Point -- a single geographic location.
               Type: compound
               Short Name: grngpoin

FIGURE 14-1   Page of the CSDGM defining the Spatial Domain compound in the Identification Information section. From Federal Geographic Data Committee, "Content Standard for Digital Geospatial Metadata," FGDC-STD-001-1998 (revised June 1998) (Washington, D.C.: Federal Geographic Data Committee).

Citation information also includes the time of publication, if known, and an element called Geospatial Data Presentation Form, which is taken from an authority list that includes such terms as "map," "globe," "model," "raster digital data," "vector digital data," and "remote sensing image."

In addition to Citation, the Identification section includes required compounds for Description, Time Period of Content, Status, Spatial Domain, and Keywords, and required elements for Access Constraints and Use Constraints. The Description compound must include an abstract and a statement of purpose describing why the dataset was developed. The Status compound includes the update frequency and a status element indicating whether the dataset is complete, "in work," or planned. The Keywords compound is divided into Theme (topical), Place (geographical location), Stratum (vertical location), and Temporal, and is meant to include terms from controlled vocabularies as well as uncontrolled keywords. Each Keyword compound includes an element indicating the thesaurus from which the keyword was taken as well as an element for the keyword itself.

Time Period of Content can represent a single date and time, multiple dates and times, or a range of dates and times. The Spatial Domain compound includes mandatory north, south, east, and west bounding coordinates expressed in latitude and longitude values. Spatial domain can also optionally be represented as a G-polygon, which describes the outline of an area using sets of coordinates known as G-rings.

The Data Quality Information section includes such information as an assessment of the accuracy of attribute values in the dataset; an assessment of the logical consistency of information contained within the dataset, including any tests performed on the data; information about the completeness of the dataset; and "lineage" information about the source of the data and responsible parties.

Spatial Data Organization Information describes the spatial data model used to encode the spatial data. It has subsections for indirect and direct spatial reference. Indirect spatial reference includes such data as the names of geographic features and addressing schemes or other means through which locations are referenced, for example, street names. Direct spatial reference must be either point, vector (directed lines), or raster (grid). Point and vector information can be expressed through "Spatial Data Concepts" in the Department of Commerce Spatial Data Transfer Standard or as terms from the Department of Defense Vector Product Format.

Spatial Reference Information gives the reference for horizontal and vertical (altitude or depth) coordinates in the dataset. For example, if latitude and longitude are used as horizontal coordinates, then the latitude and longitude resolution (the minimum difference between two adjacent values) and the type of units used for values (e.g., "decimal degrees") must be specified.

The Entity and Attribute Information section specifies what geographic information is included, such as roads, features, or elevation, and how these data are represented. This section can contain either a detailed description of each attribute or a summary overview description with links to a more complete description external to the metadata record. The latter ability is provided to accommodate cases in which the dataset has good external documentation that does not have to be replicated in the metadata record.

Distribution Information indicates where the data can be obtained and what formats are available. The Metadata Reference Information section is meta-metadata about the metadata record itself, such as date and time of creation and last update, when it should be reviewed, what version of the CSDGM was used, and who is the responsible contact person.

Content Rules and Syntax

Beyond prescribing the formats for date, time, and latitude and longitude values, the CSDGM does not include content rules. Names of originators and contact agencies are free text values, with no authority or form of name recommended. In a few places, reference is made to library authorities. The authority list for Geospatial Data Presentation Form is taken in part from *Cartographic Materials: A Manual of Interpretation for AACR2* (Chicago: American Library Association, 1982), and the definition of the Theme Keyword compound refers to the list of thesauri in the *MARC Code List for Relators, Sources, and Description Conventions* (Washington, D.C.: Library of Congress, 1988). For Place Keyword Thesaurus, the Geographic Names Information System is listed as an authorized value, implying that this thesaurus is recommended, or at least expected to be commonly used.

The CSDGM does not require any particular transport syntax. However, the FGDC makes available from its website an approved XML DTD and a number of stylesheets for displaying data based on the DTD.

Extensions and Profiles

The revised 1998 version of the standard includes two appendixes giving rules for extensibility and for creating profiles of the standard. Rules for both extensions and profiles are strictly defined to ensure conformance to the structure and conventions of the CSDGM. Extensions must be formally documented and pointed to in a Metadata Extensions compound in the Metadata Reference Information section. The definition of extended elements and compounds must include all the attributes used in CSDGM definitions and four additional attributes: "Source" (the name of the entity creating the element), "Rationale" (an optional reason for the creation of the element), "Parent" (the element in CSDGM under which the new element appears), and "Child" (the elements that may appear under the new element).

Profiles are customizations of the CSDGM for use by a particular community. They may specify the subset of CSDGM elements to be used by the community and may include formally defined extensions. A profile may not change the definition or use of any existing element and must include all mandatory and mandatory-if-applicable elements of the standard. It may, however, make optional elements mandatory and restrict domain values for an element. Profiles may be formalized through the FGDC or used informally by a user community. The FGDC lists profiles that are endorsed by or under development through the FGDC on the CSDGM website (http://www.fgdc.gov/metadata/contstan.html).

The CSDGM and its profiles can be difficult standards to use. The CSDGM itself is very large, defining more than three hundred elements and compounds. The rules for determining which elements are mandatory, mandatory-if-applicable, and optional are complex. Because many elements are required, resource descriptions using CSDGM are lengthy: the two example records given in the *Content Standard for Digital Geospatial*

Metadata Workbook are each seven pages long. Because of this, several states have defined their own geospatial "metadata-lite" schemes, and a Metadata Summit meeting held in Denver in February 1996 identified a subset of CSDGM elements that is sometimes referred to as the "Denver Core."

THE NBII BIOLOGICAL METADATA STANDARD

One of the best-known profiles of the CSDGM is the Biological Data Profile, more commonly known as the NBII biological metadata standard. Developed as part of the National Biological Information Infrastructure (NBII) initiative by the Biological Data Working Group of the FGDC and the Biological Resources Division of the United States Geological Survey (USGS), the profile was formally approved by the FGDC in 1999.

The NBII is a collaborative program among federal, state, international, non-government, academic, and private industry partners to increase access to data and information about biological resources (http://www.nbii.gov). Development of a standard for biological metadata was a key focus of the program from the beginning. Because a large proportion of biological and ecological sciences data has a geospatial component, the designers of the standard wanted to build on the CSDGM and extend its applicability to biological and ecological data.

The Biological Data Profile extends the CSDGM in three main areas. First, it extends the Identification Information section to include extensive taxonomy information in a Taxonomy compound. Second, it adds an Analytical Tool compound to the Identification Information section to include information on any analytical tools applied to the data or needed to interpret the data. Third, in the Data Quality Information section, it adds information documenting the methodology used to collect the data. The profile also extends domain information for many elements to include commonly used biological terms and sources.

The development of the NBII biological metadata standard raised a major issue related to CSDGM profiles. Some biological information resources, for example, laboratory data, have no geographical component. The biological community wanted to make the Spatial Domain compounds in the CSDGM mandatory if applicable, so that they could be used when appropriate but not required for non-geographically based information. However, while the biological standard was under development, the revised 1998 version of the CSDGM was issued with its requirement that profiles must include all mandatory elements of the CSDGM. The FGDC Standards Working Group agreed to a change in profile rules, allowing conditionality requirements to be relaxed for non-geospatial datasets. However, this experience highlights a common complaint about the CSDGM—that it is monolithic and not designed for use as a modular component of other metadata schemes.

THE ECOLOGICAL METADATA LANGUAGE

In today's metadata environment, there is some benefit in being able to combine metadata elements from different schemes, taking descriptive metadata from Dublin Core, for example, rather than embedding descriptive elements in a scheme for geographic or environmental information. This is the approach being taken by the Ecological

Metadata Language (EML) project of the Knowledge Network for Biocomplexity (KNB) (http://knb.ecoinformatics.org/). KNB, based at the University of California at Santa Barbara, is dedicated to facilitating ecological and environmental research on bio-complexity by improving access to and effective use of distributed data. Observation datasets share several characteristics: they are widely dispersed among individual institutions and researchers, they are heterogeneous, and synthetic analysis tools are required for their use. EML is a modular metadata description scheme, implemented in XML, that defines descriptions of features common to observation data. An EML description can include whichever EML modules are applicable to a particular resource, and it can include descriptive segments taken from other metadata schemes as long as they are represented as XML schema.

EML itself includes modules, or sets of metadata elements, for such features as access controls and restrictions; temporal, spatial, and taxonomic coverage; person information; and citation information. On the assumption that many ecological and environmental datasets are represented in local databases as sets of relational tables, a number of EML modules describe aspects of database data, including an overall view of the dataset, the description of all attributes (variables) in a table, and the structural integrity constraints between columns in different tables. The scheme also focuses on methodological information, such as processes performed on a dataset to verify or improve the quality of the data.

Figure 14-2 shows a resource description record in EML, taken from an online display of information in the KNB search system.

THE DARWIN CORE

Another scheme concerned with observation data is the Darwin Core, developed as a minimal description of natural history collections and observation databases. The Darwin Core is a Z39.50 profile being developed by the Z39.50 Biology Implementors Group (ZBIG) and promoted by the Species Analyst, a research project of the University of Kansas Natural History Museum and Biodiversity Research Center (http://tsadev. speciesanalyst.net/).

Version 2 of the Darwin Core, currently in development, defines forty-eight elements appropriate to the description of a specimen in a museum collection. There are several elements to identify the precise location of the specimen, including its catalog number and codes for the holding institution and collection. Taxonomic information is recorded in elements for the scientific name and the full taxonomic hierarchy from kingdom to subspecies, as well as for the names of the creator of the scientific name and the individual who applied it to the organism or specimen. Another set of elements identifies the collector and the date and time of collection. Geographic elements include a hierarchy of geographic names (continent, country, state, county, locality), latitude and longitude, bounding box, elevation, and depth. Other miscellaneous elements include type of preparation (for example, as of a slide) and relationships with other items.

The Species Analyst model combines Z39.50 searching with XML-formatted retrieval sets. The geographic information in the result set can be imported into standard GIS software to map the distribution of species observation or specimen collection. The FishNet system provides a good example of the federated search and retrieval

---

Data set description

Ecological Metadata Language

Metadata Identifier:	jwalsh.17.2
Short Name:	Baltimore demographic data by block group
Title:	Baltimore demographic data by block group

Data Set Owner(s):

Individual:	**Grove**
Address:	705 Spear Street, Burlington, VT 05403 USA
Phone:	(802) 951-6771
Email Address:	mgrove@fs.fed.us
Web Address:	www.beslter.org
Role:	Originator

Abstract:

Description of Education, housing, employment, income, and population data by block group for the Gwynns Falls watershed

Keywords:

- demographics, block groups

Online Distribution information:

ftp://www.ecostudies.org/pub/besgis/rbdata/gfdemog_sp.zip

Related Metadata and Data Files:

jwalsh.18.1	provides table-entity information for package	jwalsh.17.2
jwalsh.19.1	provides eml-attribute information for Table	jwalsh.18.1
jwalsh.20.1	provides eml-physical information for Table	jwalsh.18.1
jwalsh.16.1	provides access control rules for	jwalsh.17.2
jwalsh.16.1	provides access control rules for	jwalsh.18.1
jwalsh.16.1	provides access control rules for	jwalsh.19.1
jwalsh.16.1	provides access control rules for	jwalsh.20.1

FIGURE 14-2 Resource description record in EML retrieved from the KNB search system. Retrieved from http://knb.ecoinformatics.org/ and reprinted with permission of the author.

possibilities of this model (http://www.speciesanalyst.net/fishnet/). Records from twenty-three collections of fish specimen records can be searched, retrieved, and imported into GIS manipulation software, such as ESRI's ArcView or ArcMap. The locations where the specimens were collected can then be seen plotted on a map of the geographic area.

READINGS

Federal Geographic Data Committee (home page). Available at http://www.fgdc.gov/. Accessed 30 July 2002.

> The FGDC site contains a sidebar link to "Metadata," a page of information about FGDC metadata, including a link to the CSDGM document. The NBII biological profile is also available as a link from these web pages, at http://www.fgdc.gov/standards/status/sub5_2.html.

Federal Geographic Data Committee. *Content Standard for Digital Geospatial Metadata Workbook,* version 2.0. (May 1, 2002). Available at http://www.fgdc.gov/metadata/meta_workbook.html.

> This manual contains a complete copy of the CSDGM, annotated with additional information about the intended use of selected elements.

Frondorf, Anne F., Matthew B. Jones, and Susan Stitt. "Linking the FGDC Geospatial Metadata Content Standard to the Biological/Ecological Sciences." In *Proceedings of the Third IEEE META-DATA Conference, April 6–7, 1999.* Available at http://www.computer.org/proceedings/meta/1999/papers/4/afrondorf.html.

> An account of the development of the NBII Biological Metadata Standard, written before the standard was finalized as a profile of the CSDGM.

Niemann, Brand L. "Creating and Evaluating Metadata for a Digital Library of the State of the Environment." In *Proceedings of the Third IEEE META-DATA Conference,* April 6–7, 1999. Available at http://www.computer.org/proceedings/meta/1999/papers/73/bniemann. htm.

> How a digital library of the state of the environment was built by harvesting Dublin Core and FGDC lite metadata from web pages.

USGS Biological Resources. *An Image Map of the Content Standard for Digital Geospatial Metadata,* version 2-1998 (FGDC-STD-001 June 1998). Available at http://biology.usgs.gov/fgdc.metadata/version2/.

> A graphical representation of the CSDGM, using color coding to show which sections, compounds, and elements are mandatory, mandatory if applicable, or optional.

The Data Documentation Initiative

15

The Data Documentation Initiative (DDI) is an international group of social science data producers and archivists with a focus on social science research (http://www.icpsr. umich.edu/DDI/). The term DDI refers both to the DDI Committee, which formally constitutes the DDI, and to the metadata standard the committee has developed for describing social science datasets.

Social science datasets include census data, survey results, health statistics, election returns, and similar data files characterized by large aggregations of coded information. It is noteworthy that the producers and the users of social science datasets are typically not the same. Producers are often government agencies and polling organizations, while users are often academic researchers. Datasets are typically archived in large central repositories, such as those run by the Inter-University Consortium for Political and Social Research (ICPSR) and the Roper Center for Public Opinion Research.

Because of the disconnect between data producers and users and the non-self-explanatory nature of the data, documentation is crucial. Social science datasets are typically described by documents called *codebooks*, which contain information on the structure, contents, and layout of a data file, including the definitions of variables and the meanings of coded values. The original goal of the DDI was to replace the existing standard format for electronic codebooks, OSIRIS, which had been in use since the 1970s, with a more modern format. Work began on the DDI in 1995, funded initially by the ICPSR and later by grants from the National Science Foundation (NSF). A beta version was tested in 1999 and version 1.0 was released in March 2000.

The DDI is implemented as an XML DTD and documented by a tag library. An example of an element definition from the DDI Tag Library is shown in figure 15-1.

Variable Label

<labl> 4.2.2 (Generic element A.2)

Description: A descriptive phrase which defines the variable. The length of this phrase may depend on the statistical analysis system used (e.g., some version of SAS permit 40-character labels while some versions of SPSS permit 120 characters. A "level" attribute is included to permit coding of the level to which label applies, i.e., the study level, the file level (if different from study), the record group, the variable group, or the variable level. Vendor attribute provided to allow for specification of different labels for use with different vendors' software.

Remarks: Whenever possible this element should be used instead of 4.2.15 (Variable Text, 'txt') in order to facilitate the creation of statistical analysis software labels.

Example:

<var><labl>Why No Holiday-No Money</labl></var>

- Optional
- Repeatable
- Attributes: ID, xml:lang, source, level, vendor
- Contains: #PCDATA, Link to other element(s) within the codebook.

FIGURE 15-1   Variable Label element as defined in the DDI. From the Data Documentation Initiative DDI Tag Library, available at http://www.icpsr.umich.edu/DDI/CODEBOOK/codedtd.html.

The DDI contains five major sections:

<docDscr>   Document Description contains the bibliographic description of the DDI document;

<stdyDscr>   Study Description contains information about the data collection, study, or compilation described by the DDI codebook;

<fileDscr>   Data Files Description describes the characteristics and content of the data files comprising the study;

<dataDscr>   Variable Description describes individual variables in the data file;

<otherMat>   Other Study-related Materials identifies reports, publications, and other materials related to the study.

The Document Description (<docDscr>) describes the DDI document as a whole. Its two main sections are <citation> for describing the electronic codebook and <docSrc> for describing the source document, which may be a printed codebook or an electronic codebook in some other format. In this respect, it is reminiscent of the TEI header, which contains a <sourceDesc> element for describing the source text within the

<fileDesc> element that describes the electronic text. In DDI, however, the <citation> and <docSrc> elements are at the same level within the <docDscr>.

The <citation> element can contain a title statement, a statement of responsibility, production and distribution statements, a series statement, a version statement, a bibliographic citation for referring to the DDI document, holdings information (where the DDI document is located), and a notes section for any additional information pertaining to the citation. The title statement within the citation can contain the main title (<titl>), a subtitle, parallel title, alternative titles, and ID number. DDI documentation explicitly maps individual data elements within the citation to Dublin Core elements and recommends that values for these elements be supplied.

The <docSrc> element, as noted, describes the source of the DDI document. It contains the same subelements as the <citation> element, redefined to refer to the source document. The other high-order subelements within the Document Description are <guide> and <docStatus>. The <guide> element is a textual list of terms used in the DDI document and their definitions, intended to aid the user in interpreting the DDI. The <docStatus> element textually describes the production status of the DDI document, which may be preliminary or incomplete.

The second main section, Study Description, contains information about the study producing the described social science dataset. Its six main subsections are <citation>, <stdyInfo>, <method>, <dataAccs>, <otherStdyMat>, and <notes>. The <citation> is the same wrapper and set of subelements as defined in the Document Description section, only here they pertain to the study rather than to the DDI codebook; for example, the value of the author element refers to the primary investigator of the study, not to the creator of the codebook. The Study Scope subsection (<stdyInfo>) contains information about the intellectual content of the study and its geographical and chronological coverage. Topical headings can be given as keywords in the <keyword> element or as terms from a controlled vocabulary in the <topcClas> element, in which the name of the vocabulary can be given in the "vocab" attribute and a URL for the vocabulary can be recorded in the "vocabURI" attribute.

The Methodology and Processing (<method>) subsection within the Study Description section defines elements for information about the methodology used, including extensive information about the data collection methodology, such as the mode of data collection, the nature of the research instrument, the sampling procedure, and so on. The subsection also includes appraisal information, such as the response rate and sampling error, and the status of the study. The Data Access (<dataAccs>) subsection within the Study Description section describes the location and availability of the dataset. The Other Study Description Materials <otherStdyMat) subsection can be used to identify materials related to the study being described, such as related publications, as well as other related studies.

The third main section, Data Files Description (<fileDscr>), is repeated for each file within a data collection. It has two main subsections: File Description (fileTxt) and Notes (<notes>). The File Description subsection describes the physical data file in detail, including its name, contents, structure, dimensions, data formats, processing information, and information on missing data. Notes can contain any other data about the file not specifically defined in the File Description.

The fourth main section, Variable Description (<dataDscr>), is used to describe every variable in a data file. It has three subsections: Variables Group (<varGrp>),

Variable (<var>), and Notes (<notes>). The Variables Group associates variables that share some common factor, such as different versions of the same question or different questions that address a common subject. The Variable element describes all the features of a single variable in a data file, including such information as the name of the variable, its location in the data file (e.g., starting and ending positions), what it describes, whether it is or has a weight, its data type and format, and the ranges of its valid and invalid values. If the variable represents the response to a question, there are elements for recording the question and related information, such as the interviewer's instructions.

The final main section, Other Study-related Materials (<otherMat>), is used to include or link to other materials used in the production of the study or useful in its analysis. These can include survey questionnaires, coding notes, user manuals, and even computer programs. Textual materials can be entered directly into a <txt> subelement, and data tables can be entered in the <table> subelement. Materials can also be cited and pointed to with a URL.

Figure 15-2 shows the beginning of an online display of a codebook that has been encoded according to the DDI.

In version 1 of the DDI DTD, only the title element is required. However, the DDI website does include a page of recommended elements and further recommends that specific user communities develop their own sets of recommended elements. The DDI does not prescribe content rules. A handful of element attributes have authority lists for their values defined within the DDI specification, but in general no controlled vocabularies or authority lists are required, although a stated future direction is to develop vocabularies for "as many attributes as possible." Other directions for the DDI include investigating the use of XML schema and RDF, incorporating standards for geospatial metadata, and adding crosswalks to other bibliographic schemes, such as GILS and MARC.

The ICPSR, a major archive of social science data, is a prominent supporter of the DDI format and has already marked up all the study descriptions in its catalog according to the DDI specification. Data archives and projects that have adopted DDI are listed on the DDI website. Perhaps the largest international project to use DDI is NESSTAR (Networked Social Science Tools and Resources), a joint development project of the Norwegian Social Science Data Services, the U.K. Data Archive, and the Danish Data Archive. The NESSTAR model assumes federated search and retrieval across distributed social science data repositories, with integrated tools for browsing the metadata for the datasets, analyzing and visualizing the data, and downloading subsets of data. These facilities depend on highly structured DDI metadata for resource discovery, presentation, and data analysis.

The NESSTAR project illustrates the fact that the DDI has gone far beyond its initial goal of simply replacing the obsolete OSIRIS format. The development of the XML-based DDI format has enabled new modes of interoperability, from federated search to the researcher's ability to use multiple datasets at once. At the same time, use of the DDI has raised demands for changes and extensions to the format, requiring continued investment in its maintenance. The DDI initiative is currently struggling to find an adequate level of sustained funding and may make significant changes to its organizational model in response to this. However, the DDI has already become part of the fabric of social science research, and its future as a metadata scheme appears secure.

CBS News Monthly Poll #2, August 1992 (ICPSR 6084)
(August National Poll II, Republican National Convention)

View: Part 1: Document Description
       Part 2: Study Description
       Part 3: Data Files Description
       Part 4: Variable Description
       Entire Codebook

Document Description	
Citation	
Title:	CBS News Monthly Poll #2, August 1992
Alternative Title:	August National Poll II, Republican National Convention
Identification Number:	6084
Authoring Entity:	CBS News
Producer:	Inter-university Consortium for Political and Social Research
Copyright:	Copyright ICPSR, 2000
Date of Production:	May 10, 2000
Software used in Production:	SoftQuad XMetaL
Funding Agency/Sponsor:	National Science Foundation
Grant Number:	SBR-9617813
Distributor:	Inter-university Consortium for Political and Social Research
Date of Distribution:	May 10, 2000
Version:	2nd ICPSR XML Version
Version Responsibility:	Mary Vardigan, ICPSR Editor
Notes:	This document was initially prepared for the Data Documentation Initiative Beta Test. It was then revised to comply with Version 1 of the DDI DTD.
Bibliographic Citation:	CBS News. CBS NEWS MONTHLY POLL #2, AUGUST 1992 [Codebook file]. 2nd ICPSR XML version. Ann Arbor, MI: Inter-university Consortium for Political and Social Research [producer and distributor], 2000.

FIGURE 15-2   First page of the screen display of a codebook marked up according to the DDI. From the Data Documentation Initiative website, "Marked Up Codebooks," available at http://www.icpsr.umich.edu:8080/DDI/SAMPLES/06084.xml.

READINGS

Data Documentation Initiative (home page). Available at http://www.icpsr.umich.edu/DDI/. Accessed 31 July 2002.

> The DDI website has links to the DDI DTD and tag library, background information on the DDI, and sample DDI-encoded codebooks.

Ryssevik, Jostein, and Simon Mugrave. "The Social Science Dream Machine: Resource Discovery, Analysis, and Delivery on the Web." Paper given at the IASSIST Conference, Toronto, May 1999. Available at http://www.nesstar.org/papers/iassist_0599.html.

> A discussion of the NESSTAR vision, with some reference to the use of DDI.

Administrative
Metadata

16

While descriptive metadata is intended to help in finding, discovering, and identifying an information resource, administrative metadata is intended to facilitate the management of the resource. Management functions typically include such activities as tracking an item through various stages of processing, controlling access to the resource, establishing responsibilities related to the resource, and granting permission for its use. Although this is overly simplistic, descriptive metadata can be thought of as serving the actual or potential users of a resource, while administrative metadata serves the owners or caretakers of the resource.

No clear and clean distinction exists between descriptive and administrative metadata, as most defined data elements can be used in either descriptive or administrative contexts. There is also no clear distinction between descriptive and administrative metadata schemes, and most of the descriptive schemes described earlier contain at least some elements whose function is primarily administrative. Some schemes were designed from the start to serve both descriptive and administrative functions; for example, GILS has the dual objectives of facilitating public access to government information and supporting records management. However, most schemes tend to focus on one aspect or the other, allowing us to categorize them as primarily descriptive or administrative.

Specific schemes can focus on different aspects of administrative metadata. Preservation metadata focuses on elements needed to ensure the long-term preservation and usability of a data resource. Technical metadata focuses on describing the creation and physical characteristics of digital objects, and is often a key component of preservation metadata. Rights metadata focuses on documenting and managing rights and permissions. This chapter discusses general administrative and preservation schemes; rights metadata is covered in chapter 18.

ADMINISTRATIVE SCHEMES

In contrast to the plethora of descriptive schemes, no general administrative metadata schemes have achieved the status of formal or community standards. This may be because the need for interoperability between management applications has not been as pressing as has the need for search interoperability. Organizations responsible for maintaining information resources generally have their own internal systems for managing their resources with application-specific metadata schemes. They rarely have the need to share or exchange this metadata with other organizations or to perform searching across stores of administrative metadata maintained by different organizations. Nonetheless, there are several active efforts to develop standardized sets of administrative metadata elements, two of which are mentioned here.

The Dublin Core Metadata Initiative has an activity to define administrative metadata pertinent to descriptive metadata, which is itself an information resource to be managed. (Such metadata about metadata is often inelegantly called *meta-metadata*.) The Administrative Dublin Core, or A-Core, is a scheme in very early draft stage being developed by the DCMI's Administrative Metadata Working Group. A proposal discussed at the DC-9 workshop in Tokyo (DC-2001: International Conference on Dublin Core and Metadata Applications) defines a scheme with elements falling roughly into three categories. One set of elements records actions (creation, modification, verification, etc.) made to individual descriptive metadata records, such as the type of action, the date of the action, the identities of the parties responsible for the action, and the affiliations of and contact information for the parties. A second set of elements records nontransactional information about a metadata record, such as its language, status, location, and ownership. A third set applies not to individual records but, rather, to batches of records exchanged as a unit. These elements include a code to identify the target database for which the batch is intended, a name or code for the transmitting organization, the filename, technical format (XML, HTML, etc.), bibliographic format (Dublin Core, MARC21, etc.) and character set of the record batch, and the action to be taken in respect to the batch (e.g., append, modify, delete).

The A-Core is intended to apply to the management of any type of metadata, not just Dublin Core. Like Dublin Core itself, it defines semantics and can be implemented in any syntax. However, it is noted that because certain sets of elements must be grouped together to be meaningful (for example, type of action, date of action, and responsible party), a syntax, such as XML, that allows explicit groupings is more appropriate than a syntax, such as HTML, that does not.

Another group in the early stages of defining a common set of administrative data elements is concerned with managing licensing for and access to commercially available electronic resources. The group, led by Adam Chandler at Cornell and Tim Jewell at the University of Washington, does not have a formal name but does maintain a discussion list and a website titled "A Web Hub for Developing Administrative Metadata for Electronic Resource Management" (http://www.library.cornell.edu/cts/elicensestudy/home.html). Participants note that because the current generation of integrated library systems does not offer modules for managing licensed electronic content, many libraries are developing their own database systems for this purpose. The functions provided by these systems include recording selection decisions, tracking the process of acquiring or renewing a subscription, documenting the individual resources included in aggregate products, documenting terms of access and usage restrictions, and recording periods of unavailability and other problems with online services.

Metadata efforts have thus far concentrated on standardizing terms related to access and licensing. The presumption is that a standard data dictionary of terminology will improve communication between different library departments involved in e-resource management, will enable libraries to exchange information about licensing terms and agreements among themselves, and will encourage vendors to develop systems that address library needs.

TECHNICAL METADATA

Because technical metadata documents the creation and characteristics of digital files, the nature of the relevant information varies greatly depending on the file type. Technical metadata schemes, therefore, tend to be format-specific.

One scheme that is on track for formal standardization within NISO and AIIM International is "Technical Metadata for Digital Still Images."[1] This specification, considered a draft standard for trial use until December 2003, addresses nonmoving image formats, such as TIFF, JPEG, GIF, and PDF. For each defined data element, it specifies the data type; whether the element is mandatory, mandatory if applicable, recommended, or optional; whether the element is repeatable; and whether the element is intended to be used by a system, a system manager, or an end-user. Where the data type requires use of an authority list of coded or textual values, the list is given in the specification. It also gives usage notes and references to similar elements defined in related specifications, for example, TIFF.

Metadata elements are grouped into four categories: basic parameters, image creation, performance assessment, and change history. Basic parameters include format information, such as MIME type and compression, and file information, such as file size, checksum, and orientation. Image creation elements record detailed information about image capture, whether this was done with a digital camera or by scanning from an analog source. The performance assessment elements are designed to "serve as metrics to assess the accuracy of output (today's use), and to assess the accuracy of preservation techniques, particularly migration (future use)." These include spatial metrics, such as image length and width, and nonspatial metrics, such as the number of color components per pixel. Change history elements are designed to document any editing operations performed on the image, including the responsible party, the date and time, and the software used.

The Library of Congress has defined an XML schema for the NISO/AIIM semantics, called NISO MIX, or NISO Metadata for Images in XML Schema. The schema and related tools for implementing the data dictionary are available from the Network Development and MARC Standards Office website (http://www.loc.gov/standards/mix/).

The Library of Congress's Digital Audio-Visual Preservation Prototyping project has done extensive work in defining technical metadata elements for digital audio and video (http://www.loc.gov/rr/mopic/avprot/avprhome.html). AUDIOMD: Audio Technical Metadata Extension Schema contains thirty-seven top-level elements for describing the digital audio file and, if necessary, its analog or digital source. Similarly, VIDEOMD: Video Technical Metadata Extension Schema contains thirty-six top-level elements for describing a digital video file and its analog or digital source. The project website is particularly interesting because in addition to linking to the technical metadata schemas, it links to a spreadsheet showing how these elements have been implemented in a relational database to actually manage preservation functions.

Metadata elements of both AUDIOMD and VIDEOMD are defined as XML extension schema for METS, as is the MIX schema for NISO/AIIM Technical Metadata for Digital Still Images (see chapter 17).

PRESERVATION METADATA

A growing interest in the archiving and long-term preservation of digital materials has led to much attention being devoted to metadata schemes to help manage the preservation process. In 1998, the RLG Working Group on Preservation Issues of Metadata issued a final report recommending sixteen data elements to aid in the preservation of digital masters (http://www.rlg.org/preserv/presmeta.html). Most of these are technical metadata elements relevant to still images and were later incorporated into the NISO/AIIM specification.

Around the same time, two developments increased the sophistication of analysis pertaining to preservation metadata. First, the initial draft of the Open Archival Information System (OAIS) reference model was released in 1999.[2] Developed by NASA's Consultative Committee for Space Data Systems, the OAIS provides a conceptual framework for archival systems for the long-term preservation of digital data and is in the process of being adopted as an ISO standard. Second, a number of large-scale projects were initiated to archive digital information resources, and several of them adopted (or at least studied) the OAIS model. These projects include the Networked European Deposit Library (NEDLIB), which aimed to extend national deposit systems to digital works; the CEDARS project in the United Kingdom; and the National Library of Australia's PANDORA archive. As the library community has attempted to apply its early real-world experience in archiving within the OAIS framework, metadata element sets used by these and other projects have been published and used as the basis for further analysis. The OCLC/RLG Working Group on Preservation Metadata has issued recommendations for the semantics of preservation metadata, based on elements used in NEDLIB, CEDARS, and PANDORA, and organized within the OAIS framework.[3] Although the proposed elements are untested at this time and will doubtless be superseded by more mature specifications, they do show the likely direction of future work in preservation metadata.

In the OAIS model, an *information package* is a bundle of content and metadata used to submit archivable content to a repository, disseminate content from the repository, and manage content within the repository. Information packages are aggregates of four types of information: content information, preservation description information, packaging information, and descriptive information. The OCLC/RLG Working Group recommendation is concerned with two of these categories: Content Information and Preservation Description Information. In both cases, elements are described in terms of four attributes: "name," "origin" (whether the element was used in CEDARS, NEDLIB, or NLA, or made up by the Working Group), "definition," and "purpose." Examples of data are also given. Some elements are broken down into structures of nested subelements where the actual data values belong at the lowest subelement level.

In the OAIS model, Content Information consists of the content data object itself—that is, the actual bit stream(s) being archived—and Representation Information, or metadata. The Representation Information category consists of elements describing the content data object and elements describing the hardware and software environments required to display or access the content data object. The Working Group report recommends thirteen elements to describe the content data object, discussed briefly here.

Content Data Object Descriptive Elements

The File Description element is defined as "Technical specifications of the file(s) comprising a Content Data Object" and is the main semantic category for technical metadata. A footnote explains that some applications may need to break down this element into more granular data and notes that the elements of "Technical Metadata for Digital Still Images" may be used for certain object formats. Other elements that would be considered technical metadata are Structural Type and Size.

Significant properties of the content data object are described in Functionality, used to note the functional or "look and feel" attributes of the object, and Description of Rendered Content, which describes how the object should appear to users. Three elements are defined in anticipation of the need to migrate data files to new physical formats as older formats become obsolete. Access Facilitators is an element meant to note "aids and facilitators" that need to be taken into account during the preservation process—for example, a time index linked to a movie clip. Significant Properties records which properties of the content data object must be preserved through preservation actions, and Quirks, a term taken from the National Library of Australia, documents any loss of functionality or change in "look and feel" resulting from such actions.

Underlying Abstract Form Description is supposed to contain, in human-readable terms, an explanation of how archived bit streams should be interpreted in order to render the object. Similarly, Technical Infrastructure of Complex Object is used to describe the internal structure of multipart objects, such as web pages with embedded links and files. Other elements include Access Inhibitors, for encryption, watermarking, or other similar protection mechanisms; Installation requirements; and Documentation.

The remaining elements in the Representation Information category are a set of Environment Description elements divided into three categories: elements describing the programs needed to display or access the object, elements describing the operating systems under which those programs run, and elements describing the hardware or physical equipment required. As most objects can be displayed and accessed in many environments involving multiple combinations within these three categories and as new and backward-compatible releases of hardware and software are issued frequently, the population and maintenance of the values for these data elements may not be straightforward. Individual implementations will have to determine whether to record data in these categories comprehensively, or record minimum specifications, recommended current specifications, or some other subset of data values.

Preservation Description Information

The second broad category of metadata covered by the Working Group is Preservation Description Information. Here, the recommendation organizes elements into four broad subcategories: Reference information, Context information, Provenance information, and Fixity information. Reference information is used for identification or description and includes global identifiers, identifiers local to the archive, and some method of pointing to an existing descriptive metadata record for the resource. Context information documents why the content data object was created and how it is related to other objects. Elements exist for documenting how the object is related to other manifestations of the same object (for example, a previous version) and how it is intellectually related to other objects (for example, other items in the same collection).

Provenance information documents the history of the content information. In the Working Group report, Provenance information is broken down into five categories, four of which deal with different periods in the life cycle of the object: Origin, Pre-Ingest, Ingest, and Archival Retention. In each of these categories, events can be described in terms of what happened to the object, when, and who was responsible. An archive might reformat material at the time that it is accepted for archiving, for example. This would be recorded as an Ingest event. The fifth category, Rights Management, is defined to specify the "legal uses of the Content Data Object."

Fixity information provides the ability to verify the object has not been altered in an unauthorized or undocumented manner. The recommendation defines elements for Authentication Type, Authentication Procedure, Authentication Date, and Authentication Result. If the authentication method were an MD5 checksum, for example, the Authentication Type would be "MD5," the Authentication Procedure element would contain or point to documentation describing the generation of MD5 strings, and the Authentication Result would be the checksum string itself.

The Fixity elements illustrate one way in which the OCLC/RLG Working Group recommendations support the OAIS reference model. In OAIS, it is not taken for granted that future communities will understand or have access to current technologies. Simply stating the type of authentication (e.g., MD5) is not adequate without also documenting how that type is calculated. Similarly, when giving Reference Information, it is not adequate to record the type of identifier (e.g., ISBN) without also describing or pointing to a description of how that identifier is created and assigned. The need to refer to supporting documentation is central to OAIS and occurs throughout the Working Group recommendations.

Recommendations and Issues

The OCLC/RLG Working Group's recommended metadata element sets are, like OAIS itself, intended more as a framework for developing specific metadata applications rather than as the formal specification of a metadata scheme. It is noted that different applications will want to implement certain elements at various levels of granularity; for example, a single File Description element may satisfy one application, while a more expanded set of technical metadata elements may be required for another. Datatypes of elements are not specified, leaving an application free to implement Documentation, for example, as a text string or as a pointer. No controlled vocabularies are included or recommended, nor is any transport syntax.

As actual applications attempt to apply the recommendations as a framework for their own preservation metadata, certain issues are bound to arise. One of these is the certainty that in an actual preservation archive, many objects will need to be controlled at two levels—as logical entities and as sets of individual files comprising those logical entities. For example, a web page is a logical entity that may consist of multiple physical files (bit streams), such as an HTML file and one or more embedded GIF files. A book digitized as a set of TIFF page images is another example. For some purposes, the unit that must be described and managed is the book itself, with its attributes of author, title, and complex structure. For other purposes, such as media refreshment and forward migration, each TIFF image must be managed individually. The OCLC/RLG Working Group's recommendations acknowledge these layers but do not provide an explicit framework for sorting out what elements of description pertain to each and how they relate to each other architecturally.

Another issue is that many of the recommended metadata elements appear to require rather detailed analysis of the archived content, something which it may be impractical to supply and to act on in a large-scale production situation. In any case, extensive interest and increasing investment in the long-term preservation of digital assets guarantees that preservation metadata schemes will continue to evolve.

NOTES

1. "Data Dictionary—Technical Metadata for Digital Still Images," NISO Z39.87-2002 AIIM 20-2002, available at http://www.niso.org/standards/resources/Z39_87_trial_use.pdf. Accessed 5 July 2002.
2. Consultative Committee for Space Data Systems, "Reference Model for an Open Archival Information System (OAIS)," CCSDS 650.0-R-2, Red Book, July 2001, available at http://www.ccsds.org/documents/pdf/CCSDS-650.0-R-2.pdf. Accessed 5 July 2002.
3. OCLC/RLG Working Group on Preservation Metadata, *Preservation Metadata and the OAIS Information Model: A Metadata Framework to Support the Preservation of Digital Objects,* June 2002, available at http://www.oclc.org/research/pmwg/pm_framework.pdf. Accessed 5 July 2002.

READINGS

Digital Audio-Visual Preservation Prototyping Project of the Library of Congress (home page). Available at http://www.loc.gov/rr/mopic/avprot/avprhome.html. Accessed 5 July 2002.

> This page links to the Project Document Menu, which contains links to background documents, planning documents, and documents about metadata (http://lcweb.loc.gov/rr/mopic/avprot/avlcdocs.html). These include Extension Schemas for the Metadata Encoding and Transmission Standard (see chapter 16), which in turn link to schemas and data dictionaries defining technical metadata for audio and video.

Library of Congress Digital Library Development, Core Metadata Elements, available at http://www.loc.gov/standards/metadata.html.

> This table of administrative, descriptive, and structural metadata elements used by the Library of Congress is interesting because it categorizes elements according to several vectors, including their function (access management, presentation, preservation, etc.) and the level of object to which they apply (set, aggregate, primary object, etc.).

OCLC/RLG Preservation Metadata Working Group (home page). Available at http://www.oclc.org/research/pmwg/. Accessed 5 July 2002.

> Check the "Documents" link here for the Working Group report discussed earlier and any successor documents.

17

Structural Metadata

Structural metadata describes the internal organization of a resource. In the digital environment, logical resources are often made up of multiple physical files. Structural metadata relates physical files to one another and to the structure of logical objects. For example, a book with one hundred pages might have been digitized as one hundred TIFF images, each image representing one page. Structural metadata is necessary to indicate which TIFF file is page one, page two, and so on, and also to indicate that pages 1–14 make up chapter 1, pages 15–24 make up chapter 2, and so on. With this information, an online application can be written to perform certain functions, such as displaying a table of contents, allowing the reader to go directly to page 10 or chapter 2, and turning pages forward and backward.

Structural metadata can also associate different representations of the same intellectual content. Perhaps in addition to the TIFF files in the preceding example there are JPEG display versions and thumbnails of each page. In this case, structural metadata could be used to relate these files to one another, so that, again, the user sees the appropriate display. Another use of structural metadata in a different context might be to link passages in a sound recording to equivalent passages in the script or musical notation file.

Structural metadata is important for management and preservation purposes as well as for display. A repository with responsibility for storing digital resources needs to know which objects are comprised of which files in order to perform any functions at the level of the logical object, such as ingestion, reporting, or dissemination.

In some contexts, systems for marking up text are also considered structural metadata. For example, when textual content is encoded in SGML or XML according to the TEI *Guidelines*, that markup is likely to include structural information, such as page breaks, chapter headings, and other divisions. Used in this sense, structural metadata schemes would include such specifications as the TEI *Guidelines*, the Open eBook

Publication Structure developed by the Open eBook Forum, and the DocBook specification maintained by OASIS. However, in this chapter, we will focus on schemes that do not include content or include content only optionally.

EFFECT

The EFFECT (Exchange Format For Electronic Components and Texts) format was developed by Elsevier Science in the early 1990s to support the delivery of electronic files from publishers to libraries and other remote hosts. In the EFFECT framework, electronic journal content is bundled into collections called datasets, which can be issue- or article-based. A dataset is defined in EFFECT by a "dataset.toc" file. Hierarchical levels within the dataset.toc are indicated by _tn tags, with the highest level being _t0, followed by _t1, _t2, and so on. Tags at the _t0 level define the dataset itself and include an ID number, the version of the EFFECT format being used, and the creation date and time of the dataset.

Tags at the _t1 level identify the journal title, tags at the _t2 level identify the journal issue, and tags at the_t3 level identify the article or other contribution. In the following example, a section of a dataset.toc is used to identify an article in the journal *Brain Research* volume 945, number 1. The tags _vl, _is, and _dt at the _t2 level identify the journal volume, issue, and date. At the _t3 level, the tags _ti and _pg identify the title of the article and the pages that it appears on. Authors, subjects, an abstract, keywords, and other descriptive metadata can also be provided.

The _mf (manifestation) tags identify the files that make up the article. In this example, there are two versions, one a set of TIFF page images, and one a set of "raw" ASCII text files without markup. Other formats, such as HTML, SGML, and PDF, can also be represented.

```
_t1 AAA00001 00068996

_jn Brain Research

_pu Elsevier Science

_t2 AAA00001 00068996 v0945i01

_vl 945

_is 1

_dt 20020726

_t3 AAA00001 00068996 v0945i01 00123456

_ii [SICI] . . .

_ti Increases in amino-cupric-silver staining of the supraoptic nucleus after sleep
deprivation

_pg 1-8

_mf [TIFF 6.0] 1.tif 2.tif 3.tif 4.tif 5.tif 6.tif 7.tif 8.tif

_mf [raw ASCII] 1.raw 2.raw 3.raw 4.raw 5.raw 6.raw 7.raw 8.raw
```

Although EFFECT was designed specifically to support the delivery of Elsevier Science publications, other publishers adopted EFFECT or slightly modified versions of it to disseminate their own journal publications. When "local loading" of electronic journals was prevalent, many library organizations had processing streams in place to accept and display journal content based on EFFECT format dataset.toc files.

EBIND

The Berkeley Electronic Binding Project (Ebind) was an early (1996) attempt to standardize structural metadata for resources digitized as page images. Ebind defines structural metadata using an SGML DTD based loosely on the TEI DTD. Like TEI, the Ebind DTD contains a header section for descriptive bibliographic metadata about the resource (<ebindheader>), followed by the content of the resource itself divided into front matter (<front>), body (<body>), and back matter (<back>) sections.

In Ebind, as in TEI, structural divisions are noted with <div> elements. If these are associated with names, such as part or chapter headings, this information is recorded in <head> elements. Sections in the front matter of a book might be represented as follows:

```
<front>
<div0 type="titlepage">
<div0 type="preface">
<head>Preface to the Second Edition</head>
<div0 type="contents">
<head>Table of Contents</head>
</front>
```

In this example, there are three sections within the front matter—an unnamed title page and named preface and contents pages. If corresponding page images existed, these are given as <image> subelements within <page> elements. Attributes of the <image> element include "entityref" and "idref" for identifying image files, "seqno" for the absolute sequence number of the image file within the resource, and "nativeno" for the page number appearing on the digitized page:

```
<front>
<div0 type="titlepage">
<page><image entityref="QA00001" seqno="1"></page>
<div0 type="preface">
<head>Preface to the Second Edition</head>
<page><image entityref="QA00002" seqno="2" nativeno="i"></page>
<div0 type="contents">
```

```
<head>Table of Contents</head>

<page><image entityref="QA00003" seqno="3" nativeno="ii"></page>

<page><image entityref="QA00004" seqno="4" nativeno ="iii"></page>

</front>
```

The simplicity of the Ebind format is one of its main advantages. An Ebind SGML file can easily be created by a program from minimal data entered on worksheets. The Ebind structure also offers a certain amount of flexibility: by using nested <div> elements, Ebind can accommodate an arbitrary level of hierarchy, and if a character version of the full text were available as well as page images, the text could be included in the Ebind file with appropriate TEI markup.

MOA2 AND METS

In 1995, the University of Michigan and Cornell University began a project called Making of America to digitize monographs and serials pertaining to American social history from the antebellum period through Reconstruction. In 1997, members of the Digital Library Federation (DLF) began a project called Making of America II (MOA2), funded by the National Endowment for the Humanities. MOA2 was designed to test the building of an integrated but distributed collection of digital archival materials, such as diaries, ledgers, and photo albums, specifically excluding books and serials. Led by the University of California at Berkeley's library, participants included Berkeley, Cornell University, the New York Public Library, Pennsylvania State University, and Stanford University. One major outcome of the MOA2 project was a new metadata specification also known as MOA2.

While Ebind was designed primarily to support display functionality, such as page-turning, MOA2 took a more holistic approach, integrating descriptive, administrative, and structural metadata into a single XML DTD. The DTD had four sections. The descriptive metadata section could point to an external metadata record or contain embedded descriptive metadata. The administrative metadata section defined three types of data: technical metadata about file creation and physical characteristics, intellectual property rights information, and information about the original source of the digital object. The structural metadata section organized files into their logical places as parts of structured documents. Finally, a section called "file inventory" grouped all files for a particular version of the archival object (e.g., the JPEG or thumbnail version). The listing for each individual file could contain pointers to relevant information in the administrative metadata section, or it could contain embedded administrative metadata.

In early 2001, the DLF convened a workshop to discuss the MOA2 metadata specification and how it might be modified to meet a greater range of needs. The convening group acknowledged the success of the metadata scheme in the context of the Making of America II Testbed, but noted that it lacked external linking facilities and that it was designed to work only with a narrow range of resource types and could not accommodate audio, video, or other "time-dependent" media. As a result of the workshop, work began on a successor format to MOA2, which was named the Metadata Encoding and

Transmission Standard, or METS. A beta version of METS was released as an XML schema in the summer of 2001, and version 1.0 was released in February 2002. The Library of Congress Network Development and MARC Standards Office is the maintenance agency for the scheme and hosts the official website (http://www.loc.gov/standards/mets/). A METS Editorial Board was announced in May 2002 as an agency for managing revisions to the schema.

Like MOA2, METS has sections for descriptive, administrative, and structural metadata and a file inventory. A difference, however, is that METS also has a header section containing metadata about the METS file itself, and a fifth section for recording behaviors associated with the object. Another major design difference is that the METS schema does not define any elements of descriptive or administrative metadata. Instead, it uses the technique of either pointing to an external metadata record or embedding metadata from some other (non-METS) namespace within a wrapper element. For both descriptive and administrative metadata, the use of *extension schema*, or externally defined XML metadata schema, is encouraged. In this way, METS can leverage the work of other standards groups and avoids the maintenance issues that would arise if descriptive and administrative metadata elements were internally defined. METS can be used with digital collections with widely varying needs for descriptive metadata, and it can integrate technical metadata for any file format so long as some community has defined an XML schema describing that format.

As noted, descriptive metadata in METS can be referenced by a pointer or it can be embedded within a wrapper element (<mdWrap>). As a third option, non-XML descriptive metadata can be treated as a single datastream and wrapped in a <binData> subelement within <mdWrap>. This would allow METS to carry an embedded MARC record. Extension schemas for descriptive metadata that can be embedded within METS are listed on the official website. These include MODS (an XML schema with MARC-like semantics developed by the Library of Congress) and Dublin Core. Another extension schema called GDM (Generic Descriptive Metadata) is actually the set of metadata elements that were included in the old MOA2 DTD, pulled out and defined as a stand-alone schema.

Four types of administrative metadata elements are defined within METS: <techMD> for technical metadata, <rightsMD> for intellectual property rights, <sourceMD> for information about the digital or analog source of a derivative object, and <digiprovMD> for the provenance of the digital object. Within each of these, the metadata itself can be referenced by a pointer to an external record or embedded within the METS document within an <mdWrap> element. MIX, the XML schema for the NISO Technical Metadata for Digital Still Images standard, is an extension schema listed for technical metadata.

Because METS relies on externally defined schemes for administrative and technical metadata, it is thought of primarily as a standard for structural metadata. This is carried in the file group and structural map sections. As in MOA2, the file group section (<fileSec>) groups information about related files for a single digital version of a resource within a wrapping <fileGrp> element. In the following example, we have two file groups, one for the TIFF version of a two-page pamphlet and one for the JPEG version. The "groupid" attribute of the <file> element is used to tie corresponding files together; QA000.TIFF and QB000.JPG are associated by sharing the same "groupid" value.

```
<fileGrp>
    <file MIMETYPE="image/tiff" ID="QA000" SEQ="1"
    GROUPID="1" ADMID="A1">
        <FLocat LOCTYPE="OTHER" OTHERLOCTYPE="PATH"
            xlink:type="simple"
            xlink:href="/sun6/texts/QA001.TIF"/>
    </file>
    <file MIMETYPE="image/tiff" ID="QA001" SEQ="2"
    GROUPID="2" ADMID="A1">
        <FLocat LOCTYPE="OTHER" OTHERLOCTYPE="PATH"
            xlink:type="simple"
            xlink:href="/sun6/texts/QA002.TIF"/>
    </file>
</fileGrp>
<fileGrp>
    <file MIMETYPE="image/jpeg" ID="QB000" SEQ="1"
    GROUPID="1" ADMID="A2">
        <FLocat LOCTYPE="OTHER" OTHERLOCTYPE="PATH"
            xlink:type="simple"
            xlink:href="/sun6/texts/QB001.JPG"/>
    </file>
    <file MIMETYPE="image/jpeg" ID="QB001" SEQ="2"
    GROUPID="2" ADMID="A2">
        <FLocat LOCTYPE="OTHER" OTHERLOCTYPE="PATH"
            xlink:type="simple"
            xlink:href="/sun6/texts/QB002.JPG"/>
    </file>
</fileGrp>
```

The <file> element has other optional attributes, including the MIME type of the file, size of the file in bytes, the date created, and a checksum. The "admid" attribute is used to associate information about the file given in the administrative metadata section with the information given here. The <FLocat> subelement can be used to link to the actual file.

The structural map section (<structMap>) is often called the "heart of METS" and is the only required section of the schema. It shows the hierarchical structure of logical divisions within the object and associates these with files. The following example shows a document with little internal structure—a two-page pamphlet. The value of the "label" attribute on the high-level <div> element is intended to display in any generated table of contents. The two pages of the pamphlet are represented by <div> elements nested under the <div> for the pamphlet as a whole. "Order" is the absolute sequence of the page within the document, "Orderlabel" is the page number as it appears on the document, and "label" is the way the page number should be displayed to the user. The two files corresponding to each page are identified by the value of the "fileid" attribute of the <fptr> element, which associates these pages with the files defined in the file group section by the "id" attribute of the <file> element.

```
<structMap TYPE="logical">
    <div LABEL="Final Report of the Committee" TYPE="pamphlet">
        <div LABEL="Page 1" ORDER="1" ORDERLABEL="1"
        TYPE="page">
            <fptr FILEID="QA000"/>
            <fptr FILEID="QB000"/>
        </div>
        <div LABEL="Page 2" ORDER="2" ORDERLABEL="2"
        TYPE="page">
            <fptr FILEID="QA001"/>
            <fptr FILEID="QB001"/>
        </div>
    </div>
</structMap>
```

METS can reference parts of files as well. An <area> subelement can occur within the <fptr> element and provides the ability to link to subsections of a file. "Begin" and "end" attributes specify the beginning and ending locations within the referenced file, and the "betype" attribute indicates how the begin and end points are specified, for example, as byte offsets or as MIDI or SMIL time codes.

METS has many potential uses. It can be used to transfer digital objects between repositories and to control presentation and end-user navigation of a resource. Because of its ability to encapsulate descriptive, administrative, and structural metadata for a resource, METS has also found a use as a Submission Information Package (SIP) for digital archives following the OAIS framework. Harvard University, as part of an Andrew W. Mellon Foundation study of electronic journal archiving, used METS as the basis of an SIP for publishers to contribute electronic journal issues to the university's repository.

METS is an extremely flexible format that can be implemented in many different ways, and it is indefinitely extensible through its use of extension schema. Because of this, both the development of METS application profiles documenting the use of METS elements and the development of external schema for specific METS applications are encouraged. The Library of Congress, as the METS maintenance agency, is developing a central registry system for METS application profiles.

MPEG-7

Like METS, MPEG-7 (ISO/IEC 15938) encapsulates descriptive, administrative, and structural metadata. Developed by the Motion Picture Experts Group (MPEG), an ISO/IEC Working Group, MPEG-7 is specifically focused on audio and visual content.

The ISO/IEC 15938 specification, released in 2001, is organized into seven parts:

ISO/IEC 15938-1: Systems

ISO/IEC 15938-2: Description Definition Language

ISO/IEC 15938-3: Visual

ISO/IEC 15938-4: Audio

ISO/IEC 15938-5: Multimedia Description Schemes

ISO/IEC 15938-6: Reference Software

ISO/IEC 15938-7: Conformance Testing

Part 1 addresses the coding and transmission of metadata in textual and binary XML formats in a dynamic environment in which fragments of description may be sent out of order, and full or partial updates to a description (add/delete/replace) can be sent on demand.

Part 2 defines a Description Definition Language (DDL) for defining Descriptors and Description Schemes, the basic units of MPEG-7 description. A Descriptor can be thought of as an element definition, and a Description Scheme as a related set of element definitions. The DDL is actually a version of the XML schema definition, with some extensions to add features needed by the audiovisual community.

Parts 3, 4, and 5 define Descriptors and Description Schemes for visual media, audio media, and multimedia, respectively. Each part consists primarily of elements of technical metadata appropriate to these material types. The Visual part, for example, contains twenty-five Descriptors/Description Schemes for describing video segments, moving regions, and still regions. Metadata elements define visual material in terms of color, texture, shape, motion, localization, and the characteristics of human faces.

MPEG-7 will ultimately fit into the MPEG-21 Multimedia Framework, which is still under development. Whereas MPEG-7 is intended to describe and help manage resources, MPEG-21 will describe and help manage user interaction with resources, including rights management. MPEG-21 is conceived as a family of specifications. Part 1, which lays out the vision for the multimedia framework, has already been published as an ISO/IEC technical report.[1] The drafting of the other parts has been distributed among a number of different organizations. The planned parts of the specification are:

Part 2: Digital Item Declaration

Part 3: Digital Item Identification

Part 4: Intellectual Property Management and Protection

Part 5: Rights Expression Language

Part 6: Rights Data Dictionary

Part 7: Digital Item Adaptation

Part 8: Reference Software

NOTE

1. ISO/IEC TR 21000-1:2001 Information Technology—Multimedia Framework (MPEG-21), Part 1: Vision, Technologies, and Strategy. International Organisation for Standardization (2001).

READINGS

Digital Page Imaging and SGML: An Introduction to the Electronic Binding DTD (Ebind) (home page). Available at http://sunsite.berkeley.edu/Ebind/. Accessed 22 July 2002.

> The Ebind home page has links to the downloadable DTD, sample documents in their encoded and viewable forms, and tools for Ebind use.

METS—Metadata Encoding and Transmission Standard: Official Web Site (home page). Available at http://www.loc.gov/standards/mets/. Accessed 22 July 2002.

> Links to the METS Schema, Extension Schema, and toolkits, as well as to news and announcements about METS, examples of METS-encoded documents, and a tutorial. The site will ultimately link to registries of METS application profiles and types.

The MPEG standards, being ISO standards, must be purchased from ISO. However, there is ample MPEG information freely available online:

Hunter, Jane. "MPEG-7: Behind the Scenes." *D-Lib Magazine* 5, no. 9 (September 1999). Available at http://www.dlib.org/dlib/september99/hunter/09hunter.html.

> Written while the standard was still under development, this article explains the objectives, uses, and components of MPEG-7.

The MPEG Home Page. Available at http://mpeg.telecomitalialab.com/. Accessed 22 July 2002.

> This has links to information about all the MPEG standards, including MPEG-7 and MPEG-21. See particularly, in the Documents section, "MPEG-7 Overview" (ISO/IEC JTC1/SC29/WG11 N4674).

MPEG-7 Home Page. Available at http://www.mpeg-industry.com/. Accessed 22 July 2002.

> This site is particularly useful for its tutorials on various parts of the MPEG-7 family of standards.

Rights
Metadata

18

The ease with which digital content can be made available, reproduced, and modified has sparked intense interest in digital rights management. The phrase "digital rights management" is inherently ambiguous and has been used to mean both the computer management of intellectual property rights and the management of rights in digital content. The broader definition is generally used in the context of libraries and publishing. The International DOI Foundation (IDF) has argued that a practical rights management system must incorporate the digital management of all rights, both digital and nondigital.[1] Note, however, that when capitalized, Digital Rights Management, or DRM, is often used in a very narrow sense to mean the enforcement of content protection by software.

It is widely understood that metadata is a key component of any rights management system. Many efforts are under way to define rights metadata for use in various contexts, a few of which are mentioned here.

<INDECS>

An influential, high-level look into metadata requirements for rights management was undertaken by the <indecs> (Interoperability of Data in E-Commerce Systems) project funded by the European Commission from 1998 through 2000. From the start, <indecs> took a multinational, multimedia perspective and was supported internationally by major trade associations representing record companies, music publishers, film companies, and book and journal publishers. The goal of the project was to create a framework for electronic trading of intellectual property rights in all media. The primary product was the document, *The <indecs> Metadata Framework: Principles,*

Model and Data Dictionary, published in the summer of 2000 (http://www.indecs. org/pdf/framework.pdf).

The <indecs> model is essentially a semantic model for describing intellectual property, the parties that create and trade it, and the agreements that they make about it. The assumptions are that different metadata schemes will be developed and used by specific industries (for example, music and book publishers) and that for global electronic commerce to thrive, it must be possible for this metadata to be exchanged between industries and reused in different contexts. The <indecs> project attempts to distill the potentially infinite range of descriptive elements pertaining to rights into a defined set of generic, universally applicable categories and values. Data can be exchanged between domain-specific metadata schemes if data elements are taken from or can be mapped to the <indecs> data dictionary. For example, one scheme might have an element for "contributor" and a role value for "screenplay adapter," while another has an element for "musical arranger." Translated to <indecs> terminology, these would both be specific examples of a generic category (contributor agent role) and value (modifier).

Although the <indecs> framework does not analyze any particular externally defined metadata scheme, it does posit four guiding principles for the development of "'well-formed' metadata to support effective e-commerce." The first principle, called "the principle of unique identification," states that every entity must be identified uniquely within some namespace. Because an entity is defined as "something which is identified," this can be seen as a somewhat circular argument, but the main idea is clear: unique identifiers should be used for parties and things, and values for descriptive metadata elements should be taken from named controlled vocabularies.

The second principle, called "the principle of functional granularity," requires that metadata be able to identify parts and versions of resources at any arbitrary level of granularity, as long as the practical need for such identification arises. The third principle, "the principle of designated authority," stipulates that the author of each item of metadata must be identified in a manner that can be authenticated. Finally, "the principle of appropriate access" notes that metadata must be accessible where it is needed and, at the same time, be protected from unauthorized use.

The <indecs> framework has been influential in shaping thinking about rights metadata and has been endorsed by both EDItEUR (the parent organization of the ONIX family of standards) and the IDF. The <indecs> framework is the foundation of <indecs>rrd, a consortium-based initiative to build a data dictionary of rights metadata. In 2001, the <indecs>rrd design specification was selected as the basis for the MPEG-21 Part 6 Standard for a Rights Data Dictionary (see chapter 17 of this text), and work is proceeding on the development of that standard, which is expected to be approved in 2003.

OEB

The Open eBook Forum (OeBF) is best known for developing the OEB Publication Structure, a specification for the standard markup of e-book content. The OeBF has a number of other activities, however, including the Rights and Rules Working Group, which is charged "to create an open and commercially viable standard for interoperability of digital rights management (DRM) systems, providing trusted exchange of electronic publications (ePublications) among rights holders, intermediaries, and users."[2]

Rights and Rules actually arose from the merger of the OeBF and the Electronic Book eXchange (EBX) working group. EBX had been working since 1998 on creating standards for e-book content format and for copyright protection and distribution. A draft version of the "Electronic Book Exchange System (EBX)" specification was released in 2000. It describes how "trusted" components interact in a system that protects intellectual property throughout a range of interactions between publishers, booksellers, distributors, libraries, and individual consumers.

The mechanism used for effecting this in EBX is the creation and transfer of digital objects called *vouchers*. A voucher is an XML-encoded description of permissions that accompanies the e-book file. These permissions will vary as the e-book passes from point to point in the fulfillment chain. Among the permissions an e-book voucher can specify is whether the e-book (actually the voucher) is lendable, givable, or sellable; the amount of time the holder is allowed to borrow the voucher; the maximum number of personal use copies allowed; the length of time allowed for personal use; and the amount of content allowed for personal use. The specification also defines the interaction between the reading system and the voucher server, and it defines a fairly comprehensive rights management language.

Because OeBF and EBX were sponsored by many of the same members and had overlapping interests, the two groups joined forces in the fall of 2000, and the EBX initiative was merged into OeBF, where its work is being carried on through the OeBF Rights and Rules Working Group. The group currently is working on requirements for a rights grammar, encompassing a Rights Expression Language and a Rights Data Dictionary.

It should be noted that at roughly the same time the EBX specification was released, the Association of American Publishers (AAP) released its own specification of publisher requirements for digital rights management of e-books.[3] Written by Andersen Consulting under contract to the AAP, the specification defines pricing and usage scenarios that a rights management language must support, and it encourages publishers to participate in an open e-book standards group, such as the OeBF.

ODRL AND XRML

A general model for rights management has three basic components: agents (people and organizations), intellectual property, and agreements that govern the relationship between agents and intellectual property. The <in*decs*> framework states this succinctly: "People do deals about stuff."[4] Just as bibliographic information describing intellectual property is considered metadata, information describing rights transactions or agreements can be thought of as metadata. However, the vehicles for communicating rights information are not commonly called rights metadata schemes, but rather *rights languages*. Formally these are known as Digital Rights Expression Languages (DREL) or Rights Expression Languages (REL). Two of the most prominent rights languages are the Open Digital Rights Language (ODRL) and the eXtensible rights Markup Language (XrML).

ODRL was developed by IPR Systems in Australia and is being promoted as an open standard. In the ODRL model, agents are called "parties," and intellectual property is known as "assets." ODRL depends upon external schemes to uniquely identify parties and assets, and it focuses on the expression of rights, which are represented by nine types of entities: permissions, constraints, requirements, conditions, rights holders, contexts, offers, agreements, and revocation. Permissions govern the use, reuse, transfer, and management of an asset. Thus, for example, permission might be granted to use an asset by displaying and printing it. Constraints restrict the permissions over an asset; so, for example, user constraints may limit the use permissions to a particular individual or group. Requirements are preconditions to gaining permissions, such as the payment of a fee. Conditions are events that, if they occur, will result in the termination of permission.

Permissions, constraints, requirements, conditions, and the other entities can be represented in XML. The ODRL specification includes the model defining the entities and their components, a data dictionary defining the semantics of all the elements used in the ODRL rights expression language, and the XML encoding of ODRL expressions and elements. The specification also includes a section on how additional data dictionaries can be defined.

XrML is a product of ContentGuard, a company owned by Xerox Corporation and Microsoft. In April 2002, ContentGuard announced that it was freezing development of XrML at release 2.0 and handing further development over to OASIS, an international consortium focused on developing XML-based industry standards specifications. An OASIS Rights Language Technical Committee was formed with representatives from ContentGuard, Hewlett-Packard, Microsoft, Reuters, VeriSign, and other major players in the DRM industry to advance XrML as a rights language standard. XrML was also accepted as the basis of MPEG-21 Part 5: Rights Expression Language. It seems likely that XrML will emerge as the dominant REL within the content industries.

Although XrML is more mature and more comprehensive than ODRL, the two specifications essentially cover the same territory from the same perspective. Both express the point of view of the publisher/producer rather than the author or content user, both cover usage rather than access rights, and both assume that permissions not explicitly granted are denied. In reaction to this, the research and education communities are attempting to build a digital rights management framework of their own, one that encompasses rights of access to licensed resources and that focuses on rights of users as well as those of content owners. A key deliverable of this initiative will be the development of a core set of rights management metadata for use within this context.

NOTES

1. Norman Paskin, "Position Paper for W3C Workshop on Digital Rights Management for the Web" (22–23 January 2000), available at http://www.doi.org/001219W3C.pdf. Accessed 31 July 2002.
2. Open eBook Forum Rights and Rules Working Group (web page), available at http://www.openebook.org/members/Rights-Rules/index.htm. Accessed 31 July 2002.
3. Association of American Publishers, *Digital Rights Management for Ebooks: Publisher Requirements,* version 1.0 (2000), available at http://www.publishers.org/drm.pdf. Accessed 31 July 2002.
4. Godfrey Rust and Mark Bide, *The <indecs> Metadata Framework: Principles, Model and Data Dictionary* (June 2000), p. 4, available at http://www.indecs.org/pdf/framework.pdf. Accessed 31 July 2002.

READINGS

Coyle, Karen. "Stakeholders and Standards in the E-book Ecology: Or, It's the Economics, Stupid!" *Library Hi Tech* 19, no. 4 (2001): 314–324.

> This knowledgeable and insightful article covers digital rights management as well as other standards efforts related to e-books.

Iannella, Renato. "Digital Rights Management (DRM) Architectures." *D-Lib Magazine* 7, no. 6 (June 2001). Available at http://www.dlib.org/dlib/june01/iannella/06iannella.html.

> A clear overview of two architectures for digital rights management, the "functional" architecture and the "information" architecture, written by one of the principal developers of ODRL.

Martin, Mairéad, et al. "Federated Digital Rights Management: A Proposed DRM Solution for Research and Education." *D-Lib Magazine* 8, no. 7/8 (July/August 2002). Available at http://www.dlib.org/dlib/july02/martin/07martin.html.

> A description of how some in the research networking and library communities are attempting to develop a digital rights management architecture for teaching and research that uses Internet2 middleware.

GLOSSARY

A-Core   The Administrative Dublin Core, an unapproved draft specification of the DCMI for metadata about metadata.

AACR2   *Anglo-American Cataloguing Rules*, second edition.

AACR2R   *Anglo-American Cataloguing Rules*, second edition, 1988 revision.

AAP   Association of American Publishers.

AAT   *Art and Architecture Thesaurus*, a publication of the Getty Information Institute.

actionable   In relation to an identifier or URI, a string that when clicked in a web-enabled interface will retrieve content at some address.

added entry   A nonprimary bibliographic access point in a library cataloging record, opposed to the primary access point or main entry.

ADL   Advanced Distributed Learning, an initiative of the U.S. Department of Defense.

administrative metadata   Metadata primarily intended to facilitate the management of resources.

AIIM International   The Association for Information and Image Management.

AITF   The Art Information Task Force of the College Art Association and the Getty Art History Information Program, which developed the *Categories for the Description of Works of Art*.

ALA   American Library Association.

AMC   A term used for the USMARC Format for Archival and Manuscripts Control, which became obsolete with USMARC Format Integration.

ANSI   The American National Standards Institute, an organization which accredits other standards development organizations.

application profile   *See* Profile.

APPM   *Archives, Personal Papers, and Manuscripts : A Cataloging Manual for Archival Repositories, Historical Societies, and Manuscript Libraries*, by Steven L. Hensen.

archival collection   An archives consisting of the papers of an individual.

archives   An archival collection; an organized collection of the noncurrent records of an institution, a government, an organization, or a corporate body, or the personal papers of an individual or a family, preserved in a repository for their historical value.

ARIADNE   Alliance of Remote Instructional Authoring and Distribution Networks for Europe, a collaborative project of a number of European universities to develop and distribute computer-based teaching materials.

ArtSTOR   A project of the Mellon Foundation to develop, store, and electronically distribute digital images and related scholarly materials for the study of art, architecture, and other fields in the humanities.

attribute   In SGML and XML, name-value pairs associated with elements. In Z39.50, characteristics of a search query that can be specified, such as the access point to search or truncation characteristics.   In a metadata specification, a category of information specified about an element.

attribute set   In Z39.50, a coherent set of attributes that can be used to indicate the characteristics of a search term for a particular type of query.

authority file   A compilation of authorized terms that are used by an organization or in a particular database.

BASIC   Book And Serial Industry Communications, the standards forum of the Book Industry Study Group.

Bib-1   A Z39.50 attribute set developed primarily for the searching of MARC records.

BIBLINK   A project funded by the European Commission to establish a relationship between national bibliographic agencies and publishers of electronic material.

bibliographic access point   In library cataloging, an access point for the name of an author or other agent or the title or series associated with a work.

bibliographic utility   An organization providing a national cataloging system and database.

BIC   Book Industry Communication, a U.K. organization that develops and promotes standards for electronic commerce and communication in the book and serials industry.

BICI   Book Item and Contribution Identifier, an identifier for component parts of books, such as chapters or illustrations.

BSR   The ISO Basic Semantics Register, an internationally agreed-upon compilation of data elements to facilitate systems development in a multilingual environment.

call number   A notation denoting the shelving location of material in a library.

CC:DA   Committee on Cataloging: Description and Access, an ALA committee concerned with implementation of and changes to the library cataloging rules.

CDF   Channel Definition Format, an early specification for defining channels on the Web.

CDWA *Categories for the Description of Works of Art*, a metadata scheme for describing works of art for the purpose of art historical scholarship.

CEDARS CURL Exemplars in Digital Archives, a U.K. project to explore digital preservation issues.

CEMARC Curriculum-Enhanced MARC, a term used to refer to MARC records with fields of particular interest to K–12 educators.

channel A website that automatically sends updated information for immediate display or viewing on request.

checksum A value which is computed based upon the contents of a block of data in order to detect corruption of the data.

CHIO Cultural Heritage Information Online, a CIMI initiative to demonstrate Z39.50 searching of SGML data in museum databases.

CIDOC The International Committee for Documentation of the International Council of Museums (ICOM).

CIMI Consortium for the Computer Interchange of Museum Information, an organization dedicated to standards-based delivery of digital museum information.

classification A notational scheme that groups related resources into a hierarchical structure.

clickthrough measurement A technique for Internet search services to measure how often users select specific links returned in response to their queries.

code lists In relation to MARC cataloging, authority lists of coded values required for certain data elements.

codebook A document containing information on the structure, contents, and layout of a social science data file.

composite In the ONIX specification, a named set of data elements that must occur together.

compound element In the CSDGM, a named element comprised of other data elements and/or other compound elements.

content ratings A type of metadata utilizing rating schemes maintained by some authority, such as the movie rating scheme maintained by the Motion Picture Association of America.

content rules Rules specifying how values for metadata elements are selected and/or represented.

continuing resource In AACR2, a publication that is intended to be continued for an indeterminate period, such as serials, loose-leafs, and databases.

contributed copy Cataloging records created by libraries other than the Library of Congress, used as the source of copy cataloging.

control field In a MARC record, a field with a predefined number of bytes; also known as a fixed field.

controlled vocabulary *See* Vocabulary.

copy In library cataloging, a MARC record used as the basis for copy cataloging.

copy cataloging In library cataloging, the use of an existing catalog record as the source of a new record.

CORC   Cooperative Online Resource Catalog, an OCLC system for cataloging web resources using MARC, Dublin Core, and other metadata schemes; now a part of OCLC Connexion.

crosswalk   An authoritative mapping from the metadata elements of one scheme to the elements of another.

CSDGM   Content Standard for Digital Geospatial Metadata, a specification of the FGDC.

CUSTARD   The U.S./Canadian Standards Reconciliation Project, a joint project of the Society of American Archivists and the Canadian Council on Archives to harmonize U.S. and Canadian guidelines for cataloging and finding aid creation.

Darwin Core   A Z39.50 profile developed by the ZBIG for access to natural history collections and observation databases.

data field   In a MARC record, a field with a varying number of characters; also known as a variable field.

dataset.toc   A file defining a bundle of electronic content in the EFFECT format.

DCMI   Dublin Core Metadata Initiative.

DDC   Dewey Decimal Classification.

DDI   Data Documentation Initiative, an organization of social science data producers and archivists; also the metadata standard developed by the DDI for describing social science datasets.

deep Web   Web content that is generally inaccessible to Internet search engines, including dynamically generated web pages, database content, and nontextual files, such as images and sound; also called the hidden Web.

Denver Core   A subset of the FGDC CSDGM.

descriptive metadata   Metadata primarily intended to serve the purposes of discovery, identification, and selection.

digital signature   Data used to identify and authenticate the content of a file using public-key encryption.

direct access resource   In library cataloging, a resource with a physical carrier, such as a CD-ROM or tape cartridge.

directory   In a MARC record, a series of twelve-character entries, one for each field to follow, each indicating the field tag, length, and starting position of a field.

DLF   Digital Library Federation, a membership organization of academic and research libraries.

document type definition   *See* DTD.

DOI   Digital Object Identifier, an actionable identifier for digital publications.

domain   A subject area or professional sector with common interests and metadata needs.

domain-specific term   In the DCMI, a term for which a cross-domain need has not been demonstrated, but the need within a specific community has been established.

DREL   Digital Rights Expression Language(s).

DRM   Digital Rights Management, a term used narrowly to mean enforcement of content protection by software and more broadly to mean any automated method for managing rights in digital and nondigital materials.

DTD   Document Type Definition. In SGML and XML, a set of rules indicating which elements and attributes may occur in a document and restrictions on their use.

dumb down principle   In Dublin Core, the principle that a qualified data element should be understandable to an individual or application that does not recognize the qualifier.

EAD   Encoded Archival Description.

Ebind   A structural metadata specification of the Berkeley Electronic Binding Project.

EBX   Electronic Book eXchange, a group that developed a specification for e-book content and distribution also known as EBX.

EDItEUR   An international group devoted to the promotion of electronic commerce in the book and serials sectors.

EFFECT   Exchange Format for Electronic Components and Texts, a structural metadata specification developed by Elsevier Science.

element refinement qualifier   In Dublin Core, a qualifier that limits the meaning of an element.

EML   Ecological Metadata Language, an XML-based metadata scheme for describing ecological and environmental datasets.

empty element   In SGML and XML, an element that can contain no text or subelements.

encoding scheme qualifier   In Dublin Core, a qualifier that indicates the scheme or authority list used in representing the value of an element.

entry vocabulary   An index to a controlled vocabulary.

enumerative classification   A classification system that attempts to list all possible subjects within its scope and their notations.

EPICS   EDItEUR Product Information Communication Standards, a metadata specification initially developed by EDItEUR for the exchange of book trade information, now largely superseded by ONIX.

ESRI   A company that develops and markets software for geographic information systems (GIS).

expression   In FRBR, a specific rendering of a work, such as a particular edition of a book.

extension schema   In METS, externally defined schema that can be used within METS wrapper elements.

faceted classification   A classification system in which objects are described according to a set of characteristics, or facets, instead of by their position in a hierarchy of terms.

FGDC   Federal Geographic Data Committee, a committee composed of representatives from seventeen federal agencies to promote national use of geospatial data.

finding aid   A tool used by archival repositories to describe archive and manuscript collections. Finding aids generally begin with a high-level description of provenance followed by hierarchically ordered descriptions of groupings of materials.

fixed field   *See* Control field.

fonds   An Anglo-Canadian term for an archival collection or a record group.

FRBR   Functional Requirements for Bibliographic Records, a report of the IFLA Study Group on the Functional Requirements for Bibliographic Records. Although the report discusses a number of topics, the term *FRBR* is generally used in reference to a model in which there are works, expressions, manifestations, and items.

GEM   The Gateway to Educational Materials, a project of the U.S. Department of Education and the ERIC Clearinghouse on Information and Technology at Syracuse University; also the metadata scheme used by GEM.

GIF   Graphics Interchange Format, a standard for compressed digital images.

GILS   Government Information Locator Service, or Global Information Locator Service.

GIS   Geographic Information System(s), a computer system capable of assembling, storing, manipulating, and displaying geographically referenced information.

GMD   General Material Designation, an element in AACR2 cataloging indicating the broad type of material.

hidden Web   *See* Deep Web.

HTML   Hypertext Markup Language, a markup standard for documents used on the World Wide Web.

HTTP   Hypertext Transfer Protocol, the protocol underlying the Web.

ICONCLASS   An international subject classification system for art images.

ICPSR   Inter-University Consortium for Political and Social Research, a major repository of social science datasets located at the University of Michigan.

IDF   International DOI Foundation, an organization that supports development and promotion of the DOI system.

IEC   International Electrotechnical Commission, a standards organization for electrical, electronic, and related technologies.

IEEE   Pronounced "I-triple-E," the Institute of Electrical and Electronics Engineers, an international technical professional association.

IETF   Internet Engineering Task Force, the organization that oversees standards development for the Internet.

ILS   Integrated Library System, a set of applications software products that supports library functions, such as acquisitions, circulation, cataloging, and the online catalog.

IMS   The IMS Global Learning Consortium. The acronym once stood for Instructional Management Systems.

<indecs>   Interoperability of Data in E-Commerce Systems, a project funded by the European Commission from 1998 through 2000.

indicators   In a MARC record, the first two positions of a data (or variable) field, the value of each position having a specific meaning.

information package   In the OAIS model, a bundle of content and metadata in an archival repository.

ISAD(G)   General International Standard Archival Description, a general framework for archival description developed by the International Council on Archives.

ISBD   International Standard Bibliographic Description, a set of specifications for the description of various types of materials.

ISBN   International Standard Book Number, an identifier for nonserial print publications.

ISO   International Organization for Standardization.

ISSN   International Standard Serial Number, an identifier for serial publications.

JPEG   Literally, Joint Photographic Experts Group. A standard compression method for photographic images; a digital image using JPEG compression.

KNB   Knowledge Network for Biocomplexity, an initiative dedicated to facilitating ecological and environmental research on biocomplexity by improving access to and use of distributed datasets.

LC   The Library of Congress.

LC copy   Catalog records created by the Library of Congress cataloging service, used by other libraries in copy cataloging.

LCC   Library of Congress Classification.

LCRI   Library of Congress Rule Interpretations, LC's actual implementation of the cataloging code.

LCSH   Library of Congress Subject Headings.

leader   The first twenty-four characters of a MARC record in Z39.2 format.

link analysis   A technique for identifying how often web pages are linked to from other pages; used to weight retrievals in Internet search service.

linkage   The expression of relationships between objects, such as earlier versions or derivative file formats.

locator records   A term used for metadata records in GILS.

LOM   Learning Object Metadata, generally used to refer to the IEEE LOM specification.

LTSC   The Learning Technology Standards Committee of the Institute of Electrical and Electronics Engineers (IEEE).

main entry   The primary access point of a library cataloging record, according to AACR2.

manifestation   In FRBR, "the physical embodiment of an expression of a work," or all copies of an expression produced on the same media in the same physical form.

MARC   MAchine-Readable Cataloging, a syntax for communicating cataloging records.

MARC21   The current set of specifications for how to encode MARC records, maintained by the Library of Congress.

MCF Meta Content Framework, an early specification for defining channels on the Web.

MD5 An algorithm for generating a checksum; also the checksum generated by this algorithm.

MDA Museum Documentation Association, a U.K. organization to support standards-related activities in museums. In 1997–98 the Museum Documentation Association officially changed its name to "mda" (all lowercase).

meta-metadata Metadata that describes a metadata record or element, such as who provided a value or the date of creation or update.

metadata scheme A set of metadata elements and rules for their use that has been defined for a particular purpose.

metalanguage A language used to describe other languages. SGML and XML are examples of metalanguages.

METS Metadata Encoding and Transmission Standard, a specification for structural metadata.

MIDI Musical Instrument Digital Interface, a format for digital music.

MIME type An informal name for Internet Media Types, a standard set of terms used to identify digital formats.

MIX Metadata for Images in XML Schema, an XML schema for representing the semantics for the NISO/AIIM Technical Metadata for Digital Still Images standard.

MOA2 Making of America II, a DLF-sponsored project to build a digital collection of archival materials; also the metadata specification developed for the MOA2 project.

MP3 A standard compression format for sound, formerly MPEG-1 Audio Layer 3; also a digital audio file using MP3 compression.

MPEG Motion Picture Experts Group, an organization that develops standards related to video and multimedia.

namespace The set of values that are within the scope of an identification system, or the set of elements that are defined by a metadata scheme. In XML, a set of tags identified as being defined by a particular document.

NARA National Archives and Records Administration.

NBII National Biological Information Infrastructure, a collaborative program to increase access to data and information about biological resources.

NEDLIB The Networked European Deposit Library, a project to extend national deposit systems to digital works.

NESSTAR Networked Social Science Tools and Resources, a project to develop tools for finding and using distributed social science datasets.

netcasting The prearranged updating of news, stock quotes, sports scores, and other selected information on the Web using channels; also called webcasting.

NII National Information Infrastructure, a policy initiative of the Clinton administration.

NISO National Information Standards Organization, a membership organization that develops standards for libraries and for publishing and information services.

NLA   National Library of Australia.

notation   In classification systems, an alphabetic, numeric, or alphanumeric code designating a node on a classification tree.

OAI   Open Archives Initiative, an organization that maintains a protocol for harvesting metadata from distributed repositories.

OAIS   Open Archival Information System, a reference model for archival repositories developed by NASA's Consultative Committee for Space Data Systems.

OCLC   An international not-for-profit membership organization for libraries. Also used informally to refer to a cataloging system and union catalog database run by the OCLC organization.

ODRL   Open Digital Rights Language, a Rights Expression Language developed by IPR Systems in Australia.

OEB   The Open eBook Publication Structure, a specification of the OeBF.

OeBF   Open eBook Forum.

one-to-one principle   In Dublin Core, the principle that if multiple versions of a resource exist, each should be separately and accurately described.

ONIX   Guidelines for ONline Information eXchange, a scheme developed by publishers for exchanging book trade information.

ontology   A specification that formally defines semantic relationships among concepts.

original cataloging   Library cataloging created from scratch, without using an existing catalog record as a data source.

original order   In archival documentation, the principle that the order in which materials were created must be preserved.

PANDORA   Preserving and Accessing Networked Documentary Resources of Australia, an initiative of the National Library of Australia.

parallel title   In library cataloging, the title proper in another language or script.

PDF   Portable Document Format, the file format native to Adobe Acrobat.

preservation metadata   Metadata primarily intended to help manage the process of ensuring the long-term preservation and usability of information resources.

principle of user convenience   A cataloging principle, originated by Charles Cutter, that the convenience of the user should be put before the ease of the cataloger.

profile   A formally developed specification that limits and clarifies the use of a metadata scheme for a particular user community.

provenance   The history of creation and ownership of archival materials.

PSD   Photoshop Document, the image file format native to Adobe Photoshop.

public-key encryption   An encryption scheme in which each person gets a pair of keys, a published public key and a secret private key. Messages are encrypted using the public key of the intended recipient, and must be decrypted using his private key.

qualifier   In Dublin Core and other metadata schemes, a term that restricts the meaning of an element or identifies the encoding scheme used in representing the value of the element.

RAD *Rules for Archival Description*, a document used by Canadian archivists as a guide to the formulation of content for finding aids.

RDF Resource Description Framework, a data model and specification for representing metadata in XML.

record group An archives consisting of the papers of an organization.

reference name In the ONIX specification, the complete element name.

REL Rights Expression Language(s).

remote access resource In library cataloging, material with no physical carrier, generally accessed over the Internet.

respect des fonds In archival documentation, the principle that materials with the same origin must be kept together and not mixed with other materials. Also known as "the principle of provenance."

rights metadata Metadata primarily intended to enable the management of rights related to information resources; a type of administrative metadata.

RLG Research Libraries Group, a not-for-profit membership organization of libraries, archives, museums and other cultural heritage institutions.

RLIN Research Libraries Information Network, a cataloging system and union catalog run by the Research Libraries Group.

ROADS Resource Organisation And Discovery in Subject-based Services, a project of the Electronic Libraries Programme of the Joint Information Systems Committee (JISC) in the United Kingdom.

RSS RDF Site Summary or Rich Site Summary depending on the version; the most commonly used specification for defining channels on the Web.

SAA Society of American Archivists.

schema A formally defined metadata scheme. In XML, a way of defining a document type used as an alternative to the DTD.

SCORM Sharable Content Object Reference Model, a collection of specifications for interoperable web-based learning content, developed by the ADL.

SCSI Small Computer System Interface, a standard for interfacing between computers and devices such as hard disks, printers, and scanners.

semantic unit In the BSR, a neutral semantic concept.

semantics The definition of the meaning of metadata elements, as opposed to rules for encoding or representing the values of the elements.

SGML Standard Generalized Markup Language, a metalanguage for marking up textual data.

shelflist A printed or online list in shelf order of all physical items held by a library.

short tag In the ONIX specification, a short name for an element.

SICI Serial Item and Contribution Identifier, an identifier for component parts of serials, such as issues and articles.

SIP In the OAIS framework, a Submission Information Package, a bundle of content and metadata submitted to a digital archive.

SMIL   Pronounced "smile," Synchronized Multimedia Integration Language, a language for authoring interactive audiovisual presentations.

spamming   Deliberately overloading a web page with keywords in order to affect retrieval by Internet search engines.

spider   A program used by an Internet search engine to find, gather, and index web content; also called a webcrawler.

SSA   Serial Storage Architecture, IBM's high-speed interface to disk clusters and arrays.

structural metadata   Metadata that describes the internal organization of a resource.

subelement   In SGML and XML, an element that occurs within a higher-level element (wrapper).

subfield delimiter   In a MARC record, a character that indicates the following character is a subfield code; together, the delimiter and code flag the start of a new subfield and indicate the meaning of the subfield.

subject cataloging   The assignment of topical access points.

superwork   A set of works (in IFLA terms) with a common origin, for example, all works based on Shakespeare's *Othello*.

surrogate   A secondary object meant to substitute for the original, such as a photograph of an artwork used in place of the artwork.

syntax   How a metadata scheme is structured for exchange in machine-readable form. Common syntaxes include MARC, SGML, and XML.

tag   In a MARC record, a three-character code designating the name of a field; for example, the tag "245" designates a title proper.   In SGML and XML, the name of an element, given in angle brackets.

tag library   A document that lists the names of SGML or XML elements and attributes alphabetically, along with their definitions and rules for their use.

technical metadata   Metadata primarily intended to document the creation and characteristics of digital files.

TEI   Text Encoding Initiative, an international activity that maintains the TEI *Guidelines*, a set of specifications for standardized markup of texts in SGML and XML.

TGN   *Thesaurus of Geographic Names*, a publication of the Getty Information Institute.

thesaurus   An arrangement of a controlled vocabulary in which all allowable terms are given and relationships between terms are shown.

TIFF   Tag Image File Format, a widely used format for digital image files.

UDC   Universal Decimal Classification, a scheme for classifying the whole field of knowledge.

UKOLN   The United Kingdom Office for Library and Information Networking.

ULAN   *Union List of Artist Names*, a publication of the Getty Information Institute.

UNICODE   An ISO/IEC standard for character representation designed to cover all modern written languages.

URI   Uniform Resource Identifier, a class of identifier that includes URNs and URLs.

URL   Uniform Resource Locator, the address of a resource available through HTTP and a few other protocols.

URN   Uniform Resource Name, an identifier that can be resolved to one or more URLs.

USMARC   The version of MARC implemented in the United States; renamed MARC21 in 2000.

VADS   Visual Arts Data Service, a project of the U.K. Arts and Humanities Data Service.

variable field   *See* Data field.

vocabulary   The universe of values that can be used for a particular metadata element. When there are formal limits on these values, it is a controlled vocabulary.

voucher   In EBX, an XML-encoded description of permissions that accompanies an e-book file.

VRA Core   Visual Resources Association Core Categories.

W3C   The World Wide Web Consortium, a membership organization that manages the standards process for web-related specifications, such as HTML, XML, and RDF.

webcasting   *See* Netcasting.

webcrawler   *See* Spider.

WLN   Washington Library Network, one of the earliest bibliographic utilities. WLN and OCLC merged on January 1, 1999.

work   In FRBR, an abstract intellectual or artistic creation. In the VRA Core, a physical entity, such as an artistic creation, a performance, a building, or an object of material culture.

World Wide Web Consortium   *See* W3C.

wrapper   In SGML and XML, an element within which another element or set of elements (subelements) may be nested.

XML   Extensible Markup Language, a specification developed by the W3C for the markup of structured documents on the Web.

XMP   eXtensible Metadata Platform, an Adobe specification for embedding metadata in PDF documents.

XrML   eXtensible rights Markup Language, a Rights Expression Language developed by ContentGuard.

Z tokens   Numeric identifiers that relate metadata elements in GILS and other schemes to an attribute in the Z39.50 Bib-1 attribute set.

ZBIG   Z39.50 Biology Implementors Group, the group that developed the Darwin Core.

Z39.50   An ANSI/NISO standard protocol for system-to-system search and retrieval. Also International Standard, ISO 23950: "Information Retrieval (Z39.50): Application Service Definition and Protocol Specification."

INDEX

PRISCILLA CAPLAN is assistant director for Digital Library Services at the Florida Center for Library Automation in Gainesville, Florida. She was previously assistant director for Library Systems at the University of Chicago Library and head of the Systems Development Division of the Office for Information Systems in the Harvard University Library. She holds a B.A. from Harvard University and an M.L.S. from the University of North Carolina at Chapel Hill. She is deeply interested in metadata and standards issues related to digital libraries and has been chair of the MARBI committee of the U.S. MARC Advisory Group, chair of the National Information Standards Organization (NISO) Standards Development Committee, and a member of the Dublin Core Advisory Committee.

the
ART
of
PROBLEM
SOLVING

Volume 1:
the BASICS

Sandor Lehoczky

Richard Rusczyk

Copyright © 1993, 1995, 2003, 2004, 2006, 2011, 2014, 2015, 2017, 2018 Sandor Lehoczky and Richard Rusczyk.

All Rights Reserved.

Reproduction of any part of this book without expressed permission of the authors is strictly forbidden.

For use outside the classroom of the problems contained herein, permission must be acquired from the cited sources.

ISBN-10: 0-9773045-6-6
ISBN-13: 978-0-9773045-6-1

Published by: AoPS Incorporated
                 10865 Rancho Bernardo Road Ste 100
                 San Diego, CA 92127
                 books@artofproblemsolving.com

Visit the Art of Problem Solving website at http://www.artofproblemsolving.com

Printed in the United States of America.
Seventh Edition; printed in 2018.

Editor: David Patrick

Cover image designed by Vanessa Rusczyk using KaleidoTile software.

Cover Image: "Grand Canyon from South Rim" by Ansel Adams. No permissions required; National Archive photo 79-AAF-8.

This book was produced using the LaTeX document processing system.
Diagrams created by Maria Monks using METAPOST.